Trade Unions, Employment, and Unemployment Duration

Trade Unions, Employment, and Unemployment Duration

Bertil Holmlund
Karl-Gustaf Löfgren
and
Lars Engström

CLARENDON PRESS · OXFORD
1989

Oxford University Press, Walton Street, Oxford OX2 6DP

Oxford New York Toronto
Delhi Bombay Calcutta Madras Karachi
Petaling Jaya Singapore Hong Kong Tokyo
Nairobi Dar es Salaam Cape Town
Melbourne Auckland

and associated companies in
Berlin Ibadan

Oxford is a trade mark of Oxford University Press

Published in the United States
by Oxford University Press, New York

British Library Cataloguing in Publication Data
Holmlund, Bertil
Trade unions, employment and unemployment
duration.—(FIEF studies in labour
markets and economics policy)
1. Unemployment
I. Title II. Lofgren, Karl-Gustav
III. Engstrom, Lars IV. Series
331.13'7
ISBN 0–19–828670–8

Library of Congress Cataloging in Publication Data
Holmlund, Bertil, 1947–
Trade unions, employment, and employment duration/Bertil
Holmlund, Karl-Gustaf Löfgren, and Lars Engström.
—(FIEF studies in labour markets and economic policy)
Includes bibliographies and index.
1. Labor supply. 2. Trade-unions. 3. Unemployment. 4. Wages.
I. Löfgren, Karl-Gustaf. II. Engström, Lars. III. Title.
IV. Series.
HD5707.H65   1989   331.13'7—dc19   88–35319.
ISBN 0–19–828670–8

Set by Colset Private Limited, Singapore
Printed and bound by
Bookcraft (Bath) Ltd.,
Midsomer Norton, Avon

Contents

Introduction

The performance of labour markets is crucial for the success or failure of economic policy. This is one reason why labour market studies are central to FIEF's research activities. It is appropriate to inaugurate *FIEF Studies in Labour Markets and Economic Policy* with a volume devoted to research on labour market issues. Bertil Holmlund deals with the determination of wages and employment, while Karl-Gustaf Löfgren and Lars Engström focus on the problem of the increasing length of individual unemployment spells.

Holmlund's paper is a broad survey of recent theoretical development and empirical research, a survey extended by his own original contribution. In the theoretical chapters, Holmlund considers labour demand models—the monopoly union model and the Nash bargaining model—as well as efficient bargaining models. He uses trade union models to analyse a number of policy-relevant problems, such as the effect on wages of taxes, unemployment insurance with different financing schemes, and work-sharing. His conclusions are sensitive to assumptions about union objectives, bargaining power, and properties of the labour demand curve, and he underlines the need for empirical testing.

In the following chapters, Holmlund surveys recent empirical work on employment and wage determination. What can be said about the efficiency of wage contracts in view of recent research? Is the outcome of wages and employment on the 'contract curve', or is it on the firm's labour demand curve? These are the questions that underlie Holmlund's review of the literature. Further, he reports on recent empirical research on the trade union's objective function, on bargaining power, and on employment and wage effects of union power. Finally, Holmlund turns to an empirical analysis of the determination of employment and wages in the Swedish mining and manufacturing sector (the tradeables sector). Holmlund's results indicate that employment is sensitive to wage cost, and especially to material prices, that aggregate demand does matter for employment, and that there is a high substitutability between men and man-hours. Holmlund's estimated real-wage equation reveals that wages are pushed up when unemployment benefits are raised, and pushed down when unemployment is high.

Part I concludes with commentaries by Lars Calmfors and Andrew Oswald.

One reason why there has been a substantial rise in unemployment in many European countries in the last decade is the increase of unemployment duration rather than an increasing inflow into unemployment. This makes it important to study the duration of unemployment spells. But not only that—the welfare consequences of a few being unemployed for a long period are probably worse than the consequences of many people being unemployed for short intervals.

It is this problem which is the underlying concern of Karl-Gustav Löfgren and Lars Engström's contribution to this volume. Their paper starts with an analysis of different duration concepts. They relate duration to the re-employment probability of an unemployed person, and derive the so-called 'hazard function'. They then go on to analyse the length of unemployment spells, what measure to use, and the structure of unemployment duration over different population groups and its behaviour over the business cycle.

One section of their paper is devoted to the relationship—if any —between unemployment benefits and unemployment. Unemployment can increase with improved unemployment insurance through more quits and lay-offs, longer spells of unemployment due to increased 'reservation wages', and finally through the 'entitlement effect', if people enter the labour force to qualify for benefits. The authors survey the empirical evidence.

The next problem taken up is the dependence of the re-employment probability on the duration of the spell of unemployment. Is the reservation wage falling with the duration, so that re-employment probability will increase with time, or are there more scars left by longer spells, so that the re-employment probability falls? After a comprehensive survey of the international literature on this matter, Löfgren and Engström present their own empirical analysis based on data from a northern Swedish town. A novelty in the paper is that the empirical data allow the estimation not only of a hazard function but also of the employment risks—two factors which, multiplied, yield the unemployment rate. A sample of redundant workers from the northern Swedish mining company

LKAB, who were subject to intensified employment services, are compared with a control group consisting of unemployed applying for jobs at the employment offices in the same region and period. It turns out that there are no group differences with respect to the expected duration of unemployment and no scars from duration, but that the redundant workers have experienced significantly lower unemployment risks.

Part II concludes with commentaries by Anders Björklund and Richard Layard.

Villy Bergström
Director, FIEF

PART I

Wages and Employment in Unionized Economies: Theory and Evidence

Introductory

Of all participants in economic life, the trade union is probably
least suited to purely economic analysis.

Ross (1948)

The problem of modeling trade union behaviour has proved to
be virtually intractable.

Johnson (1975)

There is nothing about the trade union as an institution that
makes its central features impossible to characterize in a
framework analogous to purposive models in economics.

Dertouzos and Pencavel (1981)

The analysis of trade union behaviour has become one of the new
growth industries in labour and macro-economics. The interest in
union topics seen in the 1980s stands in sharp contrast to the
economic profession's revealed research preferences during
previous post-war decades. George Johnson's short survey from
1975 noted a steady fall in the proportion of articles dealing with
unionism in leading US journals.[1] In the 1940s, 9 per cent dealt with
unionism, and the proportion had fallen to 5 per cent in the 1950s, to
2 per cent in the 1960s, and to just 0.4 per cent in the first four years
of the 1970s. Leading British journals ignored union issues to a
similar extent in the early 1970s: Pencavel (1977) reported that of
major articles between 1970 and 1975, less than 1 per cent could be
classified as dealing with union behaviour.[2]

Early US studies put much research effort into the analysis of
'union-relative wage effects', i.e. the role of unions in creating wage

I have benefited from many useful comments and suggestions from Lars Calmfors,
Richard Disney, Bob Flanagan, Dan Hamermesh, Per Lundborg, Andrew Oswald,
Richard Layard, John Pencavel, Matti Pohjola, and Eskil Wadensjö. The work has
received support from the Bank of Sweden Tercentenary Foundation.

[1] *American Economic Review, Journal of Political Economy,* and *Quarterly
Journal of Economics.*

[2] Pencavel considered *Economic Journal* and *Economica.*

differentials between union and non-union workers. Gregg Lewis's classic study from 1963 is the best-known example. This research was mainly econometric, without much attention paid to behavioural union models. Recent theoretical and empirical works, by contrast, have formulated models where rational unions are assumed to maximize well-defined objective functions. The bulk of recent research has in this respect ignored the 'institutionalist' criticism from Ross and others, and instead followed the approach favoured by Dunlop (1944), who argued that 'an economic theory of a trade union requires that the organization be assumed to maximize or minimize something'.

Whereas the earlier union literature was primarily micro-oriented, the research of the 1980s has emphasized the implications of unions for macro-economic behaviour. This tilt in focus has perhaps been more pronounced in Europe than in the USA, which comes as no surprise, since unionization rates are much lower (and falling) in the USA. The sharp rise in unemployment in most European countries—and the diverging trends between unemployment in Europe and the USA—have also encouraged economists' interest in institutional arrangements of labour markets, including the role of trade unions in wage and employment determination.

The present essay has two main purposes. The first is to review—selectively but in some detail—recent theoretical and empirical work on union behaviour; the second is to offer an empirical examination of post-war movements in employment and wages in the Swedish mining and manufacturing sector. This empirical investigation draws on earlier sections of the essay, and some of the predictions from the theory part are tested in the empirical section.

The essay falls into three main sections. Chapter 1 deals with theoretical issues, and focuses on the implications of some standard bargaining models. What can simple models tell us about wage and employment effects of, say, changes in taxes, unemployment benefits, or working time? Some of the results spelled out are well known, whereas other implications are less widely appreciated. The theoretical discussion serves as introduction and background for our review of recent empirical work, and offers a starting-point for the empirical investigations of Swedish data.

Chapter 2 gives a survey of recent empirical work. What is known about the efficiency of bargaining outcomes and about union objectives? Is there a relationship between union power, wage pressure, and unemployment? Almost all studies surveyed in this chapter have appeared during the last six years. Empirical studies on union behaviour have perhaps been more common in the USA than in Europe. Empirical work on union models is, however, increasing in Europe, and this research will presumably become more relevant for understanding European labour markets than studies pertaining to the USA.

Chapter 3 turns to an empirical investigation of wage and employment determination in Sweden's mining and manufacturing sector. The analysis is centred around two behavioural relationships, namely a labour demand equation and a real-wage equation. Most empirical work on Swedish wage equations has followed the Phillips curve tradition, without much attention paid to objectives pursued by unions. A bargaining approach, by contrast, regards the nominal wage outcome as caused by real objectives, presumably including the unions' interest in high real-wages and high employment. This approach has implications for econometric wage equations that do not obviously follow from a traditional Phillips curve approach. The estimates given in Chapter 3 show, among other things, how wages are affected by shifts of the labour demand schedule and by variables that influence the unions' desired trade-off between wages and employment (such as unemployment benefits).

Chapter 4 concludes the essay with a discussion of the future research agenda.

1

Theoretical Issues

1.1. Introduction

Theoretical work on union behaviour has by now covered substantial ground, and the field does not seem to have lost its excitement among economists interested in models of wage formation. The standard monopoly union model has been extended to situations involving uncertainty and intertemporal considerations, and recent progress in game theory has found applications to unionized labour markets. Whereas earlier literature primarily dealt with bargaining between unions and firms, more recent theoretical work has also been concerned with games between unions and governments.[1]

Any exposition of trade union models is bound to be selective. Our presentation makes use of union models to analyse a few recurrent topics in policy discussions. These include the relationships between taxes and wage outcomes, the role of unemployment insurance and its financing, and the potential ability of work-sharing to raise employment. These issues are also addressed in the empirical work presented in Chapter 3 below. The list of potentially important but omitted topics can certainly be made rather long. Suffice it here to mention that we have ignored the interactions between unions and governments as well as issues concerning centralization versus decentralization in wage-bargaining. Recent work on 'hysteresis' and 'insider–outsider' models are also ignored.

This chapter starts with an elementary introduction to three popular approaches: (i) the monopoly union model, (ii) the 'right-to-manage' model, and (iii) the efficient-bargaining model. In later chapters we focus primarily on partial-equilibrium wage-bargaining models, and monopoly union models in particular, as opposed to

---

[1] A special issue of *Scandinavian Journal of Economics* (2 (1985)) deals with various aspects of the economics of trade unions. The issue contains surveys by A. Oswald and J. Pencavel. Farber (1986) and Oswald (1987) also provide surveys and discussions of the economic analysis of trade union behaviour. Kennan (1986) offers a survey of the economics of strikes.

models in which both wages and employment are determined through negotiations. This emphasis on wage-bargaining conforms to the common and presumably quite realistic view that employers can exercise considerable discretion over hirings and firings.

The chapter then proceeds to analyse union wage responses to changes in prices as well as in income and payroll taxes. The analysis emphasizes that possible 'wage push' effects of tax-hikes depend on the unions' objectives and the firms' technology, but also on how tax revenues are spent. A following section deals with the implications of government subsidies to unemployment insurance, in particular when this insurance system is run by trade unions (as it is in Sweden and some other countries). Some conventional predictions from the literature no longer hold when unions can pursue insurance policies in addition to wage-setting. Finally, the prospects for achieving employment increases through work-sharing are considered. A crucial issue here is how the unions' wage demands are affected by shorter working time, and this depends in part on how working time is determined before a work-sharing policy is introduced.

Theoretical ambiguities are certainly not absent in this field, as in so many other kinds of model; specific results typically require specific assumptions about the unions' preferences or the firms' technology. This also underlines the importance of empirical work; strong assertions about policy effects are unlikely to be theoretically robust.

1.2. On the Labour Demand Curve

Consider a union organizing a given number of workers. The union may be firm-specific, industry-specific, or possibly economy-wide, and it faces one or several employers in negotiations to determine the terms of the contract. What is the nature of the bargaining outcome in such a case? One hypothesis assumes that employers are granted exclusive influence over the level of employment, even if they are weak—or even absent—in the wage negotiations. Under this assumption, profit maximization implies that employment is chosen so as to equalize the negotiated wage with the marginal revenue product of labour. The class of bargaining model where firms are on their neo-classical labour demand schedules will be

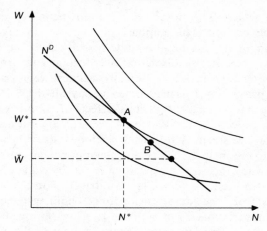

Fig. 1.1. The monopoly union

referred to as 'LD models' in this essay.

The most widely used LD model presumes that the union has complete power to enforce its wage demands in the wage negotiations. This *monopoly union* model thus characterizes wage negotiations in a highly simplified and obviously not very realistic way; the union simply calls out its desired wage and employers respond passively by setting employment. The model has already been discussed by Dunlop (1944) and Fellner (1947), and later in detail by Cartter (1959). Fig. 1.1 provides an illustration.

The union faces a binding wage–employment constraint, given by the labour demand schedule (N^D) derived from firms' profit-maximizing behaviour. The union's objective function is given by

$$\Lambda = \Lambda (w, N; X) \tag{1}$$

where w is the wage-rate, N is employment, and X is a vector of other variables that may affect union welfare. This objective function may be taken to represent the welfare of union members, but it may also be interpreted as an objective function for the 'union leader'. The function is increasing in both the wage-rate and the employment level, and union indifference curves be illustrated as in Fig. 1.1. The monopoly union's optimal wage-rate is then given by a tangency between the labour demand curve and an indifference curve, such as point A in the figure.

In case the union objective function is taken to be 'individualistic', the utilitarian form has often been applied. The union is then concerned with the sum of the members' utility levels, i.e.

$$\Lambda(\cdot) = NU(w) + (M - N)U(\bar{w}) \tag{2}$$

where $U(\cdot)$ is the individual worker's concave utility function, M is the (exogenous) number of union members, and $\bar{w}$ is the alternative wage, possibly equivalent to unemployment benefits. This objective function nests two other popular representations of union goals. One special case is maximization of the union's 'rent', the surplus on top of income available elsewhere, i.e. $R = N(w - \bar{w})$. This maximand, utilized for example by De Menil (1971), follows from (2) when the worker's utility function is linear in income. Income maximization is clearly equivalent to maximization of rents when the size of membership is exogenous.

Wage-bill maximization is equivalent to rent maximization when the alternative wage is zero. The wage-bill maximand is usually attributed to Dunlop (1944), but its origins can be traced further back: it is, for example, developed in some detail already in a 1917 dissertation by the Swedish economist Gösta Bagge. Note also that the utilitarian objective function translates into an expected utility maximand if both terms on the right-hand side of (2) are divided by M. If employment is offered by random draw, N/M represents the individual worker's probability of employment, and $(M - N)/M$ is the probability of being unemployed (or employed elsewhere). Maximization of the sum of the members' utilities is equivalent to maximization of the individual member's expected utility when the size of membership is exogenous.

The monopoly union model is open to a number of objections. One remarkable feature is the total absence of active employers in the wage negotiations. Real-world wage-bargaining appears to be very different from a situation in which the union simply calls out its desired wage, to which employers passively respond by setting employment at the appropriate level, given the wage preferred by the union. Real-world negotiations seem to involve offers and counter-offers—possibly conflicts—between unions and employers.

How then should the employers' side be introduced in the wage negotiations? The 'right-to-manage' model of Nickell and Andrews (1983) has been widely used. The model assumes that firms set employment unilaterally, after the wage negotiations have been settled. A generalized Nash bargaining solution is invoked, and the wage-rate is regarded as the outcome of a maximization of a 'Nash product' given by

$$\Omega(w) = [\Lambda(\cdot) - \Lambda_0]^\beta [\Pi(w) - \Pi_0]^{1-\beta} \qquad (3)$$

where $\Lambda(\cdot)$ is the union's utility of an agreement and Λ_0 is its 'fall back utility' or threat point, the value of opportunities available to union members in case an agreement is not reached with the employer; Λ_0 will typically depend on the level of unemployment benefits, but may also capture wages and job-finding probabilities outside the current firm or sector. Analogously, Π is firms' profit of an agreement, whereas Π_0 is firms' profits if an agreement is not reached in the negotiations; firms may for example be able to hire non-unionized workers at some cost, or they may have to bear some fixed costs even if no output is produced. This particular formulation assumes that employers are risk-neutral, which of course need not necessarily be the case.

The coefficient β in (3) captures 'the degree of union power'. The Nash solution coincides with the monopoly outcome if $\beta = 1$; the Nash bargain then maximizes $\Omega(w) = \Lambda(\cdot) - \Lambda_0$, which is equivalent to maximization of $\Lambda(\cdot)$ if Λ_0 is exogenous to the problem. The other extreme corresponds to monopsony; if $\beta = 0$ the employer could force the union to accept its fall back utility, i.e. Λ_0.

The right-to-manage model has its theoretical origins in Nash's axiomatic approach to bargaining (Nash, 1950 and 1953). The Nash solution is, however, silent about the details of the bargaining *process*, the sequence of offers and counter-offers that may lead to an agreement. But recent work on strategic-bargaining models has put the Nash solution on a more solid theoretical ground. Binmore *et al.* (1986) consider two models where the incentive to reach an agreement differ. The 'impatience model' involves incentives to agree because of time preferences. The 'exogenous-risk model' considers the possibility that the bargaining process may terminate without an agreement. Both models yield the Nash solution in the limiting case when the length of a single bargaining period approaches zero.

The power weights β and $1 - \beta$ have different interpretations in the two strategic-bargaining models. In the impatience model, β would capture the union's time preference relative to the firm's; the more impatient a player, the weaker it is. In the exogenous-risk model, the weights capture the parties' beliefs about the probability of a breakdown of the game; the higher the union's estimate of a breakdown, the lower its bargaining power.

The two strategic models suggest different interpretations of threat points. If the consequence of not reaching an immediate agreement is a delay of the outcome, the union's alternative wage includes income sources during a wage dispute. If the consequence is a breakdown of the game, the threat point captures options available to workers if they all leave the firm. The practical implications of these different interpretations will depend on particular institutional characteristics, including rules for unemployment insurance payments. In either case, the degree of labour market slack is likely to influence the union's threat point.

Fig. 1.1 illustrates a possible Nash outcome as point B on the labour demand curve. A powerless union would have to accept a wage equal to expected outside income opportunities, $\bar{w}$, possibly equivalent to unemployment benefits. As an example, consider the case where union members are risk-neutral and the union therefore cares about its members' incomes

$$\Lambda(\cdot) = Nw + (M - N)\bar{w}. \tag{4}$$

Assume also that $\Lambda_0 = M\bar{w}$, and that firms' fall back profits are zero. $\Pi(w)$ in (3) defines a maximum profit function, i.e.

$$\Pi(w) = \max_N [Q(N) - wN] \tag{5}$$

reflecting that firms are free to adjust employment unilaterally. A rise in the wage thus reduces profits as given by $\Pi_w = -N$. The first-order condition then takes the form

$$\psi(w) = \frac{\beta\Pi}{R} \frac{\partial R}{\partial w} - (1 - \beta)N = 0 \tag{6}$$

where $R = \Lambda(\cdot) - \Lambda_0$ is the union's rent, the surplus on top of income available elsewhere. We have

$$\frac{\partial R}{\partial w} = N + (w - \bar{w})N_w. \tag{7}$$

Note that the union's rent is increasing in the wage at the Nash optimum, simply reflecting the fact that union power is incomplete. The first term in (7) captures the marginal revenue to the union of a wage increase, whereas the second term reflects the marginal cost of a rise in the wage; this marginal cost is given as the difference between the negotiated wage and the expected outside wage, multiplied by the slope of the labour demand schedule.

Suppose, for simplicity, that the labour demand curve exhibits a constant elasticity with respect to the wage-rate, i.e. that the production function is Cobb–Douglas. Define this elasticity as $\epsilon = -\, wN_w/N$ and note that the ratio between the wage-bill and profits is constant in the Cobb–Douglas case, i.e. $wN/\Pi = \epsilon - 1$. The first-order condition then yields an explicit expression for the Nash wage as

$$w = [1 + \beta/(\epsilon - 1)]\bar{w} \tag{8}$$

where the monopoly wage is implied when $\beta = 1$. The 'mark-up' on the outside wage is increasing in the degree of union power and decreasing in the elasticity of labour demand.

1.3. On the Contract Curve

LD models do not produce Pareto-efficient outcomes, something that most economists find discomforting. This point is easily demonstrated by noting that the slope of a firm's iso-profit curve in the wage–employment plane is given by

$$\frac{\partial w}{\partial N} = \frac{\partial Q/\partial N - w}{N}. \tag{9}$$

The iso-profit curve is upward-sloping to the left of the labour demand curve, reaches a maximum at $\partial Q/\partial N = w$, and is downward-sloping to the right of the labour demand schedule (Fig. 1.2).

Consider the monopoly union solution at A in Fig. 1.2, corresponding to the profit-level Π_0. Clearly, there are Pareto-superior wage–employment combinations available. Point E_0 is an outcome that raises union welfare without any reduction in profits, and E_1 increases profits relative to A without reducing union welfare. Tangency points between union indifference curves and firms' iso-profit contours trace out the contract curve, characterized by the condition

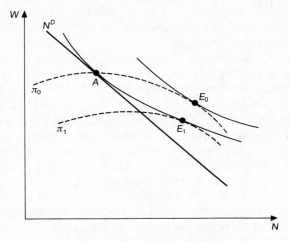

Fig. 1.2.   Efficient bargaining

$$-\frac{\partial\Lambda/\partial N}{\partial\Lambda/\partial w} = \frac{\partial Q/\partial N - w}{N} \tag{10}$$

where the left-hand side is the slope of the union's indifference curve and the right-hand side is the slope of the iso-profit function. Efficiency thus requires a wage above the firm's marginal revenue product, and employment is chosen to the right of the neo-classical labour demand schedule. The contract curve will be vertical for a risk-neutral union, but will exhibit a positive slope if the union is risk-averse. The contract curve model has been discussed in some detail in the well-known paper by McDonald and Solow (1981), but its origin can be traced back at least to Leontief (1946) and Fellner (1947).

Efficient bargains can be struck if the union and the employer bargain over both wages and employment. To arrive at determinate points on the contract curve, some specific sharing rules must be invoked. Suppose, for example, that the wage-rate *and* the employment level are chosen so as to maximize a generalized Nash bargain, such as given by expression (3) above. It is straightforward to show that a Nash bargain satisfies

$$\Lambda - \Lambda_0 = \beta(\Lambda - \Lambda_0 + \Pi - \Pi_0). \tag{11}$$

The degree of union power, captured by the parameter β, corresponds to the share of labour in the total surplus created by the wage–employment bargain.

A standard objection against the efficient-bargaining solution appeals to realism and notes that employers appear to exercise substantial discretion over employment decisions. However, the empirical evidence on efficient bargaining is limited and somewhat mixed (see Ch. 2 Sect. 3 below). Empirical objections aside, there are also incentive problems involved: the firm has always an incentive to renege *ex post* on the negotiated wage–employment contract. Consider again Fig. 1.2. The union clearly prefers outcome E_0 to outcome A. But the firm would always like to move back to the labour demand curve at any given negotiated wage–employment combination to the right of this curve. Efficient wage–employment contracts may therefore not be *enforceable* unless the union is sufficiently strong to force the employer to stick to the pre-committed employment level.[2]

There are, however, circumstances under which efficient bargains are on the labour demand curve. Fellner (1947) pointed out (p. 515) that 'when the indifference map of the union consists of horizontal lines . . . the outcome of the bargain will lie along the contract curve, even if the contract relates merely to the wage rate'. Oswald (1984 and 1985) has explored this possibility in detail, and also offered empirical tests (Carruth *et al.*, 1986). The basic argument is sketched by means of Fig. 1.3. Suppose that lay-offs are made according to seniority, i.e. 'last in—first out', and that the union wage is determined by the member with median seniority (the 'median voter'). N_s is the median voter's seniority position; the median voter is always employed when employment is above N_s, but becomes unemployed when employment falls below N_s. Union indifference curves become horizontal lines to the right of N_s ($I_0 < I_1 < I_2$), because the median worker is always employed and he is then only concerned with his wage.

---

[2] Profit-sharing may be one way of obtaining efficient bargaining outcomes even if employment decisions rest with the employers. This requires that the union and the firm bargain over both wages and the share of profits that is transferred to workers. See Pohjola (1987). Strand (1986) considers a repeated game where the monopoly solution and the efficient-bargaining solution are obtained as special cases. Cf. also Manning (1987), who develops the idea of sequential bargaining. In Manning's model there is first a bargain about the wage (or employment), and then a bargain about employment (or the wage).

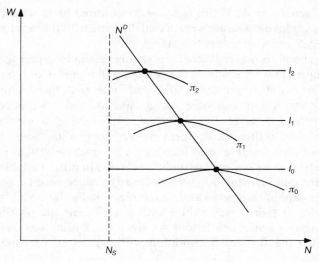

Fig. 1.3.   The seniority model

Fig. 1.3 also includes three iso-profit contours, Π_0, Π_1, and Π_2 (with $\Pi_0 < \Pi_1 < \Pi_2$). The latter have turning-points when crossing the labour demand curve, so tangency points between iso-profit contours and union indifference curves are in fact on the labour demand curve. Efficient bargains are thus achieved even if employment decisions rest with the employers. The wage–employment outcome depends on the particular bargaining solution. One may, for example, assume that profits are driven to zero, or that rents are shared according to a Nash rule.

This 'flat indifference curve model' may appear extreme in its characterization of union objectives. If, for example, lay-offs occur by plant closures, the median worker in the plant will not be unaffected by employment changes.

1.4. Monopoly Unionism versus Nash Bargaining

As noted above, the monopoly union outcome can be seen as a special case of a generalized Nash bargaining solution. Does the comparative statics predictions from the special case also carry over to the general case? If this is so, as conjectured by Oswald (1985), one might invoke Occam's razor and dispense with the more general model as one with excess baggage.

In general, however, there is no strong reason to expect the same qualitative predictions from the two types of model. Consider again the first-order condition in (6), and note that this include the monopoly union outcome as a special case. Suppose that employment is given by $N = N(w, Z)$, where Z is a vector of variables affecting employment as well as profits. Some labour demand shift variables may increase employment as well as profits; the output price is a case in point. Increases in other variables may increase employment but simultaneously reduce profits; the user cost of capital may serve as an example. Finally, increases in, say, the price of energy may reduce both employment and profits. The comparative statics predictions are given in the usual way by differentiating the first-order condition with respect to parameters of interest:

$$\frac{\partial \psi}{\partial Z} = \frac{\beta \Pi}{R} \frac{\partial^2 R}{\partial w \partial Z} + \frac{\beta \partial R}{\partial w} \frac{\partial (\Pi/R)}{\partial Z} - (1 - \beta) \frac{\partial N}{\partial Z}. \qquad (12)$$

It is clear that only the first term matters in the monopoly union case; the wage response is then given by how a change in an exogenous variable affects the union's marginal costs and benefits of a wage increase. In a Nash bargain case, on the other hand, the wage outcome is also affected by how the ratio between profits and rents is changed (the second term), and by how employment is influenced at a given wage (the third term). (Recall that $\Pi_w = -N$; the employment level captures the marginal cost to the *firm* of a wage-hike.)

Consider, as an example, a rise in the output price. Under plausible assumptions, this raises the (net) marginal benefit to the union of a wage increase, so the first term in (12) is positive. But the last term in (12) is negative, tending to offset the wage-increasing effect; the marginal cost to the firm of a wage-hike is increased by a rise in the output price. Profits are certainly raised by higher output prices, but so are rents when employment is increased at a given wage; the effect on the ratio between profits and rents is indeterminate. In general, variables that influence wages via the firms' labour demand schedule have ambiguous wage effects without the imposition of additional structure on technology and preferences.

On the one hand, a favourable demand shift, such as a rise in the output price, typically raises the marginal benefit to the union of a wage increase. However, a rise in employment induced by a higher output price also gives the firm stronger incentives to save on labour costs, and this tends to lower wages.

The wage response to a labour demand shift is determined solely by how the ratio between profits and rents changes in the special case when the wage elasticity of labour demand is constant. This follows directly from inspection of the first-order condition, which can be written as

$$\psi = \beta \frac{\Pi}{R} [\{U(\bar{w}) - U(w)\}\epsilon + wU'(w)]$$
$$- (1 - \beta)w = 0 \qquad (13)$$

in the utilitarian case. Equation (13) also confirms the well-known result that iso-elastic labour demand shifts have *no* effect on the utilitarian monopoly union's optimal wage-rate; the first-order condition for the monopoly case is then given by the expression within brackets, and the level of employment does not belong to this expression. (However, this wage rigidity result for the utilitarian case does not hold for more general objective functions.)

Consider now a change in a variable that influences the expected outside wage, $\bar{w}$. The wage response is given by the sign of

$$\frac{\partial \psi}{\partial \bar{w}} = \frac{\beta \Pi}{R} \frac{\partial^2 R}{\partial w \partial \bar{w}} + \frac{\beta \partial R}{\partial w} \frac{\partial (\Pi/R)}{\partial \bar{w}} \qquad (14)$$

The first term captures the monopoly union effect, and this is typically positive; higher unemployment benefits, for example, normally raise the marginal cost to the union of a wage increase, and this tends to push up wages. But higher benefits also reduce the union's rent, and the ratio between profits and rents is therefore increased; the wage-increasing effect is thus reinforced by a positive second term, capturing that higher benefits raise the union's threat point and therefore make the union less interested in reaching an agreement.

In conclusion, the Occam's razor argument for using monopoly union models, rather than Nash bargaining solutions, is valid when focusing on variables that influence wages via the union's outside income opportunities. However, there are no particular reasons to expect the same qualitative predictions from the two models when there are changes on the demand side. Unambiguous predictions from the monopoly union model will in general require specific assumptions about the labour demand function and the union's objective function; predictions from Nash bargaining models typically require introduction of additional restrictions.

1.5. Union Wage Responses to Changes in Prices and Taxes

It is frequently asserted that wages are pushed up by higher income taxes. After all, don't unions care about workers' real take-home pay? They almost certainly do, but they may also be concerned with members' employment opportunities. If that is the case, the effects of higher income taxes become less obvious. The discussion below takes at a look at the mechanisms involved and notes some equivalences between changes in taxes and changes in prices.

Our discussion of wage responses to price- and tax-changes is divided into four parts. The first part discusses the relationships between wage demands and changes in output and consumer prices, the second deals with income taxes, and the third part deals with payroll taxes. The fourth part recognizes that taxes also involve government spending; taxes may for example be returned to workers as transfers. Tax-transfer packages may have very different effects from those of taxes without associated income subsidies.

1.5.1. Wage Responses to Price Changes

Consider the standard case where the utilitarian union cares about employment and the utility of workers' real-wages and real alternative income, the latter taken as unemployment benefits (B) for simplicity. The objective function is

$$\Lambda(\cdot) = NU(w/p) + (M - N)V(B/p) \qquad (15)$$

where p is the consumer price, and $V(\cdot)$ is the utility function pertaining to unemployment. The first-order condition is

$$\Lambda_w = (U - V)N_w + \frac{N}{P} U'(\cdot) = 0 \qquad (16)$$

which can be rewritten as

$$\Lambda_w = [V(B/p) - U(w/p)]\epsilon + \frac{w}{P} U'(w/p) = 0 \qquad (17)$$

where $\epsilon = -wN_w/N$ is the elasticity of labour demand with respect to the wage. The first term of (17) captures the marginal cost to the union of a wage-hike, and the second term captures the marginal benefit.

Suppose that the labour demand elasticity is constant (as it would be if the production function were Cobb–Douglas). It is then immediately obvious from (17) that the nominal wage is linearly homogeneous in consumer prices and the benefit level; equiproportional increases in p and B would raise w in the same proportion, so *real* wages would remain unchanged. (Linear homogeneity can be verified by multiplying p, B, and w by a scalar and noting that the equality is preserved.)

As long as the nominal benefit level is kept fixed, a rise in the consumer price is accompanied by a less than proportional increase in the wage. The union is willing to accept some real-wage reduction as an adjustment to the fall in real unemployment pay. Suppose now that the labour demand elasticity is variable, and let q denote firms' output price. It is real-product wages that matter for employment, and we write the labour demand elasticity as $\epsilon = \epsilon(w/q)$. It then follows that the nominal wage is linearly homogeneous in the consumer price, the benefit level, and the output price. Equiproportional increases in output and consumer prices, at a given nominal benefit level, would then induce the union to accept some real-wage reduction. This has of course nothing to do with 'money illusion' on part of the union.

1.5.2 Wage Responses to Changes in Income Taxes

Some predictions from the section above show up immediately when we turn to wage responses to tax-changes. Consider the simplest case with a proportional income tax, and let t denote the constant marginal and average tax-rate. The relevant objective function becomes

$$\Lambda(\cdot) = NU[w(1 - t)/p] + (M - N)V[B(1 - t)/p]. \qquad (18)$$

Let T_a denote the income tax mark-up on the average net wage, i.e. $T_a \equiv 1/(1 - t)$. Following the earlier exposition, it should be clear that the nominal wage is linearly homogeneous in the benefit level, the output price, and the 'tax–price index' (pT_a). A rise in the tax-rate thus raises the wage to the extent that a rise in the consumer price raises the wage. In general, a 'wage-push' response to higher taxes should be expected, but exceptions are easy to find. For example, suppose that the utility functions are state-independent with constant relative degree of risk aversion (δ), i.e.

$$U(\cdot) = \frac{w(1 - t)^{1 - \delta}}{1 - \delta} \text{ and } V(\cdot) = \frac{B(1 - t)^{1 - \delta}}{1 - \delta}$$

The optimal union wage is then given as

$$w = B \left[\frac{\epsilon}{\epsilon - (1 - \delta)} \right]^{\frac{1}{1 - \delta}} \tag{19}$$

so increases in income taxes or consumer prices have *no* effect on the nominal wage outcome. The wage is linearly homogeneous in B and q, and if ϵ is constant there will also be a constant wage-benefit mark-up determined by the parameters ϵ and δ. (Incidentally, utility functions with constant degree of risk aversion have been quite popular in empirical work on union behaviour.)

Real-world progressive tax systems are often difficult to characterize by a few parameters. However, it may be useful to consider the different effects in operation when the parameters of a linear progressive tax are changed. Suppose that the objective function takes the form

$$\Lambda(\cdot) = NU(w - T_1) + (M - N)V(B - T_2) \tag{20}$$

where the consumer price has been normalized to unity, and T_1 and T_2 are linear tax functions: $T_1 = a + t_m w$, and $T_2 = a + t_m B$. The constant marginal tax-rate is denoted by t_m, and the tax system is progressive if $a < 0$ (in the sense that the average tax-rate decreases with income). One not very realistic assumption underlying (20) is that some union members are employed during the whole 'contract period', whereas other members are unemployed during the same period.

The union's desired wage is given by the first-order condition:

$$\frac{\partial \Lambda}{\partial w} = (U - V)N_w + (1 - t_m)NU' = 0. \tag{21}$$

The first term captures the marginal cost to the union of a wage increase, and the last term captures the marginal benefit from raising the wage. The parameters of the tax system influence both the marginal cost and the marginal benefit of wage increases, and this produces effects working in opposite directions.

Consider a situation where unemployment benefits are taxed as ordinary wage income. The wage effect of a rise in the marginal tax-rate then takes the sign of

$$\frac{\partial \Lambda_w}{\partial t_m} = (BV' - wU') \frac{\partial N}{\partial w} - NU' - (1 - t_m)wNU''. \quad (22)$$

The first term is in general ambiguous in sign, but would be positive if benefits were excluded from taxation. On the one hand, a higher marginal tax reduces the marginal cost of a wage increase by reducing net income during employment; on the other hand, a higher tax also reduces net income during unemployment, and it is a priori unclear how the utility difference between workers in employment and unemployment is affected.

The second term in (22) is negative, reflecting that a higher marginal tax reduces the gain to the union of further wage increases; wage-hikes have become more expensive at the margin, and this shifts the union's desired wage–employment trade-off in favour of higher employment. There is, however, also an effect that tends to raise the marginal benefit of a wage increase, and this is captured by the third term. By the concavity of the utility function, wage increases are valued more at lower incomes, and the higher tax produces exactly this effect; net income during employment falls and this involves incentives to push for higher wages.

Higher marginal tax-rates thus have ambiguous wage effects. Clear predictions are obtained in some special cases. For example, it turns out that a rise in the marginal tax-rate has *no* effect on a *risk-neutral* union's desired wage. However, if benefits were excluded from taxation, a higher marginal tax would increase a risk-neutral union's optimal wage by reducing the value of employment relative to the value of unemployment.

Consider now a shift of the intercept of the tax function, holding constant the marginal tax-rate:

$$\frac{\partial \Lambda_w}{\partial a} = (V' - U')N_w - (1 - t_m)NU''. \quad (23)$$

The last term is positive by the concavity of the utility function; the marginal benefit of a wage increase is raised when net income during employment is lowered. The first term is negative under the plausible assumption that an increase in net income is valued more by an unemployed worker than by an employed one. Again, the net effect is ambiguous without additional restrictions on preferences or the elasticity of the labour demand function.[3]

In conclusion, it should be emphasized that specific predictions about union wage responses to tax-changes require specific assumptions about union objective functions and/or tax functions. A summary statistic, such as the average tax-rate, is unlikely to capture all information of relevance when the tax system is progressive.

1.5.3. Wage Responses to Changes in Payroll Taxes

The profit-maximizing firm's employment decision is determined by the real product-wage, adjusted for wage taxes levied on employers, i.e. $N = N[w(1 + s)/q]$, where s is the payroll tax-rate and q is the output price. A rise in the payroll tax-rate is equivalent to a reduction in the output price. The labour demand schedule shifts inward, as illustrated in Fig. 1.4. How do union wage demands adjust to a payroll tax-increase? The initial position is at A, and A_1, A_2, and A_3 represent three conceivable reactions to an adverse shift in labour demand. Point A_1 corresponds to complete nominal wage rigidity; employment takes the whole burden of adjustment. Point A_3 is the other extreme, involving complete nominal wage flexibility and no change in employment; in the terminology of the tax incidence literature, the tax is completely shifted back on wages. Point A_2 in Fig. 1.4 shows an intermediate case with some, albeit incomplete, wage adjustment; labour costs increase and employment is reduced.

Consider a utilitarian union facing a labour demand constraint $N = N[w(1 + s)]$, where the output price is normalized to unity and the capital stock is fixed. Recall the first-order condition (17) above, with the consumer price normalized to unity, and suppose that technology is of the CES variety with constant returns to scale and $\epsilon = \sigma/S^x$, where σ is the elasticity of substitution between

---

[3] The comparative statics exercises above refer to a utilitarian union facing a linear tax schedule. Various other objective and tax functions are conceivable, and Hersoug (1984) has worked out the comparative statics results for a number of other cases.

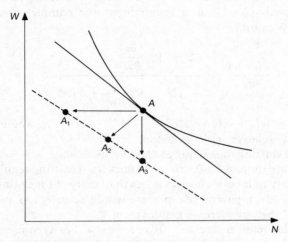

Fig. 1.4. Wage responses to tax changes

labour and capital and S^{κ} is the share of capital in value added. We have already noted that shifts of the labour demand function, induced, for example, by a payroll tax increase, has *no* effect on the preferred wage when the elasticity of labour demand is constant, i.e. when the production function is Cobb–Douglas (with $\epsilon = 1/S^{\kappa}$). The 'wage preference path' in Fig. 1.4 is then horizontal; labour costs will increase by the full amount of the tax and only employment is adjusted downwards.

In general, the wage response to a rise in the payroll tax is given by

$$\frac{\partial w}{\partial s} = \frac{(U - V)}{\Lambda_{ww}} \frac{\partial \epsilon}{\partial s} \tag{24}$$

where the second-order condition ($\Lambda_{ww} < 0$) is fulfilled by assumption. Noting that $\epsilon = \sigma/S^{\kappa}$, with $\partial S^{\kappa}/\partial w \gtrless 0$ as $\sigma \gtrless 1$, we have $\partial \epsilon/\partial s \gtrless 0$ as $\sigma \lessgtr 1$, i.e.

$$\frac{\partial w}{\partial s} \gtrless 0 \text{ as } \sigma \gtrless 1. \tag{25}$$

The desired wage is reduced (increased) when the payroll tax raises (lowers) the elasticity of labour demand at the initial wage; this corresponds to an elasticity of substitution less than (greater than) unity.

Let $w_c \equiv w(1 + s)$ denote the labour cost. Evaluating at $s = 0$ we have $\partial lnw/\partial s = -1$ as a requirement for complete backward shifting. We obtain

$$\frac{\partial(ln\ w)}{\partial s} = \frac{(U - V)\dfrac{\partial\epsilon}{\partial w_c}}{-(U - V)\dfrac{\partial\epsilon}{\partial w_c} + H(\cdot)}$$

where $H = wU'' - (\epsilon - 1)U' = -U'\{\delta + \epsilon - 1\}$, where δ is the degree of relative risk aversion, $\delta = -wU''/U'$. Complete backward shifting thus requires $H = 0$, involving $\delta + \epsilon = 1$. Since risk aversion implies $\delta > 0$, complete backward shifting requires that the elasticity of labour demand is less than unity at the optimum. (If $\delta + \epsilon < 1$ holds, a payroll tax increase would actually *reduce* labour costs, and thereby increase employment.)

In the risk-neutral case ($\delta = 0$) we have $\epsilon = 1$ as a requirement for complete backward shifting. But that is only possible in the absence of unemployment benefits in union objectives, i.e. when the union maximizes the wage-bill. Inspection of the first-order condition for the rent-maximizing union reveals that $\epsilon = 1/(1 - r)$ must hold, where $r \equiv B/w$ is the replacement ratio. Clearly, $\epsilon = 1$ requires $B = 0$.

The examples illustrate how the wage responses depend on objective functions as well as firms' technology. A combination of two popular functions—the utilitarian-objective function and the Cobb–Douglas production function—yields strong predictions about nominal wage rigidity. However, the empirical literature has suggested that the elasticity of substitution between labour and capital lies somewhere in the range between one-half and unity, and this suggests that a utilitarian union will respond to payroll tax increases by accepting some wage reduction. Available estimates of union (members'?) relative risk aversion are few (see ch. 2 below). However, they imply a location of δ in the range between 0.8 and 4; the presumption, therefore, is that higher payroll taxes will raise labour costs and reduce employment to the extent that wages are set by a utilitarian union.

1.5.4. Taxes and Transfers

The taxes considered above involved no benefits for union members. However, the tax proceeds may to some extent be returned to union members in one way or another. A tax used to finance transfers is the obvious example. In the following we deal with a wage tax levied on employers, where the tax proceeds are returned to employed workers; social insurance taxes used to finance pensions related to previous earnings have such features.

Let ω denote the income transfer financed by a tax (s) on wages. The aggregate budget restriction is then $\omega = sw$. A centralized all-encompassing union can obviously influence the transfer by its own wage policy. A 'small' union, on the other hand, regards the transfer as exogenous to its wage demands; it recognizes the existence of an economy-wide budget restriction but cannot through its own wage policy significantly influence the average wage in the economy.

Consider first the 'large' utilitarian union with the objective function

$$\Lambda = NU(w + sw) + (M - N)V(B) \qquad (27)$$

where the budget restriction $\omega = sw$ has been substituted into the utility function. Note that the wage cost, $w_c = w(1 + s)$, enters the utility function in this case. But employment and wage costs are related through the labour demand function, so we may write $w_c = \psi(N)$, and substitue $\psi(N)$ into the union's objective function. The payroll tax-rate then drops out, and will thus not affect the *employment* level preferred by the union. This is equivalent to 'complete backward shifting'; the wage is reduced by the full amount of the tax. This effect does not depend on firms' technology; the elasticity of labour demand with respect to the wage may be constant, or it may increase or decrease with changes in labour costs. This outcome is caused by the union's substitution of 'transfer income' for wage income. A higher payroll tax raises employers' contributions to the transfer system. All revenues from payroll taxes are transferred to union members, and the chosen wage influences the magnitude of this transfer. The union adjusts its wage so as to equalize the net (marginal) gain from higher employer contributions with the loss in labour income.

Let us now turn to an economy with many 'small' wage-setting unions which all take the transfer as exogenous. The ith union maximizes

$$\Lambda_i = N_iU_i(w_i + \omega) + (M_i - N_i)V(B) \qquad (28)$$

treating ω as given. The first-order condition is the usual expression

$$\Lambda_{w_i} = (V - U_i)\epsilon_i + w_iU'(w_i) = 0 \qquad (29)$$

and the transfer—disregarding its financing—reduces the optimal wage:

$$\frac{\partial \Lambda_w}{\partial \omega} = - \epsilon_i U_i' + w_i U_i'' < 0. \tag{30}$$

The transfer increases the utility difference between employment and unemployment, thereby increasing the marginal cost of a rise in the wage (the first term in (30)). Second, a higher transfer reduces the marginal utility of income by the concavity of the utility function; this reduces the marginal utility of higher wages, as reflected in the second term of (30).

How then is the optimal wage affected by a rise in the payroll tax used to finance the income transfer? In so far as the unions face identical labour demand conditions, they will end up with the same wage, $w_i = w$. *Ex post* we then have $\omega = sw$, where w now refers to the average wage. Substituting into the first-order condition yields

$$\Lambda_w = \{V - U(w + sw)\}\epsilon + wU'(w + sw) = 0. \tag{31}$$

From (31) we can derive

$$\frac{\partial \ell n\ w}{\partial s} = - \frac{A}{A + U'} \tag{32}$$

where $A = (V - U)(\partial \epsilon / \partial s) - \epsilon w U' + w^2 U'' < 0$, (assuming $\partial \epsilon / \partial s \geqslant 0$). We thus have $\partial \ell n w / \partial s < -1$; the wage falls by *more* than the full amount of the tax. Labour costs are thereby reduced and employment increases. This wage tax–income subsidy package has effects analogous to the TIP schemes proposed by Richard Layard (1982) and others. The wage tax raises the marginal cost of raising the wage, and the income subsidy raises the utility difference between employment and unemployment.

In conclusion, we have demonstrated that higher payroll taxes have *favourable* employment consequences if the proceeds are returned to employed union members. Recognizing that employment demand is determined, among other things, by the real-product wage, $N = N[w(1 + s)/q]$, it might be tempting to infer that a rise in the tax factor should have the same effect as a fall in the output price; this conclusion, however, overlooks that taxes may be associated with benefits for union members.

1.6. Unemployment Insurance and Union Wage Demands

In models of union wage-setting, it is typically assumed that unemployed union members receive benefits provided by the Government. This assumption is not particularly attractive when modelling economies where the unemployment insurance (UI) system is run by the trade unions. In Sweden and some other countries, the system is organized through a number of certified UI funds with voluntary membership and close ties to the trade unions. For most purposes the UI fund may be regarded as an integral part of a trade union. In fact, unemployment compensation in Sweden was initiated by trade unions. The first scheme was introduced by the typographers' union in the 1890s, and a growing number of union-affiliated UI funds were established during the following decades. Government subsidies to the UI system became available in the 1930s.

The current Swedish UI system is financed primarily through government subsidies, but in part also by premiums paid by the UI funds' members. The Government's share of total expenditures on unemployment benefits has shown a marked trend increase, from around 50–60 per cent in the early 1950s to around 90 per cent in the early 1980s. The Government subsidies are financed through general income taxes as well as general and uniform payroll taxes levied on employers.

The analysis below focuses on union wage responses to changes in unemployment benefits and government subsidies to the UI system. Some well-known predictions from standard theory no longer necessarily hold when the UI system is organized through the trade unions.[4]

Consider a single utilitarian union whose members have to finance some fraction of unemployment benefits paid out to members without jobs. The insurance premiums may differ between employed and unemployed members, and the union cares about (the utility value of) workers' real take-home pay, net of the premiums. The objective function then takes the form

$$\Lambda = NU(w - z_1) + (M - N)V(B - z_2) \tag{33}$$

---

[4] The analysis draws in part on Holmlund and Lundborg (1988).

where z_1 is the UI premium paid by an employed member and z_2 is the premium paid by the unemployed member. Expression (33) ignores income taxes, and the consumer price is normalized to unity; it will be assumed that the single union treats income-tax rates as exogenous to its wage choice.

Government subsidies to the UI system are approximated by a linear scheme

$$G = G_0 + G_1(M - N)B \quad 0 < G_1 < 1 \qquad (34)$$

where G_0 is a lump-sum grant and G_1 is the marginal subsidy rate, i.e. the marginal increase in government subsidies produced by a rise in benefits. Noting that total paid-out benefits are financed by government subsidies (G) as well as premiums, i.e.

$$(M - N)B = G + z_1N + z_2(M - N) \qquad (35)$$

we have the budget restriction for the UI fund as

$$(1 - G_1)(M - N)B - G_0 = z_1N + z_2(M - N). \qquad (36)$$

Since the UI fund is an integral part of the trade union, the union's wage demand must recognize the restriction implied by (36). B, G_0, and G_1 are regarded as parameters set by the Government, but premiums are determined by the union. There are several conceivable 'premium rules', in theory as well as in practice. In Sweden, unions in general differentiate premiums paid by employed and unemployed members. Unemployed workers typically paid no premiums during the 1950s, but the UI funds have gradually moved away from this practice. We consider first a 'flexible' premium system in which the union chooses z_1 and z_2 (as well as the wage-rate) so as to maximize the objective function. Next, we analyse 'rigid' premium rules, involving schemes where unemployed union members pay *no* UI premiums as well as schemes where employed and unemployed members pay the *same* premium.

One may ask why a union would ever consider a rigid premium rule; it seems obvious that flexibility is always to be preferred from the union members' point of view. There may, however, be reasons, outside the simple models dealt with here, for some degree of rigidity; examples are administrative costs, costs of changing premiums, and moral-hazard problems in job search.

1.6.1. Flexible Premium Rule

The union's problem is to choose the wage-rate (w) as well as premiums (z_1, z_2) so as to maximize (33), recognizing the labour demand constraint, $N(w)$, as well as the UI budget constraint (36). The Lagrangian for the problem is

$$L = \Lambda(z_1, z_2, w) + \lambda[G_0 + z_1 N + z_2 (M - N) \\ - (1 - G_1)(M - N)B] \tag{37}$$

where λ is the multiplier associated with the UI budget restriction. The first-order conditions are given by

$$z_1: \quad - NU'(\cdot) + \lambda N = 0 \tag{38a}$$

$$z_2: \quad - (M - N)V'(\cdot) + \lambda(M - N) = 0 \tag{38b}$$

$$\begin{aligned} w: \quad & (U - V)N_w + NU'(\cdot) \\ & + \lambda[z_1 - z_2 \\ & + (1 - G_1)B]N_w = 0 \end{aligned} \tag{38c}$$

$$\begin{aligned} \lambda: \quad & G_0 + z_1 N + z_2(M - N) \\ & - (1 - G_1)(M - N)B = 0. \end{aligned} \tag{38d}$$

From the first-order conditions we have $U'(\cdot) = V'(\cdot) = \lambda$, where λ is the value of a small increase in the lump-sum grant to the UI fund. The union equates the marginal utility of income when employed to the marginal utility of income when unemployed. This is an obvious implication of an optimal insurance policy. If the utility functions are state-independent, it is clear that we obtain equalization of *incomes* in the two states, i.e. $w - z_1 = B - z_2$.

The comparative statics predictions are obtained in the usual way by differentiation of the system. Consider first the wage response to a rise in G_0, the lump-sum grant to the UI fund. Straightforward calculations yield

$$\frac{\partial w}{\partial G_0} = \frac{1}{D_1} [(M - N)V''(N + L_{\lambda w})NU''] \tag{39}$$

where D_1 is the determinant of the system, negative by the second-order condition for maximum. The sign of (39) is thus determined by the sign of $(N + L_{\lambda w})$. Using (38a) we can rewrite (38c) as

$$(N + L_{\lambda w})U' = (V - U)N_w \tag{40}$$

so $(N + L_{\lambda w}) \geq 0$ as $U \geq V$. The union *reduces* the wage when offered an increase in the lump-sum grant to its UI fund as long as the interior solution involves a positive utility differential between employment and unemployment. This is referred to as the 'income effect'. Employment therefore increases, and premiums for both employed and unemployed members fall. If union members have linear utility functions, or if the functions are concave but state-independent, the optimal arrangement involves full utility equalization across employment and unemployment. A rise in G_0 has then *no* effect on the union's desired wage.

Consider now an increase in G_1, the marginal subsidy rate. A rise in G_1 implies that union members finance a lower fraction of increases in the amount of paid-out benefits. The wage response involves two terms, an income effect as well as a 'substitution effect':

$$\frac{\partial w}{\partial G_1} = \left(\frac{\partial w}{\partial G_1}\right)_c + (M - N)B \frac{\partial w}{\partial G_0} \gtreqless 0. \tag{41}$$

The first term captures the income-compensated wage effect. A rise in G_1 lowers the 'price' of wage increases; the union finances a lower fraction of increases in benefits associated with an employment-reducing rise in the wage. The union responds by raising the wage, provided that the lump-sum grant is adjusted so as to keep utility constant. A rise in G_1 also involves an income effect that tends to moderate wage demands; note that $\partial w/\partial G_0 < 0$ by earlier assumptions. The net effect on the desired wage is thus ambiguous.

Standard union models predict that a rise in unemployment benefits raises the optimal wage-rate. A higher benefit level reduces the utility difference between employment and unemployment, and this makes the union more inclined to push for higher wages. This implication does not unambiguously follow from a model in which the union can pursue an optimal insurance policy. The wage response to an increase in the benefit level can be derived as

$$\frac{\partial w}{\partial B} = G_1 \left[(1/B)\left(\frac{\partial w}{\partial G_1}\right)_c + (M - N) \frac{\partial w}{\partial G_0} \right] \tag{42}$$

The first term is positive and captures the reduced marginal cost of a wage increase. The second term is negative, capturing the income effect; a rise in benefits involves a positive income subsidy when

$G_1 > 0$. Comparing (41) and (42), it is obvious that the following 'symmetry property' holds:

$$\frac{\partial \ell n w}{\partial \ell n B} = \frac{\partial \ell n w}{\partial \ell n G_1} \tag{43}$$

The elasticity of the wage with respect to a rise in the benefit level is equal to the elasticity of the wage with respect to a rise in the marginal subsidy rate.

1.6.2. Rigid-Premium Rules

Suppose that employed workers pay a premium, z, whereas unemployed members do not pay any U I premiums at all. The first-order conditions are then given by:

$$z: \quad -NU'(\cdot) + \lambda N = 0 \tag{44a}$$

$$w: \quad (U - V)N_w + NU'(\cdot) + \lambda[z + (1 - G_1)B]N_w = 0 \tag{44b}$$

$$\lambda: \quad G_0 + zN - (1 - G_1)(M - N)B = 0. \tag{44c}$$

The wage response to a rise in the lump-sum grant takes the sign of

$$\frac{\partial w}{\partial G_0} = \frac{1}{D_2} NU''[\{z + (1 - G_1)B\}N_w + N] \tag{45}$$

where D_2 is the determinant of the system, positive by the second-order condition for maximum. It follows that the expression in the bracket of (45) is positive as $U > V$; we thus have $\partial w/\partial G_0 \leq 0$ as $U'' \leq 0$. The intuition is as follows. When the lump-sum grant is raised, employed members receive an income subsidy in the form of lower premiums. This raises the utility difference between employment and unemployment, and reduces the marginal utility of a wage increase (by the concavity of the utility function).

The wage response to a rise in the marginal subsidy rate is given by

$$\frac{\partial w}{\partial G_1} = \frac{1}{D_2} (-N^2 U' B N_w) + (M - N)B \frac{\partial w}{\partial G_0}. \tag{46}$$

The first term is positive, capturing the substitution effect; a rise in the marginal subsidy rate reduces the price of wage increases, and this effect tends to push up wages. There is also an offsetting income effect, however. The second term in (46) is negative, and the net effect is thus in general ambiguous. Evaluating at $G_0 \approx (1 - G_1) \approx 0$ we have

$$\text{sign } \frac{\partial w}{\partial G_1} = \text{sign}[(1 - u)\epsilon - u\delta] \qquad (47)$$

where δ is the degree of relative risk aversion and u is the unemployment rate. The sign is likely to be positive for 'realistic' values of ϵ, δ, and u. For example, suppose that $0.5 \leq \epsilon \leq 1$ and $1 \leq \delta \leq 4$. Values of ϵ and δ within these bounds always imply $\partial w/\partial G_1 > 0$ for $u < 0.11$. Note also that the smaller G_1 is, the smaller the income effect; this strengthens the case for our sign prediction.

An increase in the benefit level is likely to raise the union's desired wage. We have

$$\frac{\partial w}{\partial B} = - \frac{N_w}{D_2} [V' - (1 - G_1)U']N^2$$
$$- (1 - G)(M - N) \frac{\partial w}{\partial G_0}. \qquad (48)$$

The second term is positive, capturing that a rise in the benefit level reduces income when employed (as long as $G_1 < 1$). This (income) effect induces the union to push for a higher wage. The first term is also positive under reasonable assumptions; $V'(\cdot) \geq U'(\cdot)$ and $G_1 > 0$ are sufficient conditions.

Consider finally a premium rule according to which employed and unemployed union members pay *the same* U I premium. The first-order conditions are:

$$z: \quad -NU'(\cdot) - (M - N)V'(\cdot) + \lambda M = 0 \qquad (49a)$$

$$w: \quad (U - V)N_w + NU'(\cdot) + \lambda(1 - G_1)BN_w = 0 \qquad (49b)$$

$$\lambda: \quad G_0 + zM - (1 - G_1)(M - N)B = 0. \qquad (49c)$$

(49a) implies $\lambda = (1 - u)U'(\cdot) + uV'(\cdot)$, where $u = (M - N)/M$ is the unemployment rate; the value of a small grant to the U I fund equals the unemployment-weighted average of marginal utilities of employed and unemployed workers. Predictions concerning wage responses to changes in benefits and subsidy parameters are more difficult to obtain in this case. For example, a rise in the lump-sum grant will reduce premiums for both employed and unemployed workers, and the wage response is in general ambiguous. Similar ambiguities arise when considering the effects of a higher marginal subsidy rate or a higher benefit level, although plausible parameter values suggest that a positive wage response is the most likely outcome.

1.6.3. Other Implications

The models considered above add new comparative statics features to the standard model of a utilitarian union. Recall that iso-elastic labour demand shifts have no wage effects in the standard model. This implication need not carry over to a model where the union runs its own UI scheme. Consider for example the case where no UI premiums are paid by unemployed workers. The first-order conditions can be rewritten as

$$z: \quad U'(\cdot) + \lambda = 0 \tag{50a}$$

$$w: \quad \epsilon[V - U - \lambda(z + (1 - G_1)B] + wU'(\cdot) = 0 \tag{50b}$$

$$\lambda: \quad G_0 + zN - (1 - G_1)(M - N)B = 0. \tag{50c}$$

Suppose that a particular variable in the labour demand function, Z_i, say, shifts labour demand outwards at any given wage, $\partial N/\partial Z_i > 0$. It is clear from the first-order conditions that

$$\frac{\partial w}{\partial Z_i} = [z + (1 - G_1)B] \, \frac{\partial N}{\partial Z_i} * \frac{\partial w}{\partial G_0} \tag{51}$$

holds, so the wage response to an outward labour-demand shift takes in this case the same sign as the wage response to an increase in the lump-sum UI subsidy. In fact, a favourable demand shift leads to a *lower* wage-rate. This may seem implausible, but the intuition is not difficult. An outward labour demand shift reduces premiums paid by employed workers, and this has effects analogous to an income subsidy (or a lump-sum grant to the UI fund); the marginal utility of income falls and the utility difference between employment and unemployment increases. Other rigid premium rules may imply lower premiums for both employed and unemployed workers when there is a favourable demand shift, and this makes the wage outcome less predictable.

Consider changes in two demand shift variables, Z_i and Z_j. From (51) follows the equality

$$\frac{\partial w/\partial Z}{\partial w/\partial z_j} = \frac{\partial N/\partial Z_i}{\partial N/\partial Z_j} . \qquad (52)$$

The ratio between the wage effects equals the ratio between the employment effects; this property of the model does not depend on the particular premium rule. This reflects that the wage-rate is affected by the location of the labour demand schedule, irrespective of whether a particular shift involves an increase or a decrease in firms' profits. This implication does not follow from a wage-bargaining model of the Nash type, and it will be exploited in our empirical work.

The size of membership does not affect the union's desired wage in the standard utilitarian monopoly model. However, the number of members (M) does not drop out of the first-order conditions when the union runs its own UI scheme. Inspection of (50a–c) reveals that the wage response to an increase in membership has a sign that is opposite to the sign of the wage response to a higher lump-sum grant. In this case, therefore, we have $\partial w/\partial M > 0$. The reason is that a rise in membership implies higher unemployment at any given wage-rate, and this is bound to raise UI premiums for employed workers. For reasons already given, the optimal response is to raise the wage. Other institutional premium arrangements may have different implications; if for example each member pays the same premium, a rise in membership will reduce net income for both employed and unemployed workers.

In conclusion, we have explored union wage policies in a setting where the union runs its own UI scheme. Higher subsidies to the UI system may well reduce union wage demands, provided that the subsidies are lump-sum. On the other hand, subsidies tied to actual unemployment experience are likely to increase wage demands, although this effect cannot in general be established. The presumption is that higher benefits induce the union to push for higher wages, but this effect is also ambiguous in general. Some predictions from standard models need not carry over to the 'UI union' considered here. For example, iso-elastic shifts in labour demand, or changes in membership, will influence workers' net income via the UI budget restriction, and this will in general affect wage-setting.

1.7. Work-Hours, Wages, and Employment

A decade of rising European unemployment has increased the interest in work-sharing as a potential device to put more workers into jobs. With some notable exceptions, the economics profession seems to have been sceptical towards work-sharing proposals. The scepticism has different sources, one being Keynesian in spirit. This view argues that a reduction in work-hours, if accompanied by a fall in wage income, will reduce the demand for goods and thereby also reduce the demand for labour. Other critics of work-sharing have focused on wage responses. If employment is determined by real wages, as is conventionally assumed, then the question of wage responses to imposed changes in working time becomes crucial. If work-sharing leads unions to push for higher wages, the scope for employment increases is of course reduced. The analysis below focuses on this issue of wage responses to changes in work-hours. The topics addressed have been analysed by, among others, Hoel (1984) and Calmfors (1985). Our exposition spells out some known results, and adds some new.

Consider a labour demand schedule, $N = N(w, h)$, where the wage-rate as well as working time is exogenous to the firm. The employment effect of a change in work-hours, at a *given* wage-rate, is in general indeterminate, but it is instructive to consider some special cases. For example, if hours and workers are perfect substitutes in production, $Q = Q(Nh)$, and if the profit function is of the form

$$\Pi = Q(\cdot) - wNh \tag{53}$$

we have $(\partial \ell nN/\partial \ell nh) = -1$; a reduction in work-hours produces an increase in employment of the same relative magnitude. If the production function is of the type $Q = A N^{\alpha} h^{\beta}$, we have

$$\frac{\partial \ell nN}{\partial \ell nh} = -\frac{1 - \beta}{1 - \alpha} \tag{54}$$

which is less than unity (in absolute value) when $\alpha < \beta$, and greater than unity (in absolute value) when $\alpha > \beta$. Clearly, $(\partial \ell nN/\partial \ell nh) \geq 0$ as $\beta \geq 1$. We shall focus on the case where $(\partial \ell nN/\partial \ell nh) = -1$. It should be noted that perfect substitutability in production does not imply $(\partial \ell nN/\partial \ell nh) = -1$ when there are fixed per-worker costs. A reduction in work-hours will then raise labour costs per hour, which dampens the employment-increasing effect.

The wage response to an exogenous reduction in work-hours depends on how work-hours are initially determined. We may consider situations in which working time is determined by (i) the individual employed worker, (ii) the union, and (iii) the firm. Suppose first that the *employed worker* determines work hours in order to maximize

$$U = U(wh, h) \qquad (55)$$

where the utility function is increasing in earnings ($U_1 > 0$), and decreasing in work hours (i.e. increasing in leisure, $U_2 < 0$). The union recognizes that the employed worker chooses work-hours so as to maximize his utility. The first-order condition for the union's optimal wage takes the form

$$\Lambda_w = (U - V) \frac{dN}{dw} + NhU_1(\cdot) \qquad (56)$$

where we have recognized the fact that small changes in work-hours leave the employed worker's utility unaffected when hours are determined optimally by the worker; the union cares about the worker's indirect utility. Note also that $N = N(w, h\ (w))$ and therefore

$$\frac{dN}{dw} = \frac{dN}{\partial w} + \frac{\partial N}{\partial h} \frac{\partial h}{\partial w} . \qquad (57)$$

A wage increase reduces employment via the usual 'direct' effect, captured by the first term in (57). There is, however, also an 'indirect' effect, captured by the second term in (57). The latter effect is due to the employed worker's supply response to a wage increase; if the worker's supply curve is forward-sloping, the 'total' employment effect of a wage increase is greater than the partial effect. The higher the worker's supply elasticity, the higher the (total) elasticity of employment with respect to the wage (assuming $\partial N/\partial h < 0$). Expression (56) can be rewritten in elasticity form. Let ϵ^* denote the total employment elasticity of a wage increase, i.e.

$\epsilon^* = \epsilon^D + \epsilon^S$, where $\epsilon^D = -wN_w/N$ is the usual labour demand elasticity, and $\epsilon^S = wh_w/h$ is the labour supply elasticity. The first-order condition can then be expressed as

$$\Lambda_w = (V - U)\epsilon^* + whU_1(\cdot) = 0 \tag{58}$$

when workers and hours are perfect substitutes. Suppose that the employment elasticity ϵ^* is unaffected by changes in work-hours. The wage response to a change in work-hours then takes the sign of

$$\frac{\partial \Lambda_w}{\partial h} = w[U_1 + h(wU_{11} + U_{21})] \tag{59}$$

where we have used the envelope result that first-order changes in work-hours do not affect the employed worker's utility at his optimum. The first term in the bracket reflects that a rise in hours increases the marginal utility of a wage increase; the higher the number of work-hours, the higher the increase in earnings produced by a wage-hike. The term wU_{11} captures that the marginal utility of a wage increase falls when income is higher, by the concavity of the utility function. The third effect, captured by U_{21}, can take either sign; a rise in work-hours may or may not increase the worker's marginal utility of income.

Can expression (59) be signed? Note that the first-order condition for optimal individual labour supply is

$$U_h = wU_1(\cdot) + U_2(\cdot) \tag{60}$$

and the hours response to a wage increase takes the sign of

$$\frac{\partial U_h}{\partial w} = U_1(\cdot) + h(wU_{11} + U_{21}). \tag{61}$$

Comparing (59) and (61) reveals

$$\text{sign } \frac{\partial w}{\partial h} = \text{sign} \left[\frac{\partial h}{\partial w} \right]_s$$

where $[\partial h/\partial w]_s$ is the slope of the worker's labour supply schedule. The wage response to an exogenous reduction in working time is thus negative if the worker's supply curve is forward-sloping, and positive if the supply curve is backward-sloping. The union adjusts the wage so as to achieve a wage–hours path resembling the hours–wage path preferred by the individual worker.

Consider now a situation where the *union* determines working time. The union's optimal wage–employment combination is given by

$$\Lambda_w = (U - V)N_w + NhU_1(\cdot) = 0 \tag{62}$$

$$\Lambda_h = (U - V)N_h + wNU_1(\cdot) + NU_2(\cdot) = 0. \tag{63}$$

Noting that the first-order condition for optimal individual labour supply is $\psi \equiv wU_1(\cdot) + U_2(\cdot) = 0$, it is clear that (63) implies $\psi > 0$ when $N_h < 0$. The union prefers a shorter working time than the individual employed worker, the reason being that the union recognizes the link between its decisions on hours and firms' employment decisions. A rise in work-hours involves a cost in terms of foregone employment opportunities (the first term in (63)). By combining the two first-order conditions and using $N_h = -N/h$ we obtain:

$$\Lambda_h = (V - U)(1 - \epsilon) + hU_2(\cdot) = 0. \tag{64}$$

In order to have an interior solution in this case, the elasticity of labour demand must exceed unity.

Consider now the wage response to an exogenously imposed change in working time. In the perfect substitute case we have

$$\frac{\partial \Lambda_w}{\partial h} = (V - U)N_w \frac{1}{h} + (wU_1 + U_2)N_w$$
$$+ (wU_{11} + U_{12})Nh. \tag{65}$$

Using (63), expression (65) simplifies to

$$\frac{\partial \Lambda_w}{\partial h} = Nh(wU_{11} + U_{12}). \tag{66}$$

The sign of (66) is in general ambiguous, but is always negative if consumption and leisure are Edgeworth complements (i.e. if $U_{12} < 0$); a reduction in working time (increase in leisure) will then increase the marginal utility of consumption, and the union responds by raising the wage. Note also that the sign of (66) determines the sign of the income effect for the *individual* worker's labour supply response to a wage increase; (66) is negative if leisure is a normal good. But since the union prefers shorter work-hours than the individual worker, we cannot rule out that (66) is positive when evaluated at the *union's* desired hours, even if it is negative if evaluated at the individual worker's preferred working time.

Suppose alternatively that the *firm* determines hours per worker. The union has to obey the employment constraint, $N = N(w)$, as well as a demand function for work-hours, $h = h(w)$. The first-order condition for the optimal union wage is then

$$\Lambda_w = (U - V)N_w + \frac{NdU}{dw} = 0 \qquad (67)$$

where

$$\frac{dU}{dw} = (h + wh_w)U_1(\cdot) + h_w U_2(\cdot). \qquad (68)$$

The marginal benefit of a wage increase is here affected by firms' demand for hours. The first term in (68) captures that a wage increase will raise earnings at a given working time, but it also recognizes that there will be an induced reduction in hours which will tend to offset the rise in earnings. The last term in (68) is positive, and captures that a rise in the wage is utility-improving through its effect on leisure; in order to achieve a shorter working time the union must push for a higher wage.

The wage response to an exogenously imposed change in working time is ambiguous when firms determine initial work-hours. The derivative $\partial U/\partial h$ cannot be signed in general; the employed worker's utility remains unchanged only if work-hours happen to be optimal for the individual worker (which there is no reason to expect). On the marginal benefit side, the derivative $\partial(dU/dw)/\partial h$ is also ambiguous in sign.

In conclusion, the analysis underlines the sensitivity of the results to assumptions made about how working time is initially determined. If the individual worker is unconstrained in his labour supply decision, the wage effect depends on the slope of the worker's labour supply curve. If the union has determined the initial working time, wages are likely to rise when hours are reduced; the direct employment-increasing effect is thus to some extent offset by the union's push for higher wages. If initial hours are set by firms, the union wage-setting model offers very little information about likely wage and employment effects of work-sharing.

In practice, work-hours are presumably influenced by all three of the mechanisms considered: there surely is some scope for individual adjustment, unions have often tried to achieve a reduction in the work-week, and firms appear to exert some short-run discretion over hours. The question of how wages and employment are affected by a shorter working time is ultimately empirical, and we will return to it in the empirical work of Chapter 3 below.

1.8. Concluding Remarks

We have surveyed a few standard bargaining models and discussed some of the key implications of these models. Two major kinds of model were considered, (i) labour demand models and (ii) efficient-bargaining models. Firms have exclusive control over hirings and firings in the former type of model, whereas employment is determined by union–firm negotiations in the latter case. Labour demand models are in general inefficient, but it seems unlikely that efficient contracts are enforceable in practice. Firms always have incentives to renege *ex post* and move back to the labour demand curve, and employment reductions can typically be achieved by not replacing workers who quit. Centralized negotiations over employment are almost inconceivable; the negotiated total employment level would have to be distributed across firms and plants, and this does not seem to be a feasible operation.

Two kinds of labour demand model were compared, namely the monopoly model and the Nash bargaining (or right-to-manage) model. The comparative statics of the two models are similar with respect to changes that affect the union member's alternative income, such as changes in unemployment benefits. However, the two models have in general different wage predictions when we consider shocks to the firm's revenue function.

Wage-bargaining models yield predictions about real outcomes. Tax increases will in general influence the union's wage demand by altering its desired wage–employment trade-off. A rise in the payroll tax will under plausible assumptions raise wage costs and reduce employment; complete backward shifting of payroll taxes occurs only under very special conditions.

A union's wage demand is influenced by UI benefits, but also by the ways in which UI is financed. We have discussed a feature of UI that is found in Sweden and some other countries, namely that UI is organized through the trade unions. The effect of a government subsidy to the UI system depends on which form it takes. A rise in the marginal subsidy rate is likely to raise wage demands by reducing the marginal cost to the union of a wage increase. A lump-sum grant, by contrast, is likely to reduce the union's desired wage. The degree of progressivity of the subsidy system is thus crucial for wage outcomes.

Changes in work-hours affect employment directly via the possibility of substituting workers for hours in production. Employment is however also indirectly affected by induced wage changes. An exogenously imposed reduction in work-hours may well increase wages if hours are close to the level preferred by the union. If work-hours are set by the employed worker, the opposite prediction is more likely. Work-hours are in practice presumably influenced by unions, by individual workers, and by employers, and strong conclusions about likely wage responses to reductions in work hours are unwarranted without empirical evidence.

The theoretical models set out in this section have so far not been exposed to an impressive number of empirical tests. The past ten years or so have, however, seen a growing number of empirical studies on union behaviour, and the next section turns to a survey of recent work in this field.

2

Empirical Evidence

2.1. Introduction

A. W. Phillips's study on the relationship between unemployment and wage changes in the UK (Phillips (1958)) was followed by a minor explosion of econometric work on wage and price equations. In general, those studies did not pay much attention to the possible influence of trade unions, preoccupied as they were with the links between labour market conditions and the rate of change of money wages. One early exception was A. G. Hines (1964), who questioned the contemporary researchers' maintained hypothesis that unions were unable to affect wages independently of the state of excess demand in the labour market. According to Hines, the rejection of trade union 'pushfulness' as part of the explanation for wage inflation was not justified by a careful empirical analysis. In his own work he claimed to have established a close relationship between wage inflation and the preferred measure of union pushfulness, namely the rate of change of unionization.

To the extent that mainstream Phillips curve studies did take union influence into account, the procedures were typically *ad hoc*. Archibald (1969) characterized the prevalent practice as one of adding 'intruders' to the conventional type of Phillips curve equation. A frequent intruder was some measure of profit, justified on the ground that high profits should induce unions to push for high wages and simultaneously make employers less resistant to union wage demands.

A paper by Ashenfelter *et al.* (1972) offers an early contribution to the empirical literature on unions and wage inflation. This study focuses on the rate of change of money wages in the US manufacturing industry, and a three-equation system is specified in which wage changes, consumer price changes, and union growth are jointly determined endogenous variables. A union growth variable enters the wage equation because the 'militancy of trade union leaders is likely to be greatest when they are gaining new members'

(Ashenfelter *et al.*, 1972, p 37). Union growth is explained by social and political forces conducive to unionism, but also by consumer price changes on the argument that 'trade unions are likely to be gaining new members when prices are raising rapidly and workers are anxious to maintain their real wage without incurring the cost of mobility in the labour market' (p. 37).

Econometric work on wage formation in the 1980s shows a clear tendency to depart from early disequilibrium rationalizations of the Phillips curve, and a growing interest in explicit bargaining models. Models of the latter type have been specified and estimated in order to test particular behavioural models, or to obtain information about union objective functions, in particular with respect to the trade-off between wages and employment in union objectives.

Recent empirical literature also includes a growing number of studies where bargaining models are used to explain movements in aggregate data on employment, unemployment, and real wages. This line of research, perhaps best represented by the work of Layard and Nickell, has put applied bargaining models at the centre of urgent macro-economic issues.

The neo-classical labour demand schedule is a corner-stone in most wage-bargaining models. Although this idea is familiar enough to economists, it was conspicuously absent from much of the empirical work on employment functions in the late 1960s and the early 1970s. A standard approach related movements in employment to movements in output, suitably lagged, with no explicit role for relative factor prices. Recent work on the determinants of labour demand has, by and large, re-established the neo-classical labour demand function, although, not surprisingly, some controversies remain. The next section takes a closer look at this issue. We proceed in section 2.3 to a review of available evidence on the efficiency of employment contracts, in particular on whether the wage–employment outcome is placed on the contract curve or on the employer's labour demand curve. Section 2.4 reports on recent empirical work on union objective functions, and section 2.5 presents evidence on union bargaining power.

A certain amount of recent research has tried to estimate the effects of union pushfulness in real-wage equations; together with labour demand equations, such estimates can be used to calculate employment effects of union power. The best-known work has been done in Britain, and we discuss some of these studies in section 2.6.

2.2. Wages and Labour Demand

Union models of the L D type have made extensive use of the neo-classical labour demand schedule, involving—among other things—a negative relationship between wages and employment. Although the neo-classical labour demand function has a long history in economics, its success in empirical labour and macroeconomics has been mixed. Early empirical observations by Dunlop (1938) and Tarshis (1939) led to doubts about the presumed negative relationship. By and large, however, the neo-classical labour demand schedule has been rehabilitated by recent empirical work in labour and macro-economics. Occasionally this neo-classical comeback has led to strong—and perhaps somewhat premature—conclusions about the potential role of government policy. For example, Symons concludes from his study of the demand for labour in British manufacturing (1985) that 'government macro-economic policy can affect the level of employment in manufacturing if and only if it can affect relative prices'. Despite the clear signs of a neo-classical come-back, Symons's conclusion has no unambiguous support in recent empirical investigations.

The studies of labour demand have typically focused on either manufacturing or the aggregate labour market. Some researchers, including Neftci (1978), Sargent (1978), and Geary and Kennan (1982), have made extensive use of modern time-series methodology. The bulk of the research, however, has applied more traditional econometric methods (such as ordinary least squares or estimation by instrumental variables).

The evidence from the time-series exercises is more mixed than that produced by more traditional methods. Neftci looked at monthly data for US manufacturing and concluded that 'application of the appropriate time-series methodology reveals that real wages and employment are negatively related' (p. 283). Sargent interpreted his results—also pertaining to the USA—as 'moderately comforting to the view that the employment–real wage observations lie along a demand schedule for employment' (p. 1041). By contrast, Geary and Kennan—using data for twelve different economies—could not reject a null hypothesis of statistical independence between real wages and employment. The reasons for the diverging results are somewhat unclear. Geary and Kennan attributed the differences primarily to their superior measure of real-product wages; whereas Neftci and Sargent deflated the money wage by the consumer price index, Geary and Kennan used a wholesale price index as deflator. A recent study by Nickell and Symons (1986) takes a new look at the real-wage–employment relationship in the USA, and concludes that the results are quite sensitive to the specification of the real-wage variable. When the real (value-added) product wage is used, a negative demand-side relationship shows up, both in manufacturing and at the aggregate level.

Some time-series exercises focus rather narrowly on correlations between employment and real wages, without any allowance made for other plausible arguments of the labour demand function. Researchers following traditional econometric procedures have in general been more elaborate in this respect, paying attention to the role of capital, energy prices, and, occasionally, aggregate demand.

Conventional econometric studies of employment in manufacturing include Bruno and Sachs (1985), Symons (1985), Symons and Layard (1984), and Bruno (1986). Studies of aggregate employment in Britain include Nickell and Andrews (1983) and Layard and Nickell (1985a and 1986). Newell and Symons (1985) as well as Bean *et al.* (1986) have estimated aggregate labour demand functions for a large number of OECD economies. These studies typically treat capital as exogenous, and occasionally they include material prices among the regressors. In general the elasticity estimates are not conditional on a given level of output; a deliberate purpose has been to capture output effects as well as pure factor substitution effects.

Bruno and Sachs find that the real-product wage in manufacturing has a strong and significant negative effect on employment in eight out of the nine OECD economies they study. The average real-wage elasticity is estimated to around 0.5 in the short run and about unity in the long run. (We maintain the convention of defining the wage elasticity with a positive sign.)

The estimations undertaken by Symons, Symons and Layard, and Bruno also confirm the expected negative relationship between wages and employment. Symons uses quarterly data for the British manufacturing sector, and reports that the real wage has a slow-acting but powerful negative effect on employment; in fact, the estimated long-run elasticity is around 2 and the mean lag is over eighteen months. The evidence offered in Symons and Layard—for manufacturing employment in six major OECD economies—is broadly consistent with Symons's results for Britain, although the elasticity estimates are typically lower. Bruno's paper reports on negative wage elasticities for ten of the eleven investigated countries (the USA being the exception). The estimated long-run real-wage elasticities vary between 0.5 and 2.

Studies of aggregate employment data are in broad conformity with the studies on the manufacturing sector, although the elasticity estimates tend to be somewhat lower. Nickell and Andrews explore the determinants of the number of employees in Britain and arrive at a long-run elasticity of 0.5. The more recent work by Layard and Nickell (1986) reports a real-wage elasticity of 0.9 in Britain. Newell and Symons study sixteen OECD economies, and the real wage shows up with a negative sign in thirteen out of the sixteen estimated employment functions; the long-run elasticity of labour demand is estimated to around 0.9. Bean *et al.* estimate labour demand functions for eighteen OECD countries, and find negative wage–employment relationships in all countries except the USA. The elasticity estimates are typically between one-half and unity.

Is there any hope that government policy can increase private employment without reducing the real-product wage (or some other relative factor price that belongs to the neo-classical labour demand function)? The answer may be yes if some firms face sales constraints in the product market; a boost in aggregate demand could then bring about a rise in employment without any fall in real wages. A certain amount of research has been devoted to this issue. The typical procedure appends some aggregate-demand variables to the 'neo-classical part' of the labour demand function. The results are mixed, perhaps to some degree reflecting that researchers have varying inclinations to search for 'Keynesian' features of labour demand functions.[1]

The study by Symons reports 'as a striking implication for policy' that measures of demand (output, demand, and government spending) made no significant contribution to the explanation of movements in British manufacturing employment. Similar results

[1] As is well known, Keynes himself was more neo-classical than neo-Keynesian in the *General Theory*: 'with given organization, equipment and technique, real wages and the volume of output (and hence of employment) are uniquely correlated, so that, in general, an increase in employment can only occur to the accompaniment of a decline in the rate of real wages' (Keynes (1936, p. 17)).

are reported by Symons and Layard. Other researchers have been quite successful in detecting a role for aggregate demand. 'Pro-Keynesian' results are reported by Layard and Nickell, Bruno, and Bean *et al.* Layard and Nickell use three demand variables in the employment function: a series on the (cyclically adjusted) budget deficit, a measure of Britain's competitiveness, and a series on de-trended world trade. All three variables make a significant contribution to labour demand.

In conclusion, the role of aggregate demand in employment determination remains unsettled at the present stage of research. On the theoretical side, there is no agreement as to whether or why aggregate demand matters for employment in addition to its impact on relative prices. The possibility of non-market-clearing product markets suggests one route whereby aggregate demand may exert an independent effect on employment; the imperfect competition framework of the Layard–Nickell type offers another rationale. On the empirical side, the precise operational content of a particular aggregate-demand interpretation is unclear. The choice of proxies for aggregate demand is not without conceptual and practical problems, and it is not obvious how aggregate-demand variables should be entered into the labour demand function.

On this last point, the paper by Drazen *et al.* (1984) attempts to make some progress. The paper shows that the elasticity of labour demand is lower for sales-constrained firms than for unconstrained ones. A fall in aggregate demand is then likely to increase the fraction of firms facing sales constraints, so the aggregate labour demand elasticity should fall in slumps and rise in booms. The tests undertaken in Drazen *et al.* do not, however, give any clear support for the hypothesis of a procyclical aggregate labour demand elasticity. It remains to be seen whether the 'variable employment elasticity hypothesis' will stand up as a 'fertile field for future research', as Drazen *et al.* suggest.

2.3. Testing the Efficiency of Employment Contracts

Most empirical work on unions' role in wage determination have maintained the assumption that employers have exclusive control over employment. In general, this implies that firms are on their neo-classical labour demand schedule, and wage–employment outcomes

on the contract curve are ruled out. Efforts to discriminate between
L D models and efficient-bargaining models are scarce, despite the
potential practical importance of the issues involved. For example,
all estimates (and guesstimates) of welfare costs associated with the
existence of trade unions are conditional on the assumption that
firms are on their wage-taking labour demand curves. Under
efficient bargaining, employers and workers leave no gains from
trade unexploited, and conventional calculations of union-induced
'distortions' become suspect. (This is not to say that pairwise
efficient union–employer bargains necessarily imply social
efficiency. The welfare economics in this field is in its infancy.)

Attempts to discriminate between L D models and efficient-
bargaining models have made use of the basic condition for Pareto
efficiency: the marginal rate of substitution between wages and
employment must be the same for the union and for the firm. In
other words, the efficient contract equates the slope of the union
indifference curve and the slope of the firm's iso-profit curve.

Let $\Lambda = \Lambda(w, N)$ be the union's objective function and let
$\Pi = Q(N) - wN$ be the firm's profit. Recall the basic efficiency
requirement

$$\frac{\partial\Lambda(\cdot)/\partial N}{\partial\Lambda(\cdot)/\partial w} = \frac{w - \partial Q/\partial N}{N} \tag{69a}$$

where the left-hand side is the slope of the union's indifference curve
and the right-hand side is the slope of the iso-profit function (both
expressed as positive numbers). Efficiency implies that the wage is
above the firm's marginal revenue product, and employment is thus
chosen to the right of the neo-classical labour demand curve.
Rearranging (69a) yields

$$\frac{\partial Q}{\partial N} = w - \xi N \tag{69b}$$

where $\xi \equiv [(\partial\Lambda/\partial N)/(\partial\Lambda/\partial w)]$ is the marginal rate of substitution
between employment and wages in the union's objective function.

Expression (69b) is crucial for discriminating between L D models
and efficient-bargaining models. If, for example, the monopoly
union model is an appropriate characterization, we have
$w = \partial Q/\partial N$ and the term $- \xi N$ should be dropped from (69b). The
first-order condition for the efficient-bargaining model thus nests
the L D model as a special case, and tests may therefore focus on

whether the term $-\xi N$ can be omitted from this first-order condition.

MaCurdy and Pencavel (1986) apply this methodology to pooled time-series and cross-section data for the International Typographical Union in the USA. In a first step, production functions for the newspaper industry were estimated, yielding measures of the marginal revenue product of labour. A number of different specifications for ξ were examined, making ξ a function of the current wage, a measure of the average wage, and the level of employment. The equation was estimated by (nonlinear) 2SLS, treating the employment level and the wage-rate as endogenous. City dummies and time trends were used as instruments. A consistent finding was that restrictions that omitted the term $-\xi N$ were rejected at conventional levels of significance. This study thus lends some support to the efficient-bargaining model relative to LD models, at least for this particular union and industry.

Brown and Ashenfelter (1986) also focus on the first-order condition of an efficient-bargaining model. The basic idea is to translate the first-order condition into an estimable employment equation, and test whether measures of workers' alternative wages significantly enter this equation. To be specific, consider a marginal revenue product schedule of the form

$$\ell n Q'(N) = \alpha_0 + \alpha_1 \ell n N \tag{70}$$

with $\alpha_1 < 0$. Suppose also that the union attempts to maximize the individual worker's expected utility. Pareto efficiency then requires

$$Q'(N) = w + \frac{U(\bar{w}) - U(w)}{U'(w)} \tag{71}$$

and the corresponding employment equation (i.e. the equation for the contract curve) is obtained by combining (70) and (71) and taking Taylor approximations,

$$\ell n N \approx -(\alpha_0/\alpha_1) + (1/\alpha_1)\ell n \bar{w} - \frac{\delta}{2\alpha_1} [\ell n (w/\bar{w})]^2 \tag{72}$$

where $\delta = -wU''(\cdot)/U'(\cdot)$ measures the degree of relative risk aversion. Note that the last term in (72) drops out if the union is risk-neutral (i.e. $\delta = 0$); the employment level is then determined by the outside wage but is independent of the contract wage. Equation (72) is suggested as a test for the efficiency of employment contracts.

Negative and significant coefficients for the outside wage is taken as evidence in favour of efficient bargaining.

Although apparently straightforward, estimation of an employment function like (72) raises difficult identification problems. The contract curve defines efficient wage–employment combinations, and identification requires variables that influence the bargaining outcome without affecting the contract curve. Brown and Ashenfelter argue that income-smoothing arrangements may link the contract wage to its lagged values without there being any corresponding lags in the effects of contract wages on efficient employment. A similar argument is invoked for current and lagged consumer prices, and identification is thus achieved by using lagged contract wages and current and lagged consumer prices as instruments for the current contract wage.

Another problem, noted by MaCurdy and Pencavel, is that tests that focus on the alternative wage in the employment function rule out objective functions where the marginal rate of substitution between wages and employment is independent of the alternative wage. Under such circumstances, tests for efficiency cannot be based on whether the alternative wage is absent or present in the first-order condition. It is also easy to show that some union objective functions yield first-order conditions for the *monopoly model* that include the contract wage as well as the outside wage. This makes it difficult to discriminate between behavioural models by testing for the absence or presence of alternative wages in the first-order conditions.

The empirical results reported by Brown and Ashenfelter are not very conclusive; the results depend very much on which data on employment and alternative wages are used. There is some tendency, however, for both the outside wage and the contract wage to matter for employment. The authors' final conclusion is unlikely to invite objections: 'It seems clear that further research will be required before any of the simple contracting models of employment determination that we have examined here are likely to be useful tools in the analysis of public policies toward the labour market.'

Bean and Turnbull (1987) have undertaken a study similar to that of Brown and Ashenfelter. Bean and Turnbull attempt to estimate a contract curve for the British coal industry. They find that 'outside variables'—unemployment benefits and manufacturing wages—are important in determining the level of employment.

It is notable that no study (as far as we know) has tried to discriminate between contracting models by means of the models' reduced forms. This appears as the most natural procedure, provided that it is possible to derive conflicting comparative statics predictions from the different behavioural models. Progress along this avenue is likely to require specific bargaining models, for example of the Nash type, and specific objective functions as well. It remains to be seen whether tests can be devised without imposing overly restrictive assumptions.

2.4. Evidence on Union Objectives

The empirical literature has seen three major approaches to the problem of estimating parameters of union objective functions and testing particular hypotheses about union objectives. One approach involves unrestricted reduced-form estimation of wage and employment equations, without imposing any specific assumptions about functional forms. A second line of research has imposed certain assumptions with respect to union preferences and the firm's labour demand schedule, and solved for the reduced-form wage and employment equations that are implied by the first-order condition for a utility-maximizing monopoly union. For some specifications it is possible to identify structural parameters by estimating the reduced-form equations. The third approach, finally, estimates structural parameters by estimating the first-order condition for union utility maximization. Examples of empirical studies following the different approaches are given below.

2.4.1. Unrestricted Reduced-Form Estimation

Carruth *et al.* (1986) have adopted reduced-form estimation to test a 'flat indifference curve' model of union behaviour. The basic idea is that seniority rules may effectively shelter senior workers from the threat of unemployment. Lay-offs associated with adverse shifts in demand will affect the welfare of junior workers, possibly with no consequences for the worker in the middle of the hierarchy. If the union maximizes the median worker's welfare, and this worker is secure in his job, the union's maximand becomes a function of the wage, with no role for employment.

If the union ignores unemployed members' welfare, a change in the level of unemployment benefits (or some other measure of the alternative wage) has no impact on union preferences, as opposed to the standard utilitarian case where higher benefits twist the union's indifference curves in the wage–employment space. Does this also imply that the wage outcome is independent of outside income opportunities? That depends on which assumptions about the bargaining solution one is willing to make. Carruth *et al.* postulate utility maximization against a profit constraint. This solution yields reduced-form wage and employment equations that *exclude* the outside wage. In fact, the model implies efficient-bargaining outcomes placed on the labour demand curve, as was illustrated in Fig. 1.3 above.

Carruth *et al.* reject the flat indifference curve model when confronting it with post-war data on wages and employment from the British coal and steel industries. The alternative wage is represented by two variables, the unemployment rate and the unemployment benefit level, and a null hypothesis of joint insignificance of these variables is not accepted.

Carruth *et al.* take their results as evidence against the flat indifference curve hypothesis. But it is straightforward to see that flat union indifference curves in a Nash bargaining model produce reduced-form equations that *include* the outside wage. (Indeed, this is also pointed out in Oswald (1984).) For example, suppose that the Nash bargain solves

$$\max_{w} \; \Omega(w) = (w - \bar{w})^{\beta} \Pi^{1-\beta}. \tag{73}$$

The union cares about the wage-rate and places no value on employment. But because the outside wage influences the union's threat point, it does not drop out of the first-order condition and the associated reduced-form wage and employment equations. The results obtained by Carruth *et al.* can not therefore be taken as evidence against flat union indifference curves as long as the threat point is affected by outside income opportunities.

2.4.2. *Restricted Reduced-Form Estimation*

This approach involves specification of explicit functional forms for the union's objective function and the firm's labour demand schedule. For some specifications it may be possible to identify structural parameters by estimating the reduced form implied by the union's utility maximization. A relatively convenient expression for the union's objectives is the Stone–Geary function

$$\Lambda = (w - w_0)^\theta (N - N_0)^{1-\theta} \qquad (74)$$

where w_0 and N_0 measure 'reference' levels of wages and employment, and θ captures the relative weight placed on wages (above the reference level) relative to employment (above the reference level). Suppose that this objective function is combined with a linear labour demand function

$$N = \alpha_0 + \alpha_1(w/q) + \alpha_2 Z \qquad (75)$$

where q is the output price and Z is a vector of other variables influencing labour demand. Maximization of the union's objective function against the labour demand constraint yields the reduced-form equations

$$w = \Pi_0 + \Pi_1 q + \Pi_2 Z \qquad (76)$$

$$N = \Pi_3 + \Pi_4 q + \Pi_5 Z \qquad (77)$$

where the Π_i coefficients are nonlinear configurations of structural parameters. Simultaneous estimation of the reduced-form equations allows identification of parameters characterizing preferences and the labour demand function.

This approach can be extended in several directions. For example, the reference wage can be related to observable variables, such as lagged wages or some 'comparison wage', that influence union preferences. The Stone–Geary formulation also nests wage-bill maximization and rent maximization as special cases; the former maximand appears when $\theta = 0.5$ and $w_0 = N_0 = 0$; the latter appears when $\theta = 0.5$, $N_0 = 0$, and w_0 measures outside income opportunities.

If one is willing to assume that union objectives take the form

$$\Lambda = (\ell n w - \tilde{w}_0)^\theta (\ell n N - \tilde{N}_0)^{1-\theta} \qquad (78)$$

this general approach is also able to handle labour demand schedules that are linear in the logarithms; the reduced-form equations take the same form as (76) and (77) above, with the variables expressed in logarithms.

This general line of research was first pursued by Dertouzos and Pencavel (1981), using data for the International Typographical Union in the USA. It has also been applied in empirical work on the Swedish labour market by Pencavel (1985) and Pencavel and Holmlund (1988). The tests undertaken by Dertouzos and Pencavel reject the wage bill and rent maximization hypotheses compared to a more general specification.

Pencavel and Holmlund (1988) attempt to incorporate work-hours in union objectives and firms' employment decisions. They postulate an objective function of the form

$$\Lambda = [\ell n\{(1 - t)wh/p\} - \beta\ell nh - \widetilde{w}_0]^\theta[\ell nN]^{1-\theta} \qquad (79)$$

where t is the income tax rate, p is the consumer price, and h is hours of work. If β is zero, no weight is attached to hours of work (holding earnings constant) in the union's objectives; if β is unity, wage-*rates* and not earnings are the relevant argument of the objective function. The reference real wage ($\widetilde{w}_0$) is specified as a function of (the logarithm of) lagged real wages, thus allowing the union's current real-wage aspirations to be affected by previous wages analogous to some models of dynamic consumption behaviour.

The union is assumed to maximize against two equations characterizing firms' decisions on labour input, both linear in logarithms. The first equation characterizes the demand for workers, the second the demand for hours per worker. The reduced form includes a real-wage equation, and equations for the number of workers and work-hours. In these equations, the parameter θ captures the union's relative aversion to variations in employment. Consider an exogenous shift of the employment demand function, for example, due to higher energy and raw-material prices. In the reduced-form equations, the larger (in absolute value) the elasticity of real wages with respect to the shift variable and the smaller (in absolute value) the elasticity of employment, the larger is θ. A higher value of θ thus corresponds to greater cyclical earnings variability and smaller employment variability in response to exogenous shifts in the employment demand function. In fact, θ corresponds to a measure of relative aversion to variations in employment:

$$\theta = \frac{- (\ell nN) [\partial^2\Lambda/\partial(\ell nN)^2]}{\partial\Lambda/\partial(\ell nN)} \qquad (80)$$

Pencavel and Holmlund apply their model to the Swedish mining and manufacturing sector and estimate θ to 0.15. The implications of this estimate can be illustrated by tracing through the consequences of, say, an increase in energy and raw-material prices of 10 per cent. The estimated employment demand function reveals considerable responsiveness to changes in energy prices; in fact, the impact of a rise in material prices by 10 per cent is to reduce employment by 13 per cent. However, this employment-decreasing effect will cause unions to moderate their wage demands. How much their wage demands will change depends on the wage elasticity of employment and on the union's relative aversion to variations in employment (θ). Given the estimates of these parameters, the rise in energy prices will reduce real (consumption) wages by 3 per cent, and employment will fall, not by 13 per cent, but only by 6 per cent.

The employment-reducing effect of higher material prices would be even smaller if the unions were more averse to variations in employment. For example, suppose θ were 0.75 (instead of 0.15 as estimated). Then, given the same values of the other parameters, a 10 per cent increase in material prices would result in a 15 per cent drop in real wages and only a 2 per cent reduction in employment.

As for other parameters of the union objective function, the estimate of β lies between zero and unity, which implies that hours may neither be eliminated from the objective function nor simply added to wage-rates to form earnings; hours of work seem to have a role in union objectives that is distinct from earnings. The estimated reference wage function indicates a rising reference level for the unions' wage goals with respect to past real wages. However, the estimates reject a hypothesis according to which the unions care about wage *changes* rather than levels; the utility-enhancing effect of a rise in current wages is greater than the utility-decreasing effect of the same percentage increase in wages experienced last year.

In conclusion, the main advantage of restricted reduced-form estimation is convenience, as long as the reduced-form equations are linear in the exogenous variables. The alleged disadvantage of this approach is that it postulates union objective functions without obvious links to the welfare of individual union members. However, objective functions of the utilitarian or expected-utility type are in general unable to yield simple, explicit reduced-form expressions. Researchers have therefore adopted estimations of the first-order conditions, an approach to which we now turn.

2.4.3. Estimation of First-Order Conditions

Despite its popularity in theoretical studies, the expected utility (or utilitarian) hypothesis has not been subject to tests in the empirical literature on trade union behaviour. Several empirical studies have, however, *imposed* these kinds of objective function in order to obtain estimates of individual union members' degree of risk aversion. The typical procedure postulates individual utility functions with constant relative degree of risk aversion. Recall that the first-order condition for a wage-setting utilitarian union is given by

$$\Lambda_w = N(w)U'(w) + [U(w) - V(B)]N_w = 0. \qquad (81)$$

Suppose that the labour demand curve is linear with wage slope $N_w = \alpha_1$, and let the utility functions be given by

$$U(w) = \frac{w^{1-\delta}}{1-\delta}, \ V(B) = \frac{B^{1-\delta}}{1-\delta} \qquad (82)$$

where the parameter δ represents the union members' degree of relative risk aversion. The first-order condition for the utility-maximizing union is then

$$Nw^{-\delta} + \frac{\alpha_1}{1-\delta}(w^{1-\delta} - B^{1-\delta}) = 0. \qquad (83)$$

By adding suitable assumptions about the stochastic properties of the model, the first-order condition can be estimated jointly with a linear labour demand function. This produces estimates of structural parameters of interest, including the wage slope of the labour demand function (α_1) and the coefficient of relative risk aversion (δ). Needless to say, the validity of these estimates is conditional on the model being correct, including the form of the labour demand function. The wage-increasing effect of, say, higher unemployment benefits is *presumed* but not tested in this approach.

Studies of interest include Farber (1978*a* and 1978*b*), Carruth and Oswald (1985), and Forslund (1986). Farber studies post-war data for miners in the USA, whereas Carruth and Oswald focus on miners' wages in post-war Britain. Forslund deals with aggregate data on wages and employment for the private sector in Sweden.

Estimates of union members' degree of relative risk aversion are given in all these studies. Farber finds substantial risk aversion, with δ being between 3 and 4. Carruth and Oswald report much smaller, but highly significant, risk aversion ($\delta = 0.8$). Forslund's estimate of the degree of relative risk aversion is very high ($\delta = 4.4$). All studies thus unambiguously reject rent (or wage-bill) maximization as an appropriate characterization of union objectives.

Estimates of parameters of the unions' objective function can be used to calculate the elasticity of substitution between real wages and employment in union objectives. Forslund's preliminary results for Sweden indicate that an increase in employment by 1 per cent can be accompanied by a wage reduction of 2 per cent without any reduction in the union member's expected utility. This relative valuation of employment is higher than typically suggested by estimates from Britain and the USA.

The general procedure of estimating first-order conditions can of course be applied to a variety of union objective functions. Pencavel (1984*a* and 1984*b*) focuses on versions of the so-called 'addilog function', taken to represent the preferences of the union leader. A study by Hersoug *et al.* (1987) applies a similar union objective function to Norwegian data, but solves explicitly for the union's optimal wage-rate.

2.5. Estimating the Degree of Union Power

Do unions make a difference for wage outcomes? This is presumed in theoretical union models, but also in most empirical studies of wage-bargaining. For example, available (scanty) evidence on union objectives is mainly based on tests that are conditional on the validity of the monopoly union assumption. The recent growth in empirical studies on union behaviour has typically not involved estimations of the degree of union power; an exception is the recent study by Svejnar (1986). His framework is efficient Nash bargaining, i.e.

$$\max_{w,\,N} \Omega(w,\,N) = (\Lambda - L_0)^\beta (\Pi - \Pi_0) \tag{84}$$

where $\Lambda(w) = w^{1-\delta}/(1 - \delta)$, δ being the degree of relative risk aversion. The union's threat point is analogously given by $\Lambda_0(\bar{w}) = \bar{w}^{1-\delta}/(1 - \delta)$. An expected utility-maximizing union thus cares about

$$\Lambda - \Lambda_0 = \frac{N}{M} \frac{(w^{1-\delta} - \bar{w}^{1-\delta})}{1 - \delta}. \tag{85}$$

The firm's profit from agreement is $\Pi = Q(N) - wN - C$, where C is non-labour costs of production. The efficient wage–employment bargain satisfies

$$\frac{\partial Q}{\partial N} = \frac{\bar{w}^{1-\delta} - \delta w^{1-\delta}}{(1 - \delta)w^\delta}. \tag{86}$$

When workers are risk-neutral we have $\delta = 0$ and consequently $\partial Q/\partial N = \bar{w}$; the marginal product of labour is set equal to the union's outside wage, yielding a vertical contract curve. Risk aversion ($\delta > 0$) implies a positively sloped contract curve, and risk loving implies that the contract curve is negatively sloped.

Under risk neutrality, the wage equation can be written as

$$w = \bar{w} + \frac{\beta\Pi(N^*)}{N^*} \tag{87}$$

where N^* is the employment level given by $\partial Q/\partial N = \bar{w}$. Given data on $\bar{w}$, Π, and N^*, the parameter β is readily estimated by OLS. Allowing for risk aversion leads to a more elaborate estimation procedure, involving specification of the form of the production function. Svejnar postulates a Cobb–Douglas technology, and is then also able to produce estimates of the degree of risk aversion.

The tests are applied to data from the mid-1950s to the late 1970s pertaining to twelve major unionized companies in the USA. Estimated values of β vary substantially, but the original Nash solution with $\beta = 1/2$ is a frequent outcome; the mean of estimated values for β is 0.46. Svejnar also explores the determinants of bargaining strength by relating β to a number of variables, including the unemployment rate and the rate of consumer price inflation. Indeed, union bargaining power is found to rise with inflation but fall with unemployment.

Although wage-bargaining models of the Nash bargaining type have been applied in many theoretical studies, the theory has in general not been closely linked to econometric estimation. The paper by Nickell and Andrews (1983) is perhaps the best-known example of the use of a Nash bargaining approach as a guide to the selection of explanatory variables in the regression equations; Hoel and Nymoen (1986) proceed along very similar lines. Nickell and Andrews's estimating wage equation is, however, a reduced form, and offers no information about the unions' objectives or bargaining strength. This use of bargaining models has become increasingly popular in applied work in labour and macro-economics, as is exemplified below.

2.6. Unemployment and Union Power: Macro-economic Evidence

Various studies of aggregate wage determination have tried to capture the influence of unions. A frequent approach has been to add some proxy for 'union militancy' to the Phillips curve type of wage equation. More recent work tries to account for movements in real wages by using variables affecting bargaining outcomes, including measures of union power. Widely used proxies for union wage pressure include (i) series on strike activity, (ii) series on union density, i.e. the proportion of employees unionized, and (iii) series on union–non-union wage differentials (often referred to as the union 'mark-up').

The best-known of recent studies of the role of unions in wage formation are those of Nickell and Andrews (1983), Minford (1983), and Layard and Nickell (1985*a*, 1985*b*, and 1986). Nickell and Andrews are most explicit about the way in which union power may influence bargaining outcomes. They apply a Nash wage-bargaining framework, and argue that union power reduces the firm's threat point 'in the sense that a strong union can impose very high costs on a firm if it refuses to strike a bargain' (Nickell and Andrews 1983, p. 518). Two proxies for union bargaining strength are used in the (real-) wage equation: union density and the union mark-up. The estimating equation is a reduced form, and it would presumably take the same form even if the union power variables were given a different motivation from the one preferred by Nickell and Andrews.

The union mark-up series used by Nickell and Andrews (as well as by Layard and Nickell in their studies of unemployment in Britain) are derived from a series of year-to-year industry cross-section regressions of the form

$$\ell n \, w_i = \alpha \, (\text{union coverage}) + X\beta \qquad (88)$$

where w_i is the wage-rate in industry i, X is a vector of variables influencing the wage (besides union power), and 'union coverage' measures the fraction of workers covered by union contracts in the industry. (Layard *et al.* (1978) describe the procedure in detail.) The union coverage coefficients (in logarithms) are used as proxies for union power in the aggregate real-wage equation.

2.6.1. Unemployment and Union Density

Let us first look at results obtained when union density is included as a measure of union power, as it is in the studies by Minford (1983) and Nickell and Andrews (1983). It is noteworthy that Nickell and Andrews and Minford arrive at estimates that are of the same order of magnitude (at least if the effects are evaluated at low unemployment rates). Nickell and Andrews's 'long-run quasi reduced form' implies the employment function

$$\ell n \, N = \text{constant} - 0.33 \, UD - 0.022 \, \ell n \, UM \ldots$$

where UD is union density (the fraction of employees that are unionized) and UM is the union mark-up. Noting that $\ell n \, N = \ell n \, (1 - u) + \ell n \, L \approx - u + \ell n \, L$, where u is the unemployment rate and L is the labour force, we have the reduced-form unemployment effect of an increase in union density

$$\frac{\partial u}{\partial UD} \approx 0.33.$$

Taken at face value, a rise in the unionization rate by 1 percentage point would imply a rise in the unemployment rate by one-third of a percentage point. Recognizing that unionization in Britain has increased by more than 10 percentage points between the late 1950s and the late 1970s, it is clear that union density may account for a substantial increase in British unemployment. Minford's estimates are rather similar in this respect. His long-run unemployment equation (which is not conditional on the path of the capital stock) is

$$\ell n \, uL = \text{constant} + 5.6 \, UD \ldots$$

so we have $\partial u/\partial UD \approx 5.6u$. Fixing u at, for example, 0.55 (which corresponds to the average male unemployment rate in Britain during the period 1970–9) yields $\partial u/\partial UD = 0.31$, rather close to the long-run effect estimated by Nickell and Andrews. Minford's specification implies that a rise in unemployment magnifies the unemployment-increasing effect of a rise in union density. At unemployment rates prevailing during the early 1980s, a rise in union density by 1 percentage point would increase the unemployment rate by almost 1 percentage point. (For a discussion of the robustness of Minford's model, see Henry *et al.* (1985).)

The use of union density series in studies of wage determination is certainly not without problems. One obvious point concerns the possible endogeneity of union membership. This can be handled by instrumenting the union density variable, which Nickell and Andrews also do. (Minford treats the variable as exogenous and reports results of exogeneity tests in defence of his procedure.) However, when it comes to 'accounting' for the rise in unemployment, it does not seem very meaningful to treat union density as exogenous if it is regarded as endogenous in estimation. This also holds for other, potentially endogenous, proxies for union power, among them series on union–non-union wage differentials.

2.6.2. Unemployment and the Union Mark-Up

Whereas Nickell and Andrews include both union density and the union mark-up to capture the influence of union power, Layard and Nickell (1985*a* and 1986) include only the latter variable. Recognizing that the union mark-up may to some extent be affected by unemployment, the variable is treated as endogenous in the estimations (by the use of instrumental variables). The coefficient is estimated with reasonable precision, with a t statistic around 4.[2]

Layard and Nickell use their full model, including a price equation, a labour demand equation, and a real-wage equation, to account for the rise in British unemployment since the mid-1950s. As

[2] Interestingly (and surprisingly?), the British union mark-up jumped substantially upward in the late 1970s, after the return to power of the Conservative party. If one has the taste for it, one might try a Thatcher dummy in the British wage equation; my hunch is that it will reduce the estimated union effect and produce a significant t(ory) coefficient. More seriously, it is certainly tempting to speculate that aggressive union wage policies may have something to do with the degree of social consensus that a government is willing and able to achieve. This brings us to issues of institutional arrangements and the role of 'corporatism' in wage formation, topics that are not addressed in this essay.

is shown in Tables 2.1 and 2.2, the rise in union power is estimated
to have increased the actual unemployment rate by around 3
percentage points, and increased NAIRU by 4 percentage points. In
fact, the rise in union power appears to account for more than half of
the estimated increase in NAIRU from 2 to 9 per cent.

TABLE 2.1. *Breakdown of the change in the male unemployment rate in
Britain, 1956–1983 (% points)*

	1956–66 to 1967–74	1967–74 to 1975–9	1975–9 to 1980–3
Employers' labour taxes	0.25	0.38	0.44
Replacement ratio	0.54	−0.09	−0.10
Union power	1.18	1.17	0.80
Real import prices	−0.58	1.47	−0.93
Mismatch	0.16	0.20	0.49
Demand factors	0.12	0.54	6.56
Incomes policy	—	−0.36	0.49
TOTAL	1.67	3.31	7.75
ACTUAL CHANGE	1.82	3.01	7.00

Source: Layard and Nickell (1986, p. 158).

TABLE 2.2. *Breakdown of the change in NAIRU, British males
1956–1983 (% points)*

	1956–66 to 1967–74	1967–74 to 1975–9	1975–9 to 1980–3
Employers' labour taxes	0.29	0.51	0.69
Replacement ratio	0.64	−0.12	−0.15
Union power	1.40	1.58	1.25
Oil production	—	−0.32	−1.73
UK import/world manufactures, price ratio	−0.29	2.02	−0.17
Mismatch	0.19	0.27	0.77
Incomes policy	—	−0.50	0.78
TOTAL	2.23	3.44	1.44

Source: Layard and Nickell (1986, p. 159).

How valid is the use of series on union–non-union wage differentials in explanations of movements in unemployment? Layard and Nickell's recognition of the possible endogeneity of the variable immediately raises questions about the determinants of changes in the union mark-up. Several studies have addressed this issue on US data, including Moore and Raisan (1980), Johnson (1984), and Pencavel and Hartsog (1984). Johnson's paper reveals a counter-cyclical pattern in movements of the union mark-up; the mark-up rises when unemployment is increasing and falls when unemployment is decreasing. This pattern is also consistent with estimations of separate Phillips curves for unionized and non-unionized workers in the USA; Ashenfelter *et al.* (1972) report that the Phillips curve in the union sector is much flatter than in the non-union sector. (Cf. also Flanagan (1976) for related US evidence.)

The cyclical pattern of the union wage premium was discussed by Lewis (1963) in his classic on unionism and relative wages in the USA. Lewis offered a 'wage rigidity hypothesis' according to which union wages were likely to be less sensitive than non-union wages to changes in labour market slack. In fact, Lewis also conjectured that union wages should be less sensitive to inflation. A counter-argument on this last point notes that unions may be able to achieve indexation of wage increases to price inflation. This should *raise* the union mark-up in periods of rapid inflation. A third hypothesis, offered by Johnson (1984), suggests that a large mark-up may in itself reduce the rate of change of the mark-up; for example, threat effects may cause non-union wages to rise faster when the mark-up is higher.

I have replicated variants of the regressions run on US data by Johnson (1984), using British data for the period 1954–83. This involves regressing the annual change in the union mark-up on (i) the unemployment rate, (ii) the rate of change of consumer prices, and (iii) the lagged value of the mark-up. The results, reported in Table 2.3, reveals that the union wage premium rises with unemployment, consistent with Lewis's wage rigidity hypothesis and Johnson's results for the USA.[3] A large mark-up tends to moderate the *change* in the mark-up, whereas the price inflation variable makes a significant contribution only when the time trend is excluded.

---

[3] The study by Beenstock and Whitbread (1987) also finds that higher unemployment raises the union mark-up.

TABLE 2.3. *Determinants of changes in the union–non-union wage differential in Britain, 1954–1983. The dependent variable is the annual change in the union mark-up. (Absolute value of* t *ratios in parentheses.)*

	(1) OLS	(2) OLS	(3) IV	(4) IV
Constant	0.067	0.066	0.066	0.065
	(3.517)	(3.434)	(3.332)	(3.364)
Unemployment rate	0.840	0.710	0.711	0.694
	(2.695)	(2.358)	(2.200)	(2.248)
Rate of change in	0.195	—	—	—
consumer prices	(1.350)			
Lagged mark-up	−0.795	−0.804	−0.804	−0.797
	(3.954)	(3.939)	(3.824)	(3.865)
Time	0.0045	0.0060	0.0060	0.0060
	(2.206)	(3.389)	(3.387)	(3.383)
R^2	0.42	0.38	0.38	0.38
DW	1.67	1.70	1.70	1.71

Note: Estimation is by O L S in cols. (1) and (2) and by instrumental variables (I V) in cols. (3) and (4). The instruments for the unemployment rate in regression (3) are: a constant, the lagged mark-up, time, the logarithm of the capital stock, three aggregate demand variables (budget deficit, competitiveness, world trade), a proxy for labour market mismatch, the benefit replacement ratio, and tax rates. In regression (4), the lagged unemployment rate is added to the list of instruments. The data are taken from the data appendix for Britain published in the unemployment issue of *Economica*, 53 (1986). Series on consumer prices (the deflator for private consumption) are taken from O E C D National Accounts.

What could be learned from this exercise? Clearly, the need to treat the union wage premium as endogenous is underlined. Whereas recent British studies view changes in the union mark-up as a crucial driving force behind the rise in unemployment, other studies have tried to explain movements in the mark-up by, *inter alia*, movements in unemployment! Obviously, the state of the art is not completely satisfactory.

In defence of Layard and Nickell's work, it should be noted that the mark-up variable is treated as endogenous in their estimations. The set of instruments include lagged values of the endogenous variables, so the procedure is valid under the assumption that the stochastic errors are serially uncorrelated. But when Layard and Nickell proceed to 'account' for the rise in British unemployment, the union mark-up is *de facto* treated as exogenous. This is not an appropriate procedure if movements in the wage premium are influenced by changes in unemployment. The regression results suggest that part of the increase in the union mark-up may have to do with the rise in unemployment. The 'autonomous' rise in the mark-up is captured by the trend in the estimated equations, not by the 'raw values' of the mark-up itself.

It is not clear how endogenization of the union wage premium would affect Layard and Nickell's estimates of unions' contribution to the rise in British unemployment. Among other things, this depends on how the wage equation is specified. Should it include the actual mark-up, or only the unemployment-adjusted autonomous component? In any event, it seems evident that future work along the lines pursued by Layard and Nickell should try to explain movements of the union mark-up as well as movements in aggregate wages. In a heavily unionized economy, aggregate wages are bound to be influenced by union wage premiums—at least at the definitional level—but explanations of aggregate wage paths in terms of changes in relative wages are clearly incomplete in important respects.

Layard and Nickell (1985*b*) have also estimated the 'Layard–Nickell model' on data for the USA, France, Germany, and Japan. In the estimating wage equations they now introduce series on industrial conflicts as proxies for movements in union power; in fact, they smooth the data by fitting the conflict series to a quintic trend. The measures of union power make significant contributions to the real-wage equations for France, Germany, and Japan—but not for the USA.

Empirical work along similar lines is reported by Newell and Symons (1985) and Bean *et al.* (1986). Newell and Symons estimate real-wage equations for sixteen OECD countries and conclude that 'union density and a variety of measures of strike activity showed no consistent effect on the wage'. Bean *et al.* report similar results in their multi-country study of the OECD area. Series of strike activity and union density were included in the wage equations, but significant effects were, in general, not found.

It seems safe to conclude that current empirical knowledge of the relationships between unemployment and union power offers little ground for strong policy recommendations. It is certainly the case that standard wage-bargaining models predict that a rise in the union's bargaining strength will increase wage pressure and thereby, ultimately, unemployment. But the empirical work has not made much progress in identifying movements in union bargaining power. Some frequently used proxy variables are likely to be endogenous to the bargaining outcomes. In adddition, the implications of, for example, high unionization rates are likely to vary across countries with different institutional arrangements.

2.7. Concluding Remarks

Econometric work on behavioural union models is still in its infancy. Although progress has been made, there is a long way to go before economists can make reliable statements about the role of unions in wage and employment determination. The 'econometrics of union behaviour' has perhaps not yet reached the same methodological sophistication as the 'econometrics of labour supply', and one reason may be that the former has been handicapped by lack of suitable data. Tests of micro-economic models of union behaviour should preferably make use of data on individual bargaining units, but such data have often not been available.

Empirical work on union models has in most cases proceeded under the assumption that employment is determined by profit-maximizing firms, and a substantial body of research has tried to estimate the sensitivity of employment to changes in real-product wages. Although labour demand elasticities tend to be estimated somewhat imprecisely, the range of recent parameter estimates is reasonably narrow; a growing number of studies place the wage elasticity of labour demand in an interval between one-half and unity.

The concept of a well-defined labour demand schedule has come under criticism from the new literature on efficient bargaining. Wage–employment outcomes on the labour demand curve are in general inefficient, and several studies have produced results that cast some doubt on labour demand models. Testing between competing models is, however, a difficult enterprise, and the tests devised so far rely on quite strong prior assumptions. One may of course also address this issue by non-econometric methods, as for example Oswald (1984) did by direct inspection of union contracts. This approach offers little support for the view that employment is determined through union–firm negotiations.

Several researchers have tried to recover information about union objectives by means of estimating wage and employment equations. These have typically been structural models based on particular parameterizations of the form of the union's objective function, and specific bargaining solutions have been assumed. Tests that have invoked the monopoly solution typically reject rent maximization. These tests may, however, be seriously misleading if the monopoly model is inappropriate.

Although the monopoly model has been widely used, almost no empirical study attempts to *test* it against some general alternative. Series on union density or union–non-union wage differentials are widely used in macro-oriented labour market models, but whether or not these measures are sensible proxies for union power is an open question. It seems safe to predict that much of the future work on union wage premiums will make use of behavioural bargaining models.

3

The Determination of Employment and Wages: Swedish Mining and Manufacturing, 1950–1985

3.1. Introduction

The theoretical sections of this essay have emphasized that many conclusions from wage-bargaining models are sensitive to specific assumptions about union objectives, the union's bargaining power, and the properties of the labour demand function. The need for empirical work is obvious, and this section will focus on the determination of employment and real wages in the Swedish mining and manufacturing sector.

Most earlier Swedish studies of wage formation have involved estimation of wage change equations, typically in the Phillips curve tradition, with wage inflation explained by unemployment (or some other measure of labour market slack) and (expected) price inflation. Researchers have occasionally estimated separate equations for contractual wage increases and 'wage drift', the latter defined as the difference between total wage increases and contractual wage increases. The role of taxes was ignored in earlier work, but has entered the scene in more recent studies. There has been no attention paid to variables that influence the union's target wage in a bargaining model, such as unemployment benefits, and with the exception of the paper by Pencavel and Holmlund (1988), there have been no investigations of the role of work-hours in wage-setting.

A bargaining approach to wage formation regards the wage outcome as driven by the unions' and the employers' objectives and constraints. Our empirical work proceeds under the maintained hypothesis that employment is determined by profit-maximizing firms. This appears to be an uncontroversial assumption, especially as long as we focus on centralized wage negotiations; employment has not been subject to negotiations between the employers' federation and the confederation of trade unions. Whether or not bargaining over employment takes place at the local firm or work-place level is more open to question. Swedish legislation on co-determination and employment security has equipped the local union with a 'voice' in matters of, for example, major reductions in employment. Although this may give the union a chance to influence the *timing* of employment changes, there is little doubt that the ultimate power to hire and fire rests with the employers.

The specification of the real-wage equation is derived from a monopoly union model. The motivation for this focus on the monopoly case, rather than on a more general bargaining model, is our desire to *test* certain theoretical restrictions implied by the monopoly union model. The restrictions appear as constraints across the labour demand equation and the wage equation, and they are consistent with several union objective functions. No attempt, however, is made to estimate particular parameters of a presumed objective function.

We proceed by looking at some basic facts about wages, hours, and employment, and some of the potential determinants. Section 3 is devoted to estimations of labour demand equations, and section 4 estimates a simultaneous-equation model of employment and wages.

3.2. The Basic Facts[1]

3.2.1. Unemployment and Employment

We begin by looking at unemployment and employment. Fig. 3.1 shows the Swedish unemployment rate according to the definitions of the labour force statistics. Although Swedish unemployment is low by international standards, there has been an upward trend since the early 1960s. This holds also for the unemployment rate for blue-collar workers, as represented by the unemployment rate for employees in manufacturing occupations (according to data from the labour force statistics), or by the unemployment rate for members of industrial UI funds ('industrikassor').

Total employment has increased substantially in Sweden during the past two decades, but employment in mining and manufacturing has shown a sharp decrease. Whereas total employment *increased*

---

[1] The variables are described in some detail in the Data Appendix beginning on p. 103.

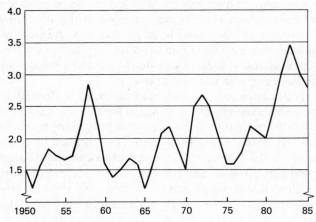

Fig. 3.1. Unemployment in Sweden, 1950–1985

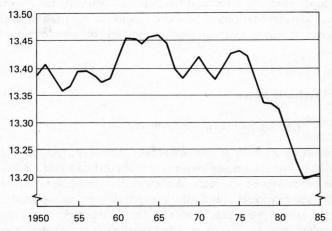

Fig. 3.2. Employment (in logs) among blue-collar workers in Swedish mining and manufacturing, 1950–85

by 16 per cent between 1965 and 1985 (implying an increase in the employment–population ratio from 0.65 to 0.70), the number of employees in manufacturing *fell* by 16 per cent during the same period. Fig. 3.2 shows employment for blue-collar workers in mining and manufacturing; the fall in employment amounts to more than 20 per cent for this group between 1965 and 1985.

3.2.2. Work-Hours

Work-hours among employees have fallen during most of the post-war period (Fig. 3.3). A production worker in Swedish industry worked on average around 2,100 hours per year in the early 1950s, but only 1,500 hours in the early 1980s. The secular reduction in working time has different sources, including longer vacations, a shorter 'standard' work-week, a rise in absenteeism, more part-time work, and a fall in overtime hours.

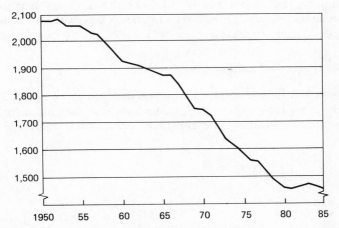

Fig. 3.3. Work-hours per year among blue-collar workers in Swedish mining and manufacturing, 1950–1985

The reduction in annual work-hours can to some extent be traced to legislative changes. These have occurred frequently, and the implementation of a particular change has often taken place gradually. The changes include laws and negotiated agreements on paid vacation; a law from 1951 extended paid vacation to three weeks, an additional increase in paid vacation took place in 1964–5 (one extra week), and in 1978 a law was passed granting all employees at least five weeks' paid vacation. The standard work-week has also been reduced, partly by laws and partly through agreements between LO (the Confederation of Trade Unions) and SAF (the Swedish Employers' Federation). The standard work-week was 48 hours in the early 1950s; it was reduced to 45 hours in the late 1950s, and further reductions (to 42.5 hours) were decided by LO–SAF in 1966. The most recent major change was the law on work-hours from 1970, implying a reduction in weekly hours from 42.5 to 40 hours during the period 1971–3. Agreements between employers and unions give workers in certain occupations a shorter work-week than the standard 40-hour week.

There have also been a number of laws granting leave of absence for various reasons (birth of children, educational reasons, etc.). Subsidies to part-time retirement have contributed to the trend decline in work-hours, and legal restrictions on overtime have presumably had some effect. In 1973 the limit on maximum overtime was reduced from 200 to 150 hours per year, but the limit was raised again to 200 hours in 1983.

3.2.3. *Wages and Labour Costs*

Let us now turn to movements of wages and labour costs (Fig. 3.4). Workers' average real-consumption wages, i.e. nominal after-tax wage-rates deflated by the consumer price index, increased on

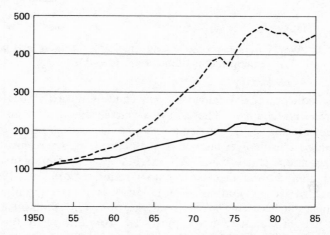

Fig. 3.4. Real-consumption wages (solid line) and real-product wages (dotted line) for blue-collar workers in Swedish mining and manufacturing, 1950–1985 (Index 1950 = 100)

average by 3 per cent per year during the period 1950–76, but this upward trend was sharply reversed in later years; real wages in 1985 were 9 per cent lower than real wages in 1976. This fall in real wages is primarily accounted for by the failure of nominal wages to keep up with price inflation; increases in income taxes do not account for much of the real-wage deterioration after 1976.

Real-product wages have increased much faster than real-consumption wages, as is seen from Fig. 3.4. (The product wage is defined as labour cost per hour, including payroll taxes, deflated by an output price index for manufacturing.) The product wage rose by almost 6 per cent per year up to 1978, and declined slightly during the years following. One source behind the more rapid increase in product wages is that consumer prices have risen almost 1 per cent faster per year than producer prices in manufacturing; another source is the rapid increase in taxes (and fees) on employers and a concomitant but less dramatic increase in income taxes on workers (see Fig. 3.5).

The wages of blue-collar workers have increased much faster than the salaries of white-collar workers during the post-war period, and there has been a dramatic reduction in wage inequality between men

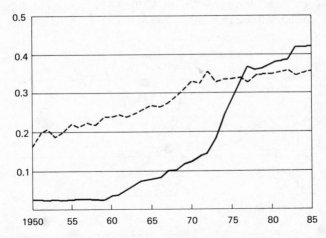

Fig. 3.5.   Payroll tax-rate (solid line) and average income tax rate (dotted line) for blue-collar workers in Swedish mining and manufacturing, 1950–1985

and women. The hourly wage of a female blue-collar worker amounted to 70 per cent of the male wage during the 1950s, but stood at 90 per cent in the early 1980s. There has also been a substantial equalization of pay between male and female white-collar workers.

3.2.4. Unemployment Insurance and Unionization

The Swedish unemployment insurance system is organized through a number of certified UI funds with close ties to the trade unions. The Government sets various rules for the UI funds, and covers a substantial fraction of the funds' expenses for unemployment benefits. Benefit levels are set by the funds, but the range of permissible levels is set by the Government. The UI funds have in general adjusted granted benefit levels to the legal maximum, sometimes with a lag.

Fig. 3.6 shows a series on maximum weekly real after-tax unemployment benefits for insured workers (i.e. workers who are members of UI funds and in addition fulfil some requirements relating to length of membership and employment during the previous year). The series shows a more erratic behaviour than the series on real wages. (Maximum benefits were constant in nominal terms for a number of years in the 1950s.) The trends are, however, rather similar, although benefits rise at a slightly faster rate, so there

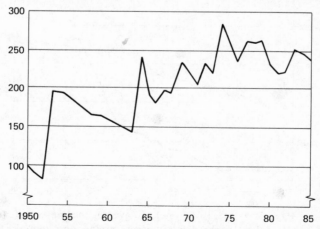

Fig. 3.6. Real weekly unemployment benefits among members of UI funds, Sweden, 1950–85 (Index 1950 = 100)

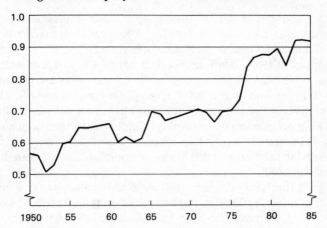

Fig. 3.7. Government share of total outlays on unemployment benefits, Sweden, 1950–1985

has been some increase in replacement ratios for insured workers.

Government subsidies to the union-affiliated U I funds have also shown a marked increase, as is evident from Fig. 3.7. Unemployment benefits were not treated as taxable income before 1974; Fig. 3.7 shows the Government's net subsidies as a fraction of net benefits. The rules of the subsidy system have undergone several changes over time. The system prevailing in the mid-1980s was progressive in the sense that the average subsidy increased with unemployment in the particular U I fund. Let G denote government subsidies and let the total amount of paid-out benefits be given by the number of unemployed $(M - N)$ times the benefit level (B). The current Swedish subsidy system can then be characterized by

$$G = [0.8 + 0.2P(\cdot)](M - N)B \qquad (89)$$

where $P(\cdot)$ is a progressive grant ('progressivbidrag'). The latter is increasing with unemployment in the U I fund, and ranges from zero (for funds with negligible unemployment) to 0.9 (for funds with more than twenty-one unemployment days per member during a year). The subsidy scheme is thus strictly proportional for U I funds with 'high' unemployment; the average and marginal (gross) subsidy rate is then 0.98. (Further details regarding the Swedish U I system are given in Björklund and Holmlund, 1986.)

Other changes in the UI system have made it successively more generous over the past two decades. The maximum benefit periods have increased, and a new unemployment benefit system was introduced in 1974, involving 'cash benefits' ('kontant arbetsmark-nadsstöd' or 'KAS') for unemployed workers who are outside the UI system (or who do not fulfil the eligibility requirements). The UI funds' coverage of the labour force has increased substantially, and a growing proportion of unemployed individuals have been covered by the UI system. Twenty-five per cent of unemployed persons were members of UI funds in 1965; this proportion had increased to 63 per cent in 1985.

The UI funds' coverage of industrial blue-collar workers has not increased much, reflecting that unionization rates have traditionally been very high among these workers. The total membership in all UI funds increased from 1.4 millions to 3.4 millions between 1963 and 1985. Membership in industrial UI funds has not shown any trend during this period, although the sharp fall in industrial employment after 1975 is accompanied by a concomitant fall in membership.

Unionization rates among Swedish employees in general have shown an upward trend during the past two decades. If union membership figures are related to the number of employees, we find unionization rates around 70 per cent in the mid-60s, but above 85 per cent in the early 80s (Kjellberg, 1983, p. 278).

3.3. The Determinants of Employment

We will now turn to an investigation into the determinants of labour demand in Swedish mining and manufacturing. We are in particular interested in the wage–employment relationship; is there strong evidence supporting the standard neo-classical prediction of a negative relationship between real-product wages and the demand for labour? The role of work-hours is also of considerable interest; to the extent that there is a case for work-sharing, this is clearly not weakened if workers and work-hours are close substitutes in production.

Suppose that there is a representative price-taking firm equipped with a gross output production function

$$Q = Q(N, h, K, M, T) \tag{90}$$

where Q is output, N is employment, h is hours per worker, K is capital, M is materials, and T is a technology parameter. The profit function takes the form

$$\Pi = qQ(\cdot) - w_c Nh - rK - mM \qquad (91)$$

where q is the output price, w_c is the hourly labour cost, r is the user cost of capital, and m is the price of materials. Working time is assumed to be exogenous to the firm's employment decision, and h refers to 'normal' hours defined as annual hours excluding overtime. No data on fixed costs of labour are available, and the profit expression reflects this limitation. We assume that output increases less than proportionally to increases in N, K, and M, so we can derive input demand functions by maximizing $\Pi(\cdot)$ with respect to the quantity of the three variable inputs. (Note that the size of the firm may be determinate even under constant returns to scale, provided that there are internal costs of adjusting the capital stock, or some other factor. Output will then increase less than proportionally to increases in input quantities.) We thus obtain the neoclassical labour demand function

$$N = N(w_c, r, m, q, h, T) \qquad (92)$$

which is homogeneous of degree zero in output and input prices. The labour demand equation will be taken to be log-linear in the empirical implementation. Ignoring dynamics and stochastic errors, we thus have

$$\ell nN = \alpha_0 + \alpha_1 \ell nh + \alpha_2 \ell n(w_c/q) + \alpha_3 \ell n(r/q) + \alpha_4 \ell n(m/q)$$
$$+ \alpha_5 T \qquad (93)$$

where T will be represented by a time trend. Note that $\alpha_1 = -1$ if workers and work-hours are perfect substitutes. Characterizing technical progress by a single trend may of course be too restrictive, and we therefore investigate how the basic results are affected by more flexible trends.

Earlier work on labour demand functions has often captured dynamics by two lagged dependent variables, and in our OLS estimations it turns out that a specification with two lags on employment consistently out-performs a specification with only one lag. The rationales for lagged dependent variables are several, including (i) adjustment costs and (ii) aggregation. For example, if the firm faces quadratic adjustment costs it turns out that the dynamic labour demand function will entail lagged employment on the right-hand side (see Nickell, 1986). Aggregation over firms or labour force categories with different adjustment costs may introduce additional lags on the dependent variable. Even if each sector is well characterized by only one lag on employment, the aggregate relationship may involve two lags on the dependent variable. (Again, see Nickell for details.)

Our estimating equations will focus on the demand for blue-collar workers. If there is some substitutability (or complementarity) between blue-collar and white-collar workers, the set of right-hand variables should include costs for both types of labour. (See Hamermesh, 1986, for a survey of the empirical literature on labour–labour substitution.) Blue-collar wages and white-collar salaries are highly collinear over the post-war period, although there has been a substantial pay compression. However, when we entered white-collar salaries as a separate argument in the labour demand equation for blue-collar workers, no significant white-collar effect could be detected.

The neo-classical labour demand function ignores the potential role of aggregate demand, at *given* real factor prices. However, if a firm is sales-constrained, a rise in aggregate demand may relax the constraint and allow employment expansion at unchanged factor prices. We have included two variables to capture aggregate-demand shifts. The first demand variable is (the log of) Swedish households' real disposable income ($\ell n\ Y$); the second is (the log of) an index of world trade in manufacturing goods ($\ell n\ WTM$).

3.3.1. Estimation Results

Table 3.1 sets out instrumental variable estimates of log-linear labour demand equations, with wages and work-hours treated as endogenous. (The OLS estimates were very similar to the instrumental-variable estimates.) The hourly labour cost is defined as $w_c \equiv w(1 + s)$, so payroll taxes (s) are accounted for. Overtime premiums are excluded from the wage-rate. The regressions in the first two columns exclude the aggregate-demand variables ($\ell n\ Y$ and $\ell n\ WTM$). This restriction is, however, clearly rejected by the data. The wage coefficients are insignificantly different from zero in the purely neo-classical specifications, but estimated with quite good precision when aggregate demand is allowed for (columns (3) and (4)). In fact, most coefficients become much better determined

TABLE 3.1. *Instrumental variable estimates of labour demand equations, Swedish mining and manufacturing, 1951–1985*

	(1)	(2)	(3)	(4)
Constant	4.368	6.325	−3.097	−2.289
	(2.873)	(3.220)	(2.182)	(1.418)
$\ell n\,(w_c/q)$	0.048	0.029	−0.295	−0.300
	(0.669)	(0.224)	(5.100)	(3.606)
$\ell n\,(r/q)$	0.057	0.033	0.039	0.034
	(3.165)	(1.454)	(3.521)	(2.714)
$\ell n\,(m/q)$	−0.673	−0.550	−0.894	−0.832
	(2.586)	(1.996)	(6.572)	(5.534)
$\ell n\,h$	−0.360	−0.562	−0.355	−0.438
	(1.771)	(1.988)	(3.232)	(2.712)
$\ell n\,N_{-1}$	1.398	1.219	0.795	0.773
	(9.315)	(6.535)	(6.687)	(6.342)
$\ell n\,N_{-2}$	−0.694	−0.655	−0.248	−0.236
	(4.332)	(4.091)	(2.357)	(2.204)
T	−0.0084	−0.0007	−0.016	−0.014
	(2.006)	(0.112)	(5.612)	(3.583)
$T^2/1000$	—	−0.395	—	−0.073
		(0.531)		(0.188)
$T^3/1000$	—	0.004	—	−0.0005
		(0.290)		(0.006)
$\ell n\,Y$	—	0.818	—	0.762
		(7.339)		(6.126)
$\ell n\,WTM$	—	0.064	—	0.076
		(2.325)		(2.530)
DW	1.680	1.484	2.086	2.098
$\overline{R}^2$	0.943	0.945	0.985	0.985
SEE	0.017	0.017	0.009	0.009

Note: Absolute values of t-statistics are in the parentheses. Wages and work hours are treated as endogenous. The instrumental variables are a constant, $\ell n(r/q)$, $\ell n(m/q)$, T, T^2, T^3, $\ell n\,Y$, $\ell n\,WTM$, $\ell n\,N_{-1}$, $\ell n\,N_{-2}$, $\ell n(w_c/q)_{-1}$, $\ell n(1+s)$, $\ell n(1-t)$, $\ell n\,h_{-1}$, $\ell n[w(1-t)/p]_{-1}$ (the real consumption wage, lagged one year) and $\ell n\,B_r$ (real weekly unemployment benefits). The DW-statistic is biased in the presence of lagged dependent variables. The test suggested by Durbin (1970) did not indicate autocorrelation. (The test involves regressing the residual on its lagged value and all variables of the estimating equation; autocorrelation is indicated if the coefficient of the lagged residual is significantly different from zero.)

when $\ell n\,Y$ and $\ell n\,WTM$ are included. We also note that a single trend seems to be sufficient to capture technical progress.

We focus on the estimates in the third column in the following discussion. The estimated wage elasticity is 0.30 in the short run and 0.65 in the long run. This rather low elasticity estimate does not sit easily with a Cobb–Douglas interpretation. (A Cobb–Douglas production function implies input demand functions with own elasticities above unity, in absolute value.) As was noted in Chapter 2, empirical work on employment demand functions has quite often produced estimates of wage elasticities below unity, and these studies have also typically adopted log-linear specifications. Aggregation over firms, some of which may be sales-constrained, may well lead to such results.

The coefficient on the user cost of capital is positive, as we should expect; a rise in r by 10 per cent raises the demand for workers by 0.4 per cent in the short run and by 0.8 per cent in the long run.[2] The demand for workers seems to be very sensitive to changes in the price of materials (i.e. intermediate consumption including raw materials and energy). Taken at face value, a rise in the price of materials by 10 per cent would reduce employment by 9 per cent in the short run. This effect may seem a little high, but the estimate is in fact in broad agreement with estimates produced by Symons and Layard (1984) using data for manufacturing employment in six major OECD economies.[3]

The unrestricted estimate of the short-run employment–hours elasticity is -0.35, and the corresponding long-run elasticity is

[2] In some alternative estimations we included the capital stock in mining and manufacturing rather than the user cost of capital. This specification was, however, clearly inferior (in terms of the standard error of the regression), and it yielded negative and/or insignificant coefficients for capital.

[3] It should be noted that the price index for materials is computed from data on the value and volume of intermediate consumption that include intra-industry transactions. This tends to inflate the coefficient on material prices, as can be seen as follows. Suppose that the observed price index can be written as a geometric average, $m = m_I^\gamma q^{1-\gamma}$, where m_I is the price of materials that are purchased from sectors outside mining mining and manufacturing and γ is the share of this 'import'; $(1 - \gamma)$ is consequently the share of intermediate consumption that represents intra-industry transactions, and it is assumed that the price of this intermediate input from the industry into itself moves at the same rate as the output price index, q. Suppose that m, rather than m_I, is used in the estimating labour demand equation. Noting that $\ell n\, m = \gamma \ell n\, m_I + (1 - \gamma)\ell nq$, we have $\dfrac{\partial \ell nN}{\partial \ell nm_I} = \alpha_4 \gamma$, where α_4 is the estimated employment elasticity of material prices, i.e. $(\partial \ell nN/\partial \ell nm) = \alpha_4$. If the share of intermediate goods purchased from sectors outside mining and manufacturing is 50%, the elasticity estimates in Table 3.1 should be halved to obtain the employment response to an 'external' shock to material prices.

– 0.77. The results are thus consistent with a production function in which workers and work-hours are close to perfect substitutes. This can be compared to related Swedish evidence based on direct estimation of production functions. Åberg (1985) estimates Cobb–Douglas production functions for mining and manufacturing, using data for the period 1963–82. He finds an output–employment elasticity of 0.75 and an output–hours elasticity of 0.73, which almost certainly are insignificant differences. (Åberg does not present information on standard errors for his estimates.) A more recent study by Anxo and Bigsten (1986) utilizes pooled cross-section and time-series data from the first quarter of 1980 to the fourth quarter of 1983. Their estimates of the output–hours elasticity fall in a rather wide range, but are typically located around unity, so it is above the output–employment elasticity. An early study by Feldstein (1967) also finds output–hours elasticities that are (substantially) above the output–employment elasticities; his estimates are, however, very imprecise. In conclusion, our estimates of hours-employment substitutability—based on a labour demand function —do not stand out as exceptional compared to results from direct production function estimation.

As already noted, a specification with two lags on the dependent variable consistently out-performs specifications with only one lag. The coefficient on the first lagged variable is around 0.8 and the coefficient on the second lag is – 0.25. Almost 50 per cent of the adjustment to a change in an exogenous variable will take place within one year.

Does the preferred specification pass conventional tests for parameter stability? Two Chow tests were undertaken, one with sample split in 1967/8 and the other checking for structural breaks after 1973. The tests do not permit rejection (at the 5 per cent level) of a null hypothesis of parameter stability across samples.[4]

---

[4] Very similar parameter estimates are obtained if the labour demand equation is estimated without imposing zero homogeneity in prices. The instrumental variable estimates are as follows:

$$\ell nN = -2.529 - 0.332\ell n\hat{w}_c + 0.032\ell nr - 0.776\ell nm + 1.033\ell nq$$
$$- 0.482\ell n\hat{h} - 0.013T + 0.778\ell nN_{-1} - 0.234\ell nN_{-2}$$
$$+ 0.800\ell nY + 0.065\ell nWTM.$$

All coefficients are significantly different from zero at conventional levels. ($\bar{R}^2 = 0.985$ and $SEE = 0.009$).

3.3.2. Functional Form Analysis

Is the log-linear specification 'superior' to other parsimonious functional forms of the labour demand equation? Carruth and Oswald
(1986) estimate a labour demand equation for Britain, and add (to
the otherwise log-linear equation) the square and the cube of the
(log) real-product wage. They find support for an S-shaped, rather
than a log-linear, labour demand curve. A replication of their
experiment on Swedish data was, however, unsuccessful in finding
support for deviations from log-linearity.

As an additional check, we applied the Box–Cox transformation.
Consider the functional form

$$\frac{y^\lambda - 1}{\lambda} = \kappa_1 + \frac{\kappa_2(X^\lambda - 1)}{\lambda} \tag{94}$$

where λ is a parameter to be estimated along with κ_1 and κ_2. This
form has linearity as a special case when $\lambda = 1$,

$$y = (\kappa_1 - \kappa_2 + 1) + \kappa_2 X \tag{95}$$

and reduces to a log-linear model when λ approaches zero:

$$\ell n\, y = \kappa_1 + \kappa_2 \ell n\, X. \tag{96}$$

Tests of particular functional forms make use of likelihood ratios
in the usual way. Can linearity be rejected? ($H_0{:}\lambda = 1$ against the
alternative $H_A{:}\lambda \neq 1$.) Can log-linearity be rejected? ($H_0{:}\lambda = 0$
against the alternative $H_A{:}\lambda \neq 0$.) Several versions of Box–Cox
transformed labour demand equations were estimated. The specifications differed with respect to the treatment of trend variables,
aggregate-demand variables, and restrictions on λ. Table 3.2 pre-
sents four regressions: $(w_c/q)^{(\lambda)}$ denotes $[(w_c/q)^{(\lambda)} - 1]/\lambda$, $(r/q)^{(\lambda)}$
denotes $[(r/q)^{(\lambda)} - 1]/\lambda$, etc. The trend variables were always
untransformed ($\lambda = 1$). As is seen, the estimated values of λ are
much closer to zero than to unity, and the unrestricted log-likelihood is very close to the restricted log-likelihood with $\lambda = 0$.
Conventional likelihood ratio tests clearly reject $H_0{:}\lambda = 1$, whereas
$H_0{:}\lambda = 0$ cannot be rejected. A null hypothesis of linearity is always
rejected; a null hypothesis of log-linearity is easily accepted.[5]

---

[5] Wages and work-hours are not instrumented in the Box–Cox regressions.

TABLE 3.2. *Labour demand equations with Box–Cox transformations, Swedish mining and manufacturing, 1950–1985*

	(1)	(2)	(3)	(4)
Constant	−2.721	−2.738	−38.353	−5.224
	(1.739)[a]	(0.662)	(5.743)	(2.165)
$(w(1+s)/q)^{(\lambda)}$[b]	−0.378	−1.112	−1.471	−0.401
	(5.530)	(4.764)	(5.626)	(4.745)
$(r/q)^{(\lambda)}$	0.072	0.278	0.420	0.674
	(4.082)	(2.922)	(3.684)	(2.846)
$(m/q)^{(\lambda)}$	−1.273	−4.713	−6.079	−1.444
	(6.460)	(5.453)	(6.427)	(5.531)
$h^{(\lambda)}$	−0.608	−2.913	−3.461	−0.902
	(3.888)	(3.992)	(4.558)	(3.954)
$N(-1)^{(\lambda)}$	0.887	0.839	0.870	0.844
	(7.745)	(7.111)	(7.633)	(7.037)
$N(-2)^{(\lambda)}$	−0.330	−0.295	−0.323	−0.299
	(3.363)	(2.878)	(3.333)	(2.909)
T	−0.023	−0.068	−0.120	−0.022
	(5.091)	(3.369)	(5.471)	(3.358)
$T^2/1000$	—	−1.569	—	0.437
		(0.955)		(0.884)
$T^3/1000$	—	2.230	—	0.069
		(0.681)		(0.678)
$Y^{(\lambda)}$	0.770	0.814	5.269	1.212
	(7.539)	(5.985)	(7.516)	(5.946)
$WTM^{(\lambda)}$	0.062	0.174	0.381	0.097
	(1.698)	(1.973)	(1.827)	(1.907)
$\hat{\lambda}$	0.030	0.130	0.150	0.040
Log-likelihood	−358.90	−357.40	−358.40	−357.58
Restricted $\quad\lambda=0$	−358.91	−357.59	−358.91	−357.59
log-likelihood $\quad\lambda=1$	−363.90	−360.59	−363.90	−360.59
DW	2.067	2.127	2.049	2.087
$\overline{R}^2$	0.983	0.983	0.983	0.983

Note: t-values are in parentheses; λ is always constrained to unity for T, T^2, and T^3, and constrained to zero for Y and WTM in regressions (3) and (4).

In conclusion, the log-linear specification of the labour demand function seems superior to obvious alternative parsimonious representations of the data. This has important implications for the union's optimal-wage policy, as was noted in the theory section.

3.4. A Simultaneous-Equation Model of Employment and Wages

The estimation results for the labour demand equations have suggested that employment is significantly affected by wages, and we now proceed to the derivation of a wage equation under the assumption that wages in Swedish mining and manufacturing are set by a centralized union. The exposition focuses on a utilitarian objective function, but some implications do not depend on this assumption. The union runs its own UI scheme, and has to obey the budget restriction of its UI fund. The labour demand curve is taken to be log-linear—an assumption that seems to fit the facts reasonably well —and the union is assumed to treat the unemployment benefit level as exogenous to its wage decision.

We take as our maintained hypothesis that the secular movements in annual hours primarily reflect individual labour supply responses to changes in wage-rates, tax-rates, and wealth. It is certainly true that legislative changes have accounted for some of the trend decline in work-hours, but it would be surprising if such legislation were unrelated to individual preferences.

Hours of work may or may not be regarded as exogenous to the union's wage choice. The exogeneity assumption makes sense if the union does not perceive a link between wages and work-hours, or if the single union's wage choice is unable significantly to affect economy-wide wage movements, the latter perhaps being crucial for legislative and other forces behind long-run movements in hours of work. In case the union takes work-hours as given, the structural-wage equation will include work-hours as one argument. On the other hand, if the union can exert indirect control over work-hours through its wage choice, and correctly perceives this possibility, hours of work do not belong to the structural-wage equation. We proceed under the assumption that the union takes work-hours as given, and we will not give estimates of a structural equation for work-hours.

Suppose that the union's objective function takes the form

$$\Lambda = NU(e/p, h) + (M - N)\tilde{V}(\cdot) \tag{97}$$

where $e = (1 - t)(wh - z)$ is net earnings, with the UI premium denoted by z and the income tax rate by t. $\tilde{V}$ is the utility of a worker who does not find employment in the sector, and it is specified as

$$\tilde{V} = (1 - \psi)U(\bar{e}/p, h) + \psi V(B_r) \tag{98}$$

where ψ is the fraction of time spent unemployed, and $(1 - \psi)$ is the fraction of time spent employed outside mining and manufacturing. Expected alternative earnings is $\bar{e} = (1 - t)(\bar{w}h - \bar{z})$, where $\bar{w}$ is the expected alternative wage, $\bar{z}$ is the UI premium outside the sector, and B_r is real after-tax benefits, $B_r = B(1 - t)/p$. In this formulation, UI premiums are not paid by unemployed workers, but this assumption is unimportant for the main features of the model. The union recognizes the UI budget restriction

$$zN = (1 - G_1)\psi(M - N)B - G_0 \qquad (99)$$

where G_1 is the marginal government subsidy rate, and G_0 is the lump-sum subsidy.

Suppose that the labour demand function has a constant wage elasticity, and write the function as $N = N(w, h, Z)$, where Z is a vector of demand shift variables. Earlier results have suggested that Z should be specified as

$$Z = Z(s, r, m, q, Y, WTM, N_{-1}, N_{-2}, T) \qquad (100)$$

with the notation of section 3 above. Maximizing the objective function with respect to w and z yields equations for the decision variables.[6] The nominal-wage equation can be written as

$$w = w(p, t, Z, h, B, G_0, G_1, \psi, \bar{w}, \bar{z}, M). \qquad (101)$$

We have already in the theory section discussed how wages are affected by variables on the right-hand side of (101). Unambiguous sign predictions are possible in a few cases, but quite often we need specific assumptions concerning union preferences, premium rules, or hours determination in order to avoid ambiguities. The variables ψ, $\bar{z}$, and $\bar{w}$ have not explicitly been dealt with, but it should be obvious that increases in ψ or $\bar{z}$, or reductions in $\bar{w}$, are likely to reduce the wage-rate by reducing union members' perceived outside earnings.

3.4.1. *The Empirical Model*

Some of the variables in (101) cannot be observed directly, so the empirical model must to some extent be formulated in terms of proxy variables. The consumer price (p) is the least problematic

---

[6] The dynamics of the labour demand relationship is not accounted for by this static optimization.

variable; we simply use the consumer price index. The income tax rate (t) is represented by a series on average income tax rates for blue-collar workers; the complications arising from the progressive tax system are thus disregarded. The two theoretical parameters of the UI subsidy system, G_0 and G_1, are not easily detected from the rather complex (and changing) subsidy rules. We include as a proxy for G_1 the average subsidy rate (G_a), measured as the ratio between the Government's net subsidies to all UI funds and the UI funds' total expenses on unemployment benefits. As unemployment benefit variable we take a series on real weekly *maximum* benefits. This is the maximum permissible daily benefit level—determined by the Government—translated into a weekly real income, recognizing that benefits became taxable in 1974. This benefit variable can reasonably be regarded as exogenous to the union.

The fraction of time spent unemployed, ψ, is correlated with movements in unemployment and vacancy rates. There are no data available on unfilled vacancies for the whole estimation period, so we are left with using the aggregate unemployment rate (RU). It may to some extent be endogenous to wage-setting in mining and manufacturing, and we therefore used its lagged value.

The expected outside wage is not easily observed in available data. Outside opportunities may include self-employment and employment in labour market programmes (including early retirement), as well as regular employment outside mining and manufacturing. We have used series on real disposable incomes of households (Y) and the total number of hours worked (HRS) in the economy, and constructed a measure of economy-wide real income per hour, $y = Y/HRS$. The logarithm of y was regressed on a quintic trend and the fitted value ($\ell n \hat{y}$) was used as proxy for expected real outside earnings. This fundamental trend variable of the wage equation captures the secular growth of workers' real-income opportunities.

Work-hours enter the wage equation via several routes. There is an effect through the labour demand schedule; earlier results suggest that longer hours will reduce employment at a given wage-rate. There are additional effects that work through the employed worker's utility function if he is employed in the sector, and also if he is employed outside the sector. No distinction will be made between 'inside hours' and 'outside hours'.

Expected outside UI premiums are not included as a separate regressor in the wage equation. Note that economy-wide UI premiums can be written as $\bar{z} = \bar{z}(G_a, RU, B)$; the premium is decreasing in the subsidy rate and increasing in the unemployment rate and the benefit level. To the extent that the UI system has any effect on wage-setting via this route—which seems rather unlikely —it should be captured by our inclusion of G_a, RU, and B, in the wage equation.

Finally, there is a potential role for the size of membership (M). This variable may influence wages if the union runs its own UI scheme, although sign predictions require assumptions about premium rules. We tried to capture movements in union member-ship by using a series on the number of members of blue-collar workers' UI funds (*industrikassor*).

The monopoly model, together with the log-linear labour demand schedule, implies certain restrictions across the wage and employ-ment equations. If we let Z_i and Z_j denote two demand shift vari-ables in the Z vector, the equality

$$\frac{\partial w/\partial Z_i}{\partial w/\partial Z_j} = \frac{\partial N/\partial Z_i}{\partial N/\partial Z_j} \tag{102}$$

must hold. The ratio between the employment effects equals the ratio between the wage effects. This follows from the fact that the wage-rate is affected by the location of the labour demand schedule, irrespective of whether a particular shift involves an increase or a decrease in the firms' profits. This implication, which does not carry over to a wage-bargaining model of the Nash type, can also be written as

$$\frac{\partial \ell n w/\partial \ell n Z_i}{\partial \ell n w/\partial \ell n Z_j} = \frac{\partial \ell n N/\partial \ell n Z_i}{\partial \ell n N/\partial \ell n Z_j} \tag{103}$$

stating that the ratio between the elasticities in the labour demand equation equals the ratio between the corresponding elasticities in the wage equation.[7]

The discussion suggests a log-linearized empirical model of the form

---

[7] These cross-equation constraints are consistent with other objective functions. Suppose that union objectives are represented by a general function, $\Lambda = g(e, N, h)$, with $g_1 > 0$, $g_2 > 0$, and $g_3 < 0$. If work-hours are taken as given, the first-order condition reads $\Lambda_w = hg_1 - (N/w)g_2\epsilon = 0$, where $\epsilon = - wN_w/N$. Iso-elastic shifts of the labour demand function preserve the 'ratio conditions' stated above.

$$\ell nN = \alpha_0 + \alpha_1 \ell n\hat{h} + \alpha_2 \ell nw + \alpha Z \tag{104}$$

$$\ell n[w(1 - t)/p] = \beta_0 + \beta_1 \ell n[p/(1 - t)] + \mu\alpha Z + \beta_2 \ell n\hat{h} \\ + \beta_3 \ell nB_r + \beta_4 \ell nG_a + \beta_5 \ell n\hat{y} \\ + \beta_6 \ell nRU_{-1} + \beta_7 \ell nM_{-1} \tag{105}$$

where Z stands for other variables that affect employment and wages:

$$\alpha Z = \alpha_2 \ell n[(1 + s)/q] + \alpha_3 \ell n(r/q) + \alpha_4 \ell n(m/q) + \alpha_5 T \\ + \alpha_6 \ell nY + \alpha_7 \ell nWTM + \alpha_8 \ell nN_{-1} + \alpha_9 \ell nN_{-2}. \tag{106}$$

The coefficient μ captures wage responses to shifts of the labour demand schedule, and its sign depends on which premium rule the union follows; μ is negative if only employed members have to pay UI premiums, but μ may well be positive under other premium arrangements. We will impose the restriction $\beta_1 = \mu\alpha_2$ in the wage equation. Employment and real wages are then invariant to equiproportional changes of the nominal variables in the system.

Wage-setting decisions are based on expectations regarding relative prices and other variables. By assumption, expected relative prices (i.e. p/q, r/q, and m/q) are based on the average of current and one-year lagged prices. Perfect foresight is assumed for taxes, benefits, UI subsidies, and the aggregate-demand variables. Workhours are predicted from an equation where the instruments include laged hours as well as the predetermined variables of the labour demand equation and the wage equation.

3.4.2. Estimation Results

Table 3.3 presents estimates of the parameters of equations (104) and (105). The model was estimated by the FIML procedure in TSP 4.0. Convergence was typically achieved after 6–7 iterations. The different columns correspond to estimations with alternative restrictions on parameters. The least restrictive form of the model appears in column (1) and the most restrictive in column (5). The restrictions implied by a monopoly union model are always imposed, and the estimated models will therefore be referred to as 'M models' in the sequel.

The FIML estimates of the parameters of the structural labour demand equation are in broad agreement with earlier instrumental-variable estimates. We also note that higher unemployment benefits

TABLE 3.3. *FIML estimates of the parameters of equations (104) and (105). Estimation period: 1951–1985*

	(1)	(2)	(3)	(4)	(5)
Labour demand					
α_0	−2.953	−3.035	−3.061	−3.288	−2.543
	(1.015)	(1.236)	(1.345)	(1.441)	(1.343)
α_1	−0.401	−0.393	−0.394	−0.428	−0.415
	(2.278)	(2.776)	(2.863)	(3.376)	(3.435)
α_2	−0.299	−0.303	−0.303	−0.312	−0.282
	(2.806)	(3.069)	(3.396)	(3.496)	(3.678)
α_3	0.040	0.040	0.039	0.040	0.037
	(2.198)	(2.799)	(2.823)	(2.823)	(2.787)
α_4	−0.924	−0.922	−0.924	−0.934	−0.791
	(3.597)	(3.705)	(3.841)	(3.881)	(4.740)
α_5	−0.015	−0.016	−0.016	−0.016	−0.016
	(3.869)	(3.970)	(4.161)	(4.502)	(4.957)
α_6	0.806	0.818	0.826	0.839	0.765
	(5.342)	(5.381)	(5.597)	(5.691)	(4.276)
α_7	0.056	0.058	0.060	0.062	0.061
	(0.685)	(0.879)	(0.977)	(1.053)	(1.244)
α_8	0.838	0.827	0.817	0.822	0.817
	(3.818)	(4.331)	(4.376)	(4.624)	(4.265)
α_9	−0.286	−0.280	−0.275	−0.273	−0.261
	(1.417)	(1.382)	(1.456)	(1.480)	(1.668)
SEE	0.008	0.008	0.008	0.008	0.008
DW	2.030	2.019	2.005	2.999	1.517
Real wages					
μ	0.119	0.205	0.261	0.314	0^c
	(0.498)	(1.384)	(3.072)	(6.029)	
β_0	−6.952	−7.190	−6.703	−7.317	−1.786
	(4.009)	(5.150)	(5.228)	(6.312)	(15.76)
β_2	0.229	0.214	0.175	0^c	0^c
	(0.775)	(0.796)	(0.801)		
β_3	0.060	0.056	0.060	0.063	0.105
	(1.948)	(2.330)	(2.278)	(2.506)	(2.906)
β_4	−0.061	0^c	0^c	0^c	0^c
	(0.699)				
β_5	0.989	0.968	0.969	0.888	0.874
	(7.845)	(8.372)	(9.337)	(28.54)	(27.93)
β_6	−0.042	−0.035	−0.032	−0.029	−0.098
	(1.354)	(1.538)	(1.474)	(1.386)	(3.886)
β_7	0.191	0.106	0^c	0^c	0^c
	(0.670)	(0.541)			
SEE	0.015	0.015	0.016	0.016	0.027
DW	1.726	1.700	1.695	1.736	0.955
$\mathscr{L}$	235.45	234.59	234.23	233.70	216.85

Notes: $\mathscr{L}$ is the value of the log-likelihood, and the parentheses contain asymptotic t values. Constrained parameters are denoted by c.

would push up wages according to these estimates; β_3 is always positive.[8] The wage effect of changes in the Government's U I subsidy rate—captured by β_4—is on the other hand *negative* (although insignificant) in the first column of Table 3.3. Although a negative sign is a theoretical possibility, as was discussed in the theory section, it is unexpected to find that β_3 and β_4 differ in sign. As was noted in the theoretical exposition, a union following an optimal insurance policy would respond to higher U I subsidies in exactly the same way as it would respond to higher U I benefits. Indeed, the model with flexible U I premiums implied a symmetry condition of the form $\beta_3 = \beta_4$. This restriction is, however, not supported by the data. Whether or not more careful specifications of the subsidy variable will lead to other conclusions remains to be seen. G_a may be a rather crude proxy for the parameters of the U I subsidy system, and its coefficient is constrained to zero in all remaining estimations.

Column (2) of Table 3.3. reports estimates of a model with only one constraint imposed, i.e. $\beta_4 = 0$. The estimated coefficients associated with work-hours and membership (β_2 and β_7) have low t-values, and are constrained to zero one by one; $B_7 = 0$ is imposed in column (3) and $\beta_2 = \beta_7 = 0$ is imposed in column (4). A likelihood-ratio test does not reject the constrained model of column (4) relative to the least restrictive model of column (1).

However, when we proceed by imposing $\mu = 0$ in column (5), a clearly inferior model is obtained. The log-likelihood value drops substantially, the standard error of the wage equation increases from 0.016 to 0.027, and the DW statistic is reduced to 0.95. Column (4) of Table 3.3 contains our preferred M model, and it implies that an outward shift of the labour demand schedule raises workers' real take-home pay.

Before proceeding to a more detailed discussion of the estimates, it is appropriate to ask whether the monopoly restrictions across the wage and labour demand equations are rejected or not. Relaxation of these restrictions requires estimation of seven additional parameters; the Z vector includes eight parameters whereas the M model needs only one parameter (μ)—in addition to the structural

---

[8] Similar results are reported by, for example, Layard and Nickell (1986) in their time-series analysis on British data. Cross-section studies on U S data (Topel, 1984, and Hamermesh and Wolfe, 1987) have, on the other hand, found that the availability of U I will *reduce* wages by reducing the wage differential required to compensate workers for unemployment risks.

parameters of the labour demand equation—to capture wage responses to labour demand shifts. The unrestricted form of the wage equation takes the form

$$\ell n[w(1 - t)/\mathrm{p}] = \beta_0' + \alpha_2'\ell n \left[\frac{p(1 + s)}{q(1 - t)} \right]$$
$$+ \alpha_3'\ell n(r/q) + \alpha_4'\ell n(m/q) + \alpha_5'T + \alpha_6'\ell nY$$
$$+ \alpha_7'\ell nWTM + \alpha_8'\ell nN_{-1} + \alpha_9'\ell nN_{-2} + \beta'X \quad (107)$$

where

$$\beta'X = \beta_2'\ell n\hat{h} + \beta_3'\ell nB_r + \beta_4'\ell nG_a + \beta_5'\ell n\hat{y} + \beta_6'\ell nRU_{-1}$$
$$+ \beta_7'\ell nM_{-1}. \quad (108)$$

Table 3.4 sets out estimates of wage equations without imposing the monopoly restrictions. These 'bargaining' wage equations will be referred to as 'B models', and they include the constraints of our preferred M model, i.e. $\beta_2' = \beta_4' = \beta_7' = 0$. Column (1) of Table 3.4 shows estimates of the least restrictive of the B models. A comparison with the preferred M model reveals a clear improvement in the log-likelihood; the relevant likelihood ratio is $LR = 2(240.48 - 233.70) = 13.56$. There are seven degrees of freedom, the 5 per cent critical value is 14.07, and the 10 per cent critical value is 12.02. The monopoly restrictions are thus not rejected at the 5 per cent level, but they are rejected at the 10 per cent level.

As is seen from the first column of Table 3.4, several of the demand shift variables are associated with very imprecisely estimated coefficients. This is in particular the case for $\ell n(r/q)$, T, and $\ell nWTM$. The two lagged employment variables have a sign pattern that is somewhat difficult to interpret. (Recall that the coefficient on ℓnN_{-1} is positive, and the coefficient on ℓnN_{-2} negative, in the structural labour demand equation.) Lagged employment in manufacturing is certainly correlated with the lagged unemployment rate, and may capture labour market slack. In column (2) of Table 3.4 we delete lagged employment from the wage equation, but obtain only a minor increase in the t value of the unemployment coefficient.

In column (3) we delete instead $\ell n(r/q)$, T, and $\ell nWTM$. These restrictions are easily accepted relative to the least restrictive B model. In column (4) we delete also the lagged employment variables. The final model has thus five estimated parameters fewer

Bertil Holmlund

TABLE 3.4. *FIML estimates of unrestricted wage equations*

	(1)	(2)	(3)	(4)
Constant	−7.675	−6.371	−6.015	−5.824
	(2.750)	(2.649)	(2.558)	(3.852)
$\ell n \left[\dfrac{p(1+s)}{q(1-t)} \right]$	−0.455	−0.285	−0.399	−0.290
	(1.215)	(1.247)	(2.039)	(2.332)
$\ell n (r/q)$	0.002	−0.009	0^c	0^c
	(0.055)	(0.409)		
$\ell n (m/q)$	−0.972	−0.764	−0.986	−0.804
	(1.484)	(1.663)	(2.455)	(5.863)
T	−0.003	−0.0004	0^c	0^c
	(0.473)	(0.056)		
$\ell n\ Y$	0.417	0.400	0.465	0.341
	(1.413)	(1.533)	(2.632)	(2.111)
$\ell n\ WTM$	0.061	0.006	0^c	0^c
	(0.687)	(0.108)		
$\ell n\ N_{-1}$	−0.336	0^c	−0.368	0^c
	(0.831)		(1.217)	
$\ell n\ N_{-2}$	0.385	0^c	0.274	0^c
	(1.345)		(1.926)	
$\ell n\ B_r$	0.048	0.062	0.051	0.062
	(1.807)	(2.388)	(2.216)	(2.977)
$\ell n\ RU_{-1}$	−0.041	−0.035	−0.048	−0.040
	(1.094)	(1.232)	(1.403)	(1.961)
$\ell n\ \hat{y}$	0.928	0.813	0.875	0.876
	(2.895)	(2.566)	(4.719)	(4.257)
$\mathscr{L}$	240.48	237.21	239.19	237.00
DW	1.910	1.764	1.746	1.728
SEE	0.013	0.014	0.013	0.014

Note: Each wage equation is estimated jointly with the labour demand equation. Asymptotic t values are in the parentheses. Constrained parameters are denoted by c.

than the least restrictive B model, and the restrictions of the final model are not rejected. The remaining variables have coefficients with respectable t values, and the alternative restrictions have not been associated with drastic changes of the estimated values of the coefficients.

The model in column (4) of Table 3.4 is our preferred B model. How does it perform relative to our preferred M model? Write the nested model as

$$\ell n[w(1 - t)/p] = \beta_0^* + \mu^* \alpha_2^* \ell n[p(1 - t)]$$
$$+ \mu^* \alpha^* Z + \beta_3^* \ell n B_r + \beta_5^* \ell n \hat{y}$$
$$+ \beta_6^* \ell n R U_{-1} + \gamma_1 \ell n \left[\frac{p(1 + s)}{q(1 - t)} \right]$$
$$+ \gamma_2 \ell n(m/q) + \gamma_3 \ell n Y \qquad (109)$$

and note that this model has the preferred M model as a special case when $\gamma_1 = \gamma_2 = \gamma_3 = 0$, and that it reduces to the preferred B model when $\mu^* = 0$. Equation (109) is estimated jointly with the labour demand equation, and Table 3.5 sets out parameters and statistics of primary interest. The nested model yields estimate of γ_1, γ_2, and γ_3 that are at least in broad agreement with those obtained when $\mu^* = 0$ is imposed. The estimates of μ^* takes a negative sign and is clearly insignificant when estimating the nested model, whereas it is positive and significant when the M restrictions are imposed. The restrictions implied by the B model are easily accepted, whereas the M restrictions are accepted at the 5 per cent level but rejected at the 10 per cent level. We take the B model in column (4) of Table 3.5 as our preferred wage equation, recognizing, however, that it is not overwhelmingly superior to the preferred M model.

Turning to the estimated coefficients of our preferred model, we first note that the wedge, $\ell n[p(1 + s)/q(1 - t)]$, is associated with a

TABLE 3.5. *Tests of alternative model restrictions*

	M model	B model	Nested model
μ^*	0.314	0^c	-0.172
	(6.029)		(0.549)
γ_1	0^c	-0.290	-0.413
		(2.332)	(1.221)
γ_2	0^c	-0.804	-1.224
		(5.863)	(1.484)
γ_3	0^c	0.341	0.534
		(2.111)	(1.448)
$\mathscr{L}$	233.70	237.00	237.50
$2(\mathscr{L}_N - \mathscr{L}_M)$	7.60		
$2(\mathscr{L}_N - \mathscr{L}_B)$		1.00	

Notes: $\mathscr{L}_M$, $\mathscr{L}_B$, and $\mathscr{L}_N$ are log-likelihood values referring to the M model, the B model, and the nested model. Asymptotic t values are in parentheses. Constrained estimates are denoted by c.

coefficient of -0.3. A rise in the payroll tax factor, $(1 + s)$, by 1 per cent would thus reduce wages by somewhat less than one-third of a percentage point, and wage costs would therefore increase (and employment decrease). If the tax ratio, $ln[(1 + s)/(1 - t)]$, and the price ratio, $ln(p/q)$, are entered separately, we obtain virtually identical coefficient estimates (-0.293 and -0.287 with t values of 2.3 and 2.0). The results confirm other evidence that taxes matter for labour costs.[9]

The estimates indicate that real wages are very responsive to relative material prices. In fact, the elasticity of real wages with respect to relative material prices is very similar to the estimated elasticity of employment with respect to the same relative price. The wage push effect of higher unemployment pay appears to be rather modest, but it is noteworthy that the estimates are robust to the inclusion or exclusion of other variables.

The unemployment elasticity of real wages is small (-0.04), but is of the same order of magnitude as the estimate for Britain reported by Layard and Nickell (1986). A specification containing the logarithm of the unemployment rate yields a slightly smaller standard error of the estimated wage equation than a specification that includes the unemployment rate itself; Layard and Nickell (1986) report similar results.[10]

The estimated wage equation can be combined with the structural labour demand equation to yield a reduced-form employment equation. Suppose, for example, that there is an increase in real material prices by 10 per cent. This reduces the demand for labour by around 9 per cent in the short run, according to the estimated labour demand equation. Wages are, however, reduced as a response to higher material prices, and this offsets in part the fall in employment. The magnitude of the offsetting effect depends on (i) the wage response to higher material prices, and (ii) the employment response to lower wages. We have estimated the former elasticity to -0.8 and the latter to 0.3 (in the short run). Employment is therefore not reduced by 9 per cent, but by 6–7 per cent.

[9] Results reported by Holmlund (1983) and Bosworth and Lawrence (1987) also suggest that higher payroll taxes lead to higher wage costs.

[10] Layard and Nickell (1986) as well as Nickell (1987) discuss in some detail the implications of the finding that 'when it comes to holding down wages, it is proportional and not absolute increases in unemployment that are important' (Layard and Nickell, 1986, p. S153.)

3.5. Concluding Remarks

We have undertaken an empirical investigation of the determinants of employment and real wages in the Swedish mining and manufacturing sector, and the major results can be summarized as follows.

(i) The demand for blue-collar workers seems to be quite responsive to relative prices. The preferred models yield estimates of the long-run wage elasticity between 0.6 and 0.7. A rise in the cost of capital raises the demand for workers, whereas increases in material prices are associated with substantial reductions in employment.

(ii) Aggregate demand matters for employment, in addition to relative prices. Indeed, the relative price effects are well determined only when aggregate-demand variables are included in the estimating labour demand equation.

(iii) The labour demand equation reveals considerable substitutability between workers and work-hours. In fact, it is impossible to reject the hypothesis that workers and work-hours are perfect substitutes; the long-run elasticity of employment with respect to work-hours is not significantly different from minus one.

(iv) The restrictions implied by a monopoly union model do not obviously violate the data. Wage outcomes are responsive to labour demand shifts, but certain types of shift seem to be more important than others. The elasticity of real wages with respect to changes in real material prices is negative and sizeable. The labour market thus exhibits some degree of real-wage flexibility; shifts of the labour demand schedule lead to adjustment in both wages and employment.

(v) There is some evidence suggesting that wages are pushed up when unemployment benefits are raised, and pushed down when unemployment is high. The benefit elasticity of real wages is, however, small, and the same holds for the unemployment elasticity.

Unsettled issues abound. For example, no distinction has been made between contractual wage increases and wage drift, and we have not offered a structural model of the determination of work-hours. Although it is rather easy to pin-point various shortcomings of the present approach, there should be little doubt that a better understanding of wage and employment determination requires further work on bargaining models, rather than a retreat to models with Walrasian auctioneers.

4

Conclusions and Appendix

The 1980s have seen a remarkable upsurge in theoretical and empirical work on the economics of trade unions. There is no obvious single explanation for this development, but the dramatic increase in unemployment since the late 1970s has almost certainly played a role: double-digit unemployment figures are difficult to reconcile with the notion of a labour market with full employment and flexible wages. A major driving force behind the interest in bargaining models has been a desire to understand the sources of wage stickiness, and the role of sticky wages in explaining employment fluctuations. The literature has also seen a variety of models with wage rigidity properties. The proliferation of efficiency wage models provides further illustration of economists' departure from market-clearing labour market models. One may here draw a parallel with the interest in unemployment seen in the 1930s. The economics profession is indeed responsive to real-world phenomena.

What directions will future work on unions take? On the theory side, a number of shortcomings of most existing models are easily identified, and this brief concluding discussion is confined to a few of these.

One problem is related to partial versus general equilibrium. The partial-equilibrium nature of most of the existing theoretical work is disturbing, especially when the models are taken to represent (wholly or partially) unionized economies with decentralized wage-setting. For example, the partial-equilibrium distinctions between labour demand models and efficient-bargaining models may not hold in a general-equilibrium model of a wholly unionized economy, as noted by Pissarides (1986) and Layard and Nickell (1987). General-equilibrium models of partially unionized economies are also under-developed. Why is there unemployment if workers have access to a competitive labour market? A few explanations have been suggested, and one of those assumes barriers to free intersectoral labour mobility (see for example McDonald and Solow, 1985).

Workers may find it worthwhile to queue for union jobs rather than take a job in the non-union sector, if non-union employment reduces the probability of obtaining a union job. Whether or not this is an appropriate characterization is, however, very much an open question.

Existing bargaining models do not, in general, make any distinction between negotiated wage-rates and actual wage outcomes. Phelps Brown (1962) once noted that 'wage drift has been conspicuous in the democracies with predominantly industry-wide settlements—in Scandinavia, the Netherlands, the United Kingdom, and Australia'. Wage drift, i.e. the difference between actual and contractual wage increases, does not fit easily into any of the conventional union models. Wage-bargaining as well as efficiency wage considerations are presumably important in wage determination at the plant level. However, to the extent that there is an economy-wide or industry-wide union, this union should take local wage-setting behaviour into account in its own wage policy. The formal modelling of the interrelationships between the determination of wage drift and contractual wage-rates is in its infancy (see Holmlund, 1986, and Holden, 1987); much more work is inevitable as a step towards empirically applicable models of wage-setting.

Theoretical work on insider–outsider models and 'membership dynamics' has attracted interest in recent years (see for example Blanchard and Summers, 1986, Lindbeck and Snower, 1986*b*, and Gottfries and Horn, 1987). The standard union model assumes that the union cares about a fixed number of workers (the union members), and that it gives equal weight to employed 'insiders' and unemployed 'outsiders'. The optimal employment level is supposed to fall short of the number of members, so corner solutions are in general ruled out. Violations of some of these assumptions can have dramatic effects. For example, if the union only cares about the employed workers' welfare, it would be opposed to employment increases! Favourable demand shifts would then lead to wage increases for the employed insiders rather than jobs for the unemployed outsiders. Dynamic 'membership models' raise difficult intertemporal considerations. If a job loss is associated with a loss of power to influence the union's wage policy, this should be taken into account when rational workers formulate their current wage demands. It seems, however, that the issues addressed in these models are relevant primarily for economies with decentralized wage-setting. With bargaining at the firm or plant level, the unemployed workers may have no natural union affiliation, and they may *de facto* lose their influence over wage-setting when losing their jobs. (Decisions on wage demands may, for example, be taken at the work-place.) An economy-wide or industry-wide union is presumably less inclined to ignore the interests of its unemployed workers.

We have noted that increases in payroll taxes are likely to raise wage costs within a standard monopoly union framework. The empirical evidence on this point is in general consistent with this prediction. However, these results are difficult to reconcile with a popular model of an economy with world market-determined output prices and a given rental rate on capital; indeed, a model with such features is also standard in the macro-economics of small open economies. The conventional wisdom takes it for granted that wages adjust in the long run, but the precise links between (myopic?) union wage demands and long-run adjustments in wages and capital are not well understood. Sweden's experience is a case in point; dramatic increases in payroll taxes have not caused major unemployment problems.

On the empirical side, the importance of using richer data sets is obvious. Much of the current empirical work exploits highly aggregate and highly collinear time series, and the estimates are often not robust to minor changes in specifications. More dis-aggregated data, pertaining to bargaining units at the firm or industry level may provide information needed for discrimination between competing models. Pooling data from different countries may also be worth considering. Cross-country comparative studies may in addition illuminate the role of alternative institutional arrangements in wage determination. The popular discussion has seen numerous claims about the virtues of centralization (or decentralization) in wage determination, but these claims are often based on ideological convictions rather than on theoretical insights or empirical results. Promising work is now emerging in this field which, it is hoped, can bring knowledge of relevance to an evaluation of the pros and cons of (de)centralization in wage-bargaining.

Appendix[1]

w	Average hourly earnings (excluding overtime pay) of blue-collar workers in mining and manufacturing. (SCB-SOS Wages.)
N	Number of blue-collar workers in mining and manufacturing. (SCB-SOS: Manufacturing.)
h	Average annual hours worked per worker, excluding overtime. (SCB-SOS: Manufacturing; Wages.)
Y	Index of Swedish households' real disposable income. (SCB: National Accounts.)
WTM	Quantum index of world manufacturing exports. (Nickell and Andrews, 1983, for the period 1950–79, thereafter chained to series on world trade in manufacturing goods published in *UN International Trade Statistics Yearbook*.)
s	Payroll tax-rate for blue-collar workers. The series include fees due from employers according to law as well as collective agreements. (For 1960 and 1965–85 this series is published in LO, *De centrala överenskommelserna mellan LO och SAF 1952–1987*. This series is linked to the series used by Holmlund, 1983.)
t	Income tax rate for a person working full-time with average blue-collar hourly earnings. (The series is obtained by using the preliminary tax tables, taking the means of tax-rates implied by the different columns of the tables (corresponding to different categories of tax-payer).)
p	Consumer price index inclusive of indirect taxes. (SCB: Prices.)
q	Output price index based on the gross output deflator in manufacturing. (SCB: National Accounts.)
m	Price index of raw materials and intermediate goods using the deflator for intermediate consumption in manufacturing. (SCB: National Accounts.)
r	Index of rental value of capital goods defined as $r = (INT + DEP)*PINV$, where $PINV$ is a price index of investment goods (SCB: National Accounts), DEP is the depreciation rate, and INT is the after-tax cost of acquiring funds to buy capital goods. The series on $(INT + DEP)$ has been provided by Villy Bergström and Jan Södersten; the methods used in the calculations are described in Bergström and Södersten (1984).

[1] The abbreviations are as follows:

AMS   Arbetsmarknadsstyrelsen (National Labour Market Board)
LO   Landsorganisationen (Confederation of Trade Unions)
SCB   Statistiska Centralbyrån (Statistics Sweden)
SOS   Sveriges Officiella Statistik (Official Statistics of Sweden)

R U Unemployment rate. For the period 1962–85 we used the economy-wide unemployment rate according to SCB's labour force statistics. For earlier years this series is chained to a series on unemployment among members of unemployment insurance funds, *R UI*. (See Hegelund *et al.*, 1975 for details about the latter series.) The two unemployment series move closely together, especially during the 1960s. We estimated an equation of the form

$$RU = \alpha + \beta RUI$$

for the period 1962–70. The regression produced an insignificant intercept ($R^2 = 0.78$), and re-estimation without intercept yielded

$$RU = 1.151RUI$$

with a t value of 31.89. A measure of RU for the period 1950–61 was obtained by multiplying RUI by 1.15.

y Index of economy-wide disposable income per hour. The variable is defined as $y = Y/HRS$, where Y is defined above and HRS is the total number of work hours in the economy. (SCB: National Accounts.) The actual variable used is predicted from the regression

$$\ell ny = 2.969 + 0.055T - 0.005T^2 + 0.363(D - 03)T^3$$
$$- 0.104(D - 04)T^4 + 0.975(D - 07)T^5$$

where $(D - 03) = 0.001$, $(D - 04) = 0.0001$ etc.

B_r Real value of the maximum weekly unemployment compensation. The variable is defined as

$$B_r = \frac{\bar{B}(1 - t)D}{p}$$

where $\bar{B}$ is the maximum daily benefit level ('maximal dagpenning'), and D is the number of weekdays covered by *UI*. ($D = 6$ for the period 1950–64, and $D = 5$ during 1965–85.) Unemployment benefits were not treated as taxable income during 1950–73; hence we have $t = 0$ for those years. Series on daily benefit levels as well as information on changes of *UI* rules are obtained from AMS.

G_a UI subsidy rate. Let G denote the total amount of government subsidies to the UI system, and let BT denote the amount of paid-out benefits. The gross subsidy rate is given as $G_a^g = G/BT$, and the corresponding net subsidy rate takes the form $G_a^n = (G_a^g - t)/(1 - t)$. Benefits were not considered as taxable income before 1974, so we have set $G_a = G_a^g$ for the period 1950–73, and $G_a = G_a^n$ for 1974–85. (Information on benefits and subsidies is provided by AMS.)

M Membership in industrial UI funds. (AMS.)

5

Comment

Andrew Oswald

Bertil Holmlund's paper is a valuable addition to the literature, offering something for the student as well as for the research specialist. It surveys much of the recent American and European research on the economics of unions, wages, and employment. It proves new theoretical results (most especially on the effects of union-organized unemployment insurance and on the consequences of variable working hours). It makes a major contribution to the empirical analysis of the Swedish labour market.

The purpose of this chapter is to discuss a number of issues raised by Holmlund's analysis. Inevitably, with a paper of this length, it is necessary to be selective. I shall concentrate on topics which seem to me both interesting and important for future research.

5.1. Efficient Bargains and Labour Demand

One of the key questions in this field is whether, when there are trade unions, equilibrium will be characterized as a point on some labour demand curve. Although Holmlund discusses this briefly, he does not tell us where he stands. On the one hand, the labour demand approach is *imposed* for all of the econometric work on Sweden. On the other, the author argues that there is evidence (MaCurdy and Pencavel, 1985, Svejnar, 1986) to suggest that this is the wrong framework, and that labour economists should embrace the efficient-bargain model.

It is possible to extend the author's econometric work to perform a simple check on the validity of the labour demand view. Following Ashenfelter and Brown (1985), and others, we may insert into the labour demand specification an alternative wage variable. There is controversy over exactly how such a variable should be defined, but obvious candidates include (i) the wage in the rest of the economy; (ii) the unemployment rate elsewhere (to measure the availability of work in other sectors); and (iii) unemployment benefits paid by the Government or other bodies. If the labour demand curve is properly specified and identified, and it and not the efficient-bargain contract curve is the 'true' relationship, the addition of (i)–(iii) should contribute no information. If, however, we find for example that wages elsewhere enter negatively and significantly, that might make us doubt the labour demand approach.

On this view, one can construct a method by which the labour demand model might be rejected. It is obvious that that could not *prove* the correctness of the contract curve analysis: classical statistical theory does not allow a hypothesis to be 'accepted' (despite what one might think from the misleading usage in some articles) but merely to be 'not rejected'. I should like to see the results of the inclusion of variables (i)–(iii).

Holmlund raises two objections to the test based upon the inclusion of the alternative wage. The first, due to MaCurdy and Pencavel (1985), is that, if the union utility function is suitably separable, the efficient-bargain model also predicts that the alternative wage will not enter the employment function. However, this is not a good objection. Nothing is proved, in any case, if the alternative wage fails to enter. The point is that the null hypothesis of the labour demand model can be rejected *if the alternative wage appears significantly* (assuming, of course, that the model is correctly identified). This test, of whether the labour demand curve can or cannot be rejected, is valid whatever the structure of the union utility function. The test teaches us something if the alternative wage is found to have a significant (negative) effect. The author's second objection is that even the monopoly union model has a first-order condition which includes the alternative wage. But this is not a conceptual difficulty, because the test itself is done on the employment function.

The other way in which to judge whether we should believe in efficient bargains of the Leontief–McDonald–Solow type is to study the industrial-relations facts of life. The theory says that pay and employment should be treated entirely *symmetrically*, because each marks out an axis of a utility diagram. I do not know any labour economist who believes that bargainers treat wages and jobs in a symmetrical way. Yet this difficulty is rarely considered by the proponents of contract curve models. Knowing that their models require the union somehow to negotiate over the number of jobs, some theorists have constructed imaginative ways in which, indirectly, the trade union might do so. Hence we have models with crew size/man–machine ratio bargaining, or with repeated games in which there are implicit understandings about employment, or with some other feature which allows covert rules about the fixing of employment. I do not doubt that all these have their place. But it does seem important to recognize that such approaches are unnatural, in the strict sense, in that they choose a complicated explanation where a simple one would do. If a union and a firm wished to negotiate about the level of employment, they could easily do so. It is straightforward to conceive of a world in which annual bargaining would cover not just the wage for the next year but also the number of employees for the next year. Yet we do not see that. The natural explanation is that the firm and the trade union do not want to negotiate about the employment level.

This leads on to the 'flat indifference curve' or 'seniority' model, which Holmlund summarizes. My prejudices are probably reasonably well known, so I wish to make only three points. First, the seniority model fits the facts and does not require that economic agents act in a strangely complicated way when a simple way would suffice. Second, Holmlund astutely points out that Carruth *et al.*'s (1986) results cannot reject a flat indifference curve model in which variables like unemployment affect the status quo or fall-back points in bargaining. Third, Holmlund argues that the model 'may appear a little extreme' because even the median worker N_s is affected by a plant closure. This is true, but does not seem to me a strong criticism. Naturally there is employment bargaining when more than half the work-force is about to be sacked. The seniority model predicts that, and there is much supporting evidence from the industrial relations literature on 'concession bargaining' (see, for example, Flanagan's 1985). In addition, it seems uncontroversial to believe that immense falls in employment are the exception rather than the rule.

5.2. Bargaining Bias

Another way to object to the flat indifference curve model is to argue that Farber (1978), Dertouzos and Pencavel (1981), Pencavel (1984), Carruth and Oswald (1985), and others have proved that

unions place some value on jobs and some on pay. There are,
however, reasons to doubt this. What these studies have done is to
assume that the monopoly union model is correct and then to
estimate, by FIML methods, the implied curvature of the indifference curves.

In order to obtain an interior maximum, the FIML program must
necessarily converge to a tangency point between a union indifference curve and a labour demand curve. Given the assumptions,
therefore, it is impossible to conclude that indifference curves are
flat.

There is a broader point along the same lines. Assume that the
'true' model has bargaining about the wage-rate, and that the union
is at w^b and below the wage w^u, which it would set unhindered.
Assume also that the union attaches some utility weight to the level
of employment.

Consider Fig. 5.1. The observed wage-rate is w^{bb}, which the
economic investigator assumes—following the methodology of
most econometric studies in the field—to be a tangency optimum for
the monopoly union. Let the fitted indifference curve be I_*. If, however, the union in its bargaining cannot get to its true optimum, w^b
actually lies upon an indifference curve I_0. This induces what might
be termed *bargaining bias*. The actual indifference curve always has
a gradient which is below that of the estimated indifference curve.
Hence, because in that region I_0 is necessarily flatter than I_*, an

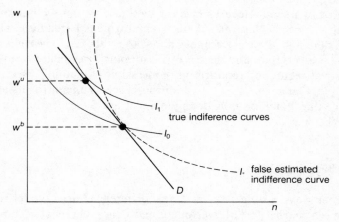

Fig. 5.1. Bargaining bias

economist who applies the monopoly union model to estimate the structure of indifference curves will overestimate the extent to which unions care about employment. The intuitive reason is an obvious one. Conventional monopoly union theory assumes that the actual wage is set no higher because the union is worried about lost jobs. In the real world of bargaining, however, it may well be that the union cares little about the loss of jobs, and that the reason pay is no higher is that the firm is strong enough to keep down the union's wage in order to ensure high profits.

5.3. The Dynamics of Employment

Chapter 3, an econometric enquiry into Swedish mining and manufacturing, was for me exceptionally interesting. As usual, it is informative to begin by studying the raw time series, and Holmlund includes these. Two things stand out. First of all, there was a large decline in blue-collar employment between the mid-1970s and the mid-1980s, and this coincided with a 10 per cent fall in real wages (see Figs. 3.2 and 3.4). At a glance, then, one might wonder whether this could be consistent with a downward-sloping demand curve for labour. Second, there is a marked regular cycle in employment in the sector. Put roughly, that cycle is five years long, and peaks in 1951, 1956, and so on. Fig. 3.1 shows the same from a different angle: the troughs in unemployment occur in 1951, 1955, 1961, 1965, 1970, 1976, 1980, and 1985. These are the stylized facts which any econometric model must explain.

In passing, it is worth noting that Britain, too, has a similar five-year cycle and has peaks in approximately the same years. The British ratio of vacancies to unemployment shows the booms as the years 1960, 1965, 1969, 1974, 1979, and 1985. It seems natural to interpret this correspondence between Sweden's cycle and Britain's cycle as an example of the importance of world trade shocks.

Table 3.1 contains Holmlund's estimated labour demand curve using annual data from 1951–85. It works remarkably well (see p. 85 n. 4, the notes to Table 3.1, and the text) and appears to be stable. Those who are sceptical of neo-classical economics for the labour market will find that the table provides food for thought.

I believe that this is how the world works—that there is a labour demand curve which shifts back and forth—so there is only a little more to be said. One reason to take the results seriously is that they are similar to those obtained from British aggregate and industry data, and broadly compatible with the estimates from other countries which are reported in the 1986 symposium issue of *Economica*. A new working paper from the Centre for Labour Economics at the London School of Economics, for example, entitled 'Wages, Prices, Employment and Output in UK Industry', by Stephen Nickell and Paul Kong of the University of Oxford, estimates similar employment functions for fourteen industries. Like Holmlund, the authors find downward-sloping labour demand curves, and effects from lagged employment, material prices, world trade, and other shocks.

One intriguing aspect of Holmlund's labour demand estimates is that the dynamic structure turns out to be the same as in many other different studies. Taking equation (3) from Table (3.1), for example, employment is described by the difference equation:

$$\ell n\, N = 0.8\, \ell n\, N_{-1} - 0.2\, \ell n\, N_{-2} + \text{other terms}$$

Compare this with the Layard and Nickell (1986) equation for the whole British economy:

$$\ell n\, N = 1.1\, \ell n\, N_{-1} - 0.4\, \ell n\, N_{-2} + \text{other terms}$$

Alternatively, consider the results of Card (1986), who used data on employment in the US airline industry to obtain on quarterly data:

$$\ell n\, N = \ell n\, N_{-1} - 0.3\, \ell n\, N_{-2} + \text{other terms}$$

Franz and Konig (1986) find, for effective hours of employment, a labour demand curve for the German economy of the form:

$$\ell n\, N = 0.8\, \ell n\, N_{-1} - 0.3\, \ell n\, N_{-2} + \text{other terms}$$

Still more recently, Holly and Smith (1987) have estimated a quarterly employment function for British non-manufacturing industry. It has the structure:

$$\ell n\, N = 1.3\, \ell n\, N_{-1} - 0.4\, \ell n\, N_{-2} + \text{other terms}$$

There are many more examples in the literature.

This similarity in dynamic structure across countries and sectors is surprising. It makes it hard to accept the standard explanation (mentioned also by Holmlund) that employment functions are auto-regressive because of adjustment costs and aggregation. My own view is that some kind of cyclical characteristic is being picked up by the two lagged dependent variables. All the above equations generate oscillations. Moreover, although I have not yet explored the issue in depth, it is worth bearing in mind that the special case

$$\ell n\, N = \ell n\, N_{-1} - 0.5\, \ell n\, N_{-2} + \text{constant}$$

produces a damped cycle of exactly eight periods (see Goldberg, 1958, p. 154). This area seems likely to repay intensive research.

5.4 Wages: Internal and External Influences

The estimated wage equations are also interesting. Table 3.4 reveals, however, that multicollinearity may be a difficulty in this sample: once extra variables are added to equation (4), the coefficients hardly alter, but the t statistics drop dramatically. Nevertheless, a number of points seems to emerge from the table.

First, the variable $\hat{y}$, which proxies real income growth in the whole economy, enters with a coefficient close to unity. Second, despite the lack of lagged dependent variables, there is little or no sign of autocorrelation. It would still be natural to try lagged dependent variables, especially as a correct dynamic optimization model (which Carruth and Oswald (1985) attempt to pursue) suggest their inclusion, but my impression is that the inclusion of $\hat{y}$ makes them empirically unnecessary. Third, there is some indication that the *change* in past employment enters negatively with a coefficient of approximately -0.3. This reminds me of a somewhat similar finding by Wabe and Leech (1978) in their article on earnings in British industry. Some may be inclined to interpret such results as evidence of a hysteresis effect (Blanchard and Summers, 1986 among others). Fourth, materials prices enter negatively and strongly, which to me is reminiscent of the powerful import price effect found in British wage equations by Carruth and Oswald (1987). Fifth, unemployment benefit levels enter with the expected positive sign.

I should like to stress two other points. The less speculative is that unemployment appears to drive down real wages in the Swedish mining and manufacturing industry. The best evidence is provided by the remarkable stability of the coefficient (approximately -0.04) across different specifications. A sceptic, however, would point to the poor t statistics. Further evidence for Sweden is urgently required.

The more controversial point I wish to make concerns the role of product demand and profitability. In a recent British survey (Blanchflower and Oswald, 1987) a representative sample of more than 1,000 managers were asked the question: 'What factors influenced the level of pay decided upon in the most recent (wage) settlement?' The most commonly given single answer was 'profitability and productivity' within the manager's establishment. Outside forces, like the 'going wage', were stressed rather less than most neo-classical theorists would have guessed.

It would have been interesting to see if lagged profits entered significantly in Holmlund's Swedish wage equation (as, for example, Carruth and Oswald (1987) found for Britain). Although Holmlund does not do that, his results allow some insight into the broad issues. The (real) product price in mining and manufacturing enters positively in the wage equation. This is in accord with the John Dunlop's belief (1944) that it is product price (not unemployment) movements that are important in explaining wage changes. Households' income, a demand shift parameter, also enters positively. Material prices enter negatively. All this appears to be consistent with the view that profitability—or at least pros- • perity—exerts an influence upon pay determination, which fits in with the idea that firms raise wages when they are doing well in the product market, and that insiders thus share in their employers' prosperity. It seems plausible to believe that some such phenomenon might explain the simultaneous drop in real wages and employment at the end of the 1970s. Presumably this industry encountered a huge slump in profits, which forced employees to accept wage reductions, and firms to cut back their workforces. This view—wage determination as the outcome of a bargain over the division of a cake—dates back at least to the work of Slichter (1950), who concluded that 'wages, within a considerable range, reflect managerial discretion, that where managements can easily pay high wages they tend to do so, and that where managements are barely breaking even, they tend to keep wages down'.

5.5. Conclusions

In these comments I have tried to stress the following points.

1.   A central issue in the field is whether equilibrium lies on a labour demand curve, but Holmlund does not tell us whether he favours this or an efficient-bargain model, nor does he test between the contract curve approach and a labour demand framework. However, those who believe in a downward-sloping demand curve will find comfort in Holmlund's excellent econometric results.

2.   There are reasons to be sceptical of the theory of efficient wage bargains.

3.   The early econometric literature probably overestimates the weight which unions give to employment. This 'bargaining bias' is a result of the monopoly union assumption that the wage is no higher because at the margin the union wants extra jobs. In reality it may be that unions would like higher pay but do not have the power to attain that.

4.   Holmlund's estimated wage and employment functions have a similar structure, and set of elasticities, to those obtained on other countries' data. This is an extra reason to take them seriously.

5.   Employment functions on almost all data sets seem to take an AR(2) structure, with a coefficient on the first lagged dependent variable of approximately unity, and a coefficient on the second lagged dependent variable of approximately -0.3. This cannot be a coincidence, and it is difficult to believe that all countries and sectors have the same adjustment costs and aggregation properties. My view is that there is something important to be explained here.

6.   I believe that wages are determined by a mixture of internal forces (past profitability, for example) and external forces (the unemployment rate in the economy, for example).

This paper by Bertil Holmlund is an example of the growing interest, among European economists especially, in the forces which shape the levels of wages and employment. It also makes clear a change of emphasis since, for example, the 1984 Stockholm symposium on the topic (reported in a special issue of the *Scandinavian Journal of Economics* in 1985). We have begun to apply, and to test empirically, the theoretical models developed earlier. It is an interesting time and, to use Holmlund's adjective, an exciting one.

6
Comment

Lars Calmfors

Bertil Holmlund's paper contains three major parts: a survey of theoretical work on union wage-setting and wage-bargaining, a survey of recent empirical work on employment and wage determination under unionization, and an attempt to estimate wage and labour demand equations for Sweden. It is an impressive piece of work, containing pedagogical surveys and an abundance of reflections, as well as his own research. The article is highly rewarding for anyone taking the time to penetrate it, but it makes hard reading. The reason is the multitude of aspects that are not organized around a main theme, and the mixture of survey material and original contributions.

The part I find the most useful is the review of recent empirical work, which has not been summarized elsewhere, provided by Chapter 2. It may provide an important input for others. Since I have no major objections to this chapter, I shall leave it aside. Instead I shall concentrate on the theoretical survey in Chapter 1 and the estimations in Chapter 3.

6.1. Theoretical Issues

One objection to Chapter 1 is that it to some extent duplicates earlier surveys by Oswald (1985), Pencavel (1985), and Farber (1986). Most of the material on monopoly unions and efficient wage contracts has been treated extensively there. However, Holmlund does consider a number of additional aspects.

Bargaining solutions are discussed at some length, and there is a useful comparison of conclusions from monopoly union and Nash

I am grateful to Anders Forslund and Peter Sellin for comments, and to Anna Thompson for the typing.

bargaining models of wage formation. There is also a quite detailed survey of how wages are affected by various methods of financing unemployment benefits, which is an area to which Holmlund himself has been the main contributor. Finally, the effects on wages of working-time reductions are reviewed in a more pedagogical way than has been done before.

Any choice of topic for a survey is, of course, subjective. *My* preference would have been to focus less on the micro-economics of union behaviour and wage-bargaining and more on the macro-economics. Unions appear to be crucial for understanding aggregate real-wage and employment determination, and there is a growing literature in the field which is in need of a review. I am thinking mainly of issues such as (i) the game between governments and unions, and the question of accommodation versus non-accommodation policies, (ii) the implications of various degrees of centralization in wage-bargaining, and (iii) the insider–outsider problem, i.e. the possibility that only the interests of employed workers are taken into account by unions. These are 'hot' issues at present in the macro-economic policy debate, and the bulk of Scandinavian contributions that have received international attention are concentrated to this field—see, for example, Calmfors (1982), Gylfason and Lindbeck (1984, 1986), Hersoug (1985), Rødseth (1985), Calmfors and Horn (1985, 1986), Söderström (1985), Gottfries and Horn (1987), Horn and Wolinsky (1985, 1987), Lindbeck and Snower (1986b, 1987), Strand (1987), Calmfors and Driffill (1988), and Horn and Persson (1988). It seems to me a pity that these issues are neglected in a survey with a Scandinavian focus. My views on this may, however, be as biased by my own research activities as are Holmlund's.

One feature of the analysis that I find disturbing is a certain lack of coherence. For instance, one main point is that an Occam's-razor argument cannot in general be used to defend the use of the monopoly union model instead of the more general Nash bargaining model: the qualitative conclusions will be the same with respect to changes that influence the union members' outside income opportunities (such as unemployment benefits) but not with respect to variables that shift the labour demand schedule. Still, Holmlund goes on to analyse the effects of price and tax changes, of various unemployment insurance systems, and of working-time reductions within the standard monopoly union model without discussing how the conclusions might be affected by the alternative assumption of bargaining.

6.2. Wages and Working-Time Reductions

To shed more light on the issue of bargaining versus monopoly union models, I shall expand Holmlund's analysis of how working-time reductions affect wages. This also provides an opportunity to discuss the generality of the results in this field. The issue is an important one, in view of the widespread demands for working-time reductions throughout Europe.

Holmlund analyses the case when working time and employment (i.e. the number of workers) are perfect substitutes, so that the marginal product of an additional hour of work is the same independently of whether the increase takes the form of longer working hours for the already employed or of additional employment of more workers. Using the monopoly union framework, Holmlund finds that the wage response to an exogenously imposed reduction of working time depends upon how hours have been determined initially. If they have been determined by individual supply, the wage per hour rises if the supply curve is backward-sloping and falls if it is forward-sloping. This is a new result.[1] If initial working time has instead been set by unions, wages will rise if leisure and consumption are Edgeworth complements (i.e. if an increase in leisure increases the marginal utility of consumption), which is a sufficient condition for leisure to be a normal good (i.e. for individuals to prefer more leisure when there is an exogenous increase in income).

A natural question to ask is whether these results carry over also to a Nash bargaining solution. Using Holmlund's notation, we shall instead assume that wages are set so as to maximize

$$\Omega = [\Lambda - \Lambda_0]^\beta \Pi^{1-\beta}. \tag{1}$$

Hence, the first-order maximization condition becomes

$$\Omega_w = \beta\Pi\Lambda_w + (1 - \beta)(\Lambda - \Lambda_0)\Pi_w$$
$$= \beta\Pi\Lambda_w - (1 - \beta)(\Lambda - \Lambda_0)Nh = 0. \tag{2}$$

[1] There is a slight inconsistency in Holmlund's exposition, since the analysis of an *exogenous* working-time reduction is partly performed with the help of equations (56) and (57) which presuppose that working time is *endogenous*. As is clear from setting $\beta = 1$ in my equation (4c), in the derivation of which h has been treated as exogenous throughout so that $N_w = dN/dw$, Holmlund's result is still correct.

Differentiation of (2) with respect to h and w gives

$$\frac{dw}{dh} = - \frac{\Omega_{wh}}{\Omega_{ww}} \tag{3}$$

where $\Omega_{ww} < 0$ by virtue of the second-order condition for a maximum. Hence sgn dw/dh = sgn Ω_{wh}, where

$$\Omega_{wh} = \beta\Pi\Lambda_{wh} + \beta\Lambda_w\Pi_h - (1-\beta)Nh\Lambda_h$$
$$- (1-\beta)(\Lambda - \Lambda_0)(N + hN_h). \tag{4}$$

But the assumption that hours and employment are perfect substitutes ensures that profits are independent of working time, i.e. $\Pi_h = 0$, and that $N_h = -N/h$. Hence (4) simplifies to

$$\Omega_{wh} = \beta\Pi\Lambda_{wh} - (1-\beta)Nh\Lambda_h \tag{4a}$$

where

$$\Lambda_{wh} = \frac{N_w}{h}(V - U) + (wU_1 + U_2)N_w + (wU_{11} + U_{12})Nh. \tag{5}$$

Now, if we assume that initial working time, too, has been set through a Nash bargain, we have

$$\Omega_h = \beta\Pi\Lambda_h + (1-\beta)(\Lambda - \Lambda_0)\Pi_h = \beta\Pi\Lambda_h$$
$$= \beta\Pi N \left[wU_1 + U_2 - \frac{1}{h}(U - V) \right] = 0. \tag{6}$$

Because the assumption that hours and employment are perfect substitutes ensures that profits are not affected by a reduction of working time, i.e. $\Pi_h = 0$, the outcome of a Nash bargaining over hours is the same as when hours are determined by a monopoly union. $\Omega_h = 0$ is thus equivalent to $\Lambda_h = 0$, and hence (4a) simplifies to

$$\Omega_{wh} = \beta\Pi Nh(wU_{11} + U_{12}). \tag{4b}$$

Thus the Nash bargaining case for wages gives the result that wages rise when working time is reduced, if consumption and leisure are Edgeworth complements and initial working time has also been determined in such a bargain. This is an analogous conclusion to that from the monopoly union model. Under the above assumptions, the choice of a bargaining versus a monopoly union model does not thus affect the results.

Consider, then, the case where initial hours have instead been determined through individual supply decisions (which, for reasons similar to those above, result in the same number of hours as if working time had been determined in a Nash bargaining between firms and individual wage-earners). Then we can impose the condition that $U_h = wU_1 + U_2 = 0$ in equation (5), which gives

$$\Lambda_{wh} = \frac{N_w}{h}(V - U) + (wU_{11} + U_{12})Nh. \qquad (5a)$$

Hence (4a) in this case simplifies to

$$\begin{aligned}
\Omega_{wh} &= \beta\Pi\left[(V - U)\frac{N_w}{h} + (wU_{11} + U_{12})Nh\right] \\
&\quad - (1 - \beta)Nh\Lambda_h = \beta\Pi N[U_1 + h(wU_{11} + U_{12})] \\
&\quad + N(1 - \beta)[N(U - V) - (\Lambda - \Lambda_0)] \\
&= \beta\Pi N[U_1 + h(wU_{11} + U_{12})] + (1 - \beta)NM(V_0 - \mathcal{V}), \quad (4c)
\end{aligned}$$

where we let V_0 denote the fall-back level of utility (in case of no agreement) for the individual worker, so that $\Lambda_0 = MV_0$.

In general, the outcome in this bargaining case thus becomes somewhat more complex than in the monopoly union case. The sign of $U_1 + h(wU_{11} + U_{12})$ determines whether the individual supply curve is forward- or backward-sloping. A backward-sloping supply curve is now a necessary and sufficient condition for wages to rise when working time falls only in the special case of $V = V_0$, i.e. when the utility level for the individual worker in the absence of an agreement equals that when unemployed. If one makes the 'impatience interpretation' of the Nash bargaining solution (see ch. 1, sect. 2), we cannot say much about the relative size of V and V_0 in general, and hence the slope of the individual supply curve for hours no longer uniquely determines the effect on wages of working-time reductions.[2]

In the above case it thus appears that the choice of a bargaining model instead of a monopoly union one does matter. It will, of course, become crucial if one drops the assumption that hours and workers are perfect substitutes, since then both profits and the sensitivity of profits to wage changes will in general be affected by working time. Abandoning the perfect-substitutability assumption also implies that the effects on wages of working-time reductions

[2] In this case the fall-back level of utility V_0 should be interpreted as the utility obtained during a labour market dispute. On the one hand, one could claim that $V_0 < V$, since unemployment benefits are not paid to striking workers. But, on the other hand, there may be disutility attached to being without regular employment.

become more complex within the monopoly union model as well, and that Holmlund's simple conclusions can no longer be drawn (see Calmfors, 1985).

6.3. Swedish wage-setting

Chapter 3 is an attempt at simultaneous estimations of labour demand and wage equations for the Swedish mining and manufacturing sector. The main focus is on wage-setting, and a number of alternative equations are tested and compared. The analysis is done meticulously, and the explanatory power of most variables that could possibly influence wages are carefully examined. A novel feature of the analysis is the attempt explicitly to test monopoly union versus bargaining models. This is done in a clever way by noting that the monopoly union model predicts that the ratios between effects on wages and effects on employment of changes in variables that shift the labour demand schedule have to be equal (equation (52)). The reason is that the wage effects occur only via labour demand. The upshot of the empirical analysis is that the bargaining model seems to do a little—but not much—better than the monopoly union model.

In Holmlund's preferred wage equation, the (after-tax) real-consumption wage depends upon the wedge between the real-consumption and the real-product wage, the relative price between the raw-material input price and the output price of the sector, real disposable income in the whole economy, unemployment, real unemployment benefits, and real disposable income per hours worked in the economy. On the whole the results look quite reasonable, but I still have some reservations.

(i) The estimations imply that a 1 percentage point rise of the wedge causes a 0.3 percentage point fall in the real-consumption wage. There is thus only a very limited amount of backward shifting onto wages of, say, an increase of payroll taxes. At the same time, a 1 percentage point rise in the relative price of raw-material inputs reduces wages by as much as 0.8 per cent. Although these differing results are in no way theoretically inconsistent, I find it hard to square them with my prior beliefs. My guess is that the large estimated sensitivity of wages to raw-material input prices reflects mainly the coincidence of the rise in the relative price of oil and the fall in the real-consumption wage from the middle of the 1970s.

(ii)   In the theoretical section, Holmlund puts heavy emphasis on the amount of government subsidization of the costs for unemployment insurance. The failure to detect such effects in the estimations makes one wonder whether this emphasis was justified.

(iii)   Holmlund finds some support for the view that aggregate goods demand may influence employment directly in addition to the indirect effects working via real factor prices: total real disposable income in the economy shows up as a significant explanatory variable. However, this result could be due to simultaneity bias in the estimations. One should expect the real-consumption wage to be an important determinant of total real disposable incomes (although the dependent wage variable refers only to blue-collar workers in mining and manufacturing, there are, of course, strong interrelations with wages for other groups). I would feel more confident about the results on aggregate demand if they had applied to other, more exogenous demand variables such as measures of fiscal and monetary policies or world trade.

(iv)   One main determinant of real wages in the manufacturing and mining sector is the real disposable income per hour worked in the whole economy. The variable is introduced as a proxy for the alternative wage for workers that become employed in other sectors. It means, however, that the wage equation does not explain wages in the *overall* economy: instead, since the elasticity is close to unity, the estimated wage equation really provides an explanation only of the *relative wage* in manufacturing and mining.

It may be instructive to compare Holmlund's regression results with alternative estimations by Anders Forslund and myself that are based on similar union and bargaining models. The main difference in the theoretical set-up is that we take explicit account of the activities of AMS (the Labour Market Board), which is a central feature of the Swedish labour market: a worker who does not receive regular employment may either become engaged in labour market programmes (retraining or relief works) or become openly unemployed. Hence the expected alternative wage is influenced both by the probability of getting a regular job elsewhere and by the conditional probability of becoming engaged in a labour market programme when not obtaining a regular job anywhere. The first probability is related to *total* unemployment (open unemployment plus the number of persons in labour market programmes), and the second to the fraction of workers outside regular employment that are involved in such programmes. We also allow for the possibility that inflationary expectations may be mistaken, by introducing the change in inflation as a possible additional explanatory variable (the naïve idea being that expected inflation equals a weighted average of today's and last year's inflation). Our dependent variable is the after-tax real-consumption wage in the whole private sector (which has been obtained by dividing total real-wage incomes by the number of hours worked).

Our regression results are shown in Table 6.1 (see also Calmfors and Forslund, 1989). As can be seen, the estimations show a stable pattern. The main differences from Holmlund are as follows.

(i) We are able to explain wages quite well with a barebones model containing only a limited number of explanatory variables. We do not have to introduce a measure of other wages in the economy. Nor do we introduce total real disposable incomes in the economy as an explanatory variable, and therefore we avoid the simultaneity problems in Holmlund's equations.

(ii) There is a significant downward influence on wages from *total* unemployment rather than just from open unemployment, as in Holmlund's estimations. Since $\log [1 + (U + AMS)/L] \approx (U + AMS)/L$, where U = open unemployment, AMS = the number of persons engaged in labour market programmes, and L = regular employment, it follows that a 1 percentage point rise in total unemployment reduces real wages by the order of magnitude of 1–2 percentage points.

(iii) $AMS/(AMS + U)$ emerges as an important explanatory variable. A rise in the share of AMS-engaged people in total unemployment from, say, 50 to 55 per cent will cause real wages to increase by 1.6–2.2 percentage points. $AMS/(AMS + U)$ may be interpreted as a measure of how accommodating are government policies, since it indicates the extent to which open unemployment has been offset through labour market programmes. Our estimation results, together with Holmlund's negative findings on government subsidization of the unemployment insurance system, strengthen my prior belief (see Calmfors, 1982, or Calmfors and Horn, 1985, 1986) that the amount of accommodation policies is a far more important determinant of wages than the set-up of the unemployment insurance system.

(iv) We introduce time trends as additional explanatory

TABLE 6.1. *Estimated wage equations (dependent variable: the (log of the) after-tax real-consumption wage for the private sector)*

	constant	$1+(U+AMS)/L$	$AMS/(AMS+U)$	$\Delta^2 P_c$	t	t^2	θ	R^2	SSE	AR(2)
1	3.17	−1.89	0.22	−1	0.032	$-5.4\cdot10^{-4}$	0	0.981	0.010	0.89
	(25.4)	(2.31)	(4.77)		(3.77)	(2.68)				
2	3.14	−2.00	0.21	−1	0.037	$-5.9\cdot10^{-4}$	−0.10	0.981	0.010	1.16
	(23.7)	(2.33)	(4.46)		(3.04)	(2.64)	(0.57)			
3	3.02	−1.04	0.17	0	0.039	$-6.9\cdot10^{-4}$	0	0.988	0.006	1.51
	(31.6)	(1.64)	(4.83)		(5.85)	(4.48)				
4	3.03	−1.42	0.18	0	0.045	$-7.2\cdot20^{-4}$	−0.19	0.987	0.007	2.92
	(28.0)	(2.02)	(4.55)		(4.42)	(3.91)	(1.31)			
5	3.01	−1.12	0.16	−0.39	0.040	$-7.2\cdot10^{-4}$	0	0.992	0.005	2.10
	(32.3)	(1.92)	(4.85)	(2.42)	(6.53)	(5.04)				
6	2.98	−1.25	0.16	−0.37	0.047	$-7.9\cdot10^{-4}$	−0.13	0.992	0.004	4.48
	(31.8)	(2.13)	(4.56)	(2.36)	(5.61)	(5.16)	(1.17)			

Notes: All variables are in logs. U = open unemployment, AMS = number of persons in labour market retraining and relief works, L = total employment (excluding labour market programmes but including the public sector), P_c = consumer price index, t = time, θ = $[(1+T_L)(1-T)]\cdot(P_c/P_Q)$ = the wedge, T_L = payroll tax-rate, T = income tax-rate, and P_Q = output price of the private sector. Estimation period 1960–85. $AR(2)$ is an F-test for residual autocorrelation up to second order.

variables in order to allow for a continuous rise in real-consumption wages due to the growth of total factor productivity and the capital stock. This feature is absent from Holmlund's wage equations in Table 3.4. Both a linear and a quadratic time trend proved significant. The latter was introduced in order to catch the decline of productivity growth from the middle of the 1970s and onwards.

(v)   We also tried real unemployment benefits and working time as explanatory variables. In contrast to Holmlund (but in conformity with most foreign studies), we could detect no significance for the former variable. Nor could we with respect to working time (which is the same result as Holmlund's).

Although there are important differences between Holmlund's and our results, these should not be overstated. The main conclusion is that empirical studies that are consistent with union-wage setting and bargaining models do indeed seem to work for Sweden.

References for Part I*

Åberg, Y. (1985). *Produktionens och sysselsättningens bestämnings-faktorer i svensk ekonomi* ['The Determinants of Output and Employment in the Swedish Economy'], Report to the Delegation for Working-Time Issues, Stockholm: Swedish Ministry of Labour.

Anxo, D., and Bigsten, A. (1986). 'Working Hours and Productivity in Swedish Manufacturing', Department of Economics, Gothenburg University (mimeo).

Archibald, G.C. (1969). 'The Phillips Curve and the Distribution of Unemployment', *American Economic Review*, 59.

Ashenfelter, O., Johnson, G.E., and Pencavel, J. (1972). 'Trade Unions and the Rate of Change of Money Wages in the U.S. Manufacturing Industry', *Review of Economic Studies*, 39.

Bagge, G. (1917). *Arbetslönens reglering genom sammanslutningar* (Wage Regulation by Unions) Stockholm: Nordiska.

Bean, C.R., Layard, P.R.G., and Nickell, S. (1986). 'The Rise in Unemployment: A Multi-Country Study', *Economica*, 53, Supplement.

—— and Turnbull, P.J. (1987). 'Employment in the British Coal Industry: A Test of the Labour Demand Model', Center for Labour Economics, London School of Economics, Discussion Paper No. 274.

Beenstock, M., and Whitbread, C. (1987). 'Explaining Changes in the Union Mark-Up for Male Manual Workers in Great Britain, 1953–83', Center for Economic Policy Research, Discussion Paper No. 158, London.

Bergström, V., and Södersten, J. (1984). 'Do Tax Allowances Stimulate Investment?', *Scandinavian Journal of Economics*, 86.

Binmore, K., Rubinstein, A., and Wolinsky, A. (1986). 'The Nash Bargaining Solution in Economic Modelling', *Rand Journal of Economics*, 17.

Björklund, A., and Holmlund, B. (1986). 'The Economics of Unemployment Insurance: The Case of Sweden', FIEF Working Paper No. 24, Stockholm.

Blanchard, O., and Summers, L. (1986). 'Hysteresis and the European Unemployment Problem', in S. Fisher (ed.), *NBER Macroeconomics Annual*, Cambridge, Mass.: MIT Press.

* For additional references, see the special issue of *Scandinavian Journal of Economics* (1985:2), Farber (1986), Kennan (1986), and Oswald (1987).

Blanchflower, D.G., and Oswald, A.J. (1987). 'Internal and External Influences Upon Pay Determination: New Survey Evidence', mimeo, London School of Economics, forthcoming in *British Journal of Industrial Relations*.

Bosworth, B., and Lawrence, R. (1987). 'Adjusting to Slower Economic Growth: The Domestic Economy', in B. Bosworth and A. Rivlin (eds.), *The Swedish Economy*, Washington, DC: Brookings Institution.

Brown, J.N., and Ashenfelter, O.C. (1986). 'Testing the Efficiency of Employment Contracts', *Journal of Political Economy*, 94, Supplement.

Bruno, M. (1986). 'Aggregate Supply and Demand Factors in OECD Unemployment: An Update', *Economica*, 53, Supplement.

—— and Sachs, J. (1985). *Economics of Worldwide Stagflation*, Oxford: Blackwell.

Calmfors, L. (1982). 'Employment Policies, Wage Formation and Trade Union Behaviour in a Small Open Economy', *Scandinavian Journal of Economics*, 84.

—— (1985). 'Work Sharing, Employment and Wages', *European Economic Review*, 27.

—— and Driffill, J. (1988). 'Bargaining Structure, Corporatism and Macroeconomic Performance', *Economic Policy*, 6.

—— and Forslund, A. (1989). 'Wage Formation in Sweden', in Calmfors, L., *Wage Formation in the Nordic Countries: Empirical Studies Based on Union and Bargaining Approaches*, SNS and Basil Blackwell.

—— and Horn, H. (1985). 'Classical Unemployment, Accommodation Policies and the Adjustment of Real Wages', *Scandinavian Journal of Economics*, 87.

—— and —— (1986). 'Employment Policies and Centralized Wage-Setting', *Economica*, 53.

Card, D. (1986). 'Efficient Contracts with Costly Adjustment', *American Economic Review*, 76.

Carruth, A.A., and Oswald, A.J. (1985). 'Miners' Wages in Post-War Britain: An Application of a Model of Trade Union Behavior', *Economic Journal*, 95.

—— and —— (1986). 'Testing for Multiple Natural Rates of Unemployment in the British Economy: A Preliminary Investigation', Centre for Labour Economics, London School of Economics, Discussion Paper No. 265.

—— —— (1987). 'Wage Inflexibility in Britain', *Oxford Bulletin of Economics and Statistics*, 49.

—— —— and Findlay, L. (1986). 'A Test of a Model of Union Behaviour: The Coal and Steel Industries in Britain', *Oxford Bulletin of Economics and Statistics*, 48.

Cartter, A.M. (1959). *Theory of Wages and Employment*, Homewood, Ill.: Irwin.

Dertouzos, J.N., and Pencavel, J.H. (1981). 'Wage and Employment Determination under Trade Unionism: The International Typographical Union', *Journal of Political Economy*, 89.

Drazen, A., Hamermesh, D.S., and Obst, N.P. (1984). 'The Variable Employment Elasticity Hypothesis: Theory and Evidence', in R. Ehrenberg (ed.), *Research in Labor Economics*, 6, Greenwich, Conn.: JAI Press.

Dunlop, J.T. (1938). 'The Movement of Real and Money Wage Rates', *Economic Journal*, 48.

—— (1944). *Wage Determination under Trade Unions*, New York: Macmillan.

Durbin, J. (1970). 'Testing for Serial Correlation in Least-Squares Regression when Some of the Regressors are Lagged Dependent Variables', *Econometrica*, 38.

Farber, H.S. (1978*a*). 'Individual Preferences and Union Wage Determination: The Case of the United Mine Workers,' *Journal of Political Economy*, 68.

—— (1978*b*). 'Bargaining Theory, Wage Outcomes, and the Occurrence of Strikes,' *American Economic Review*, 68.

—— (1986). 'The Analysis of Union Behaviour', in O. Ashenfelter and R. Layard (eds.), *Handbook of Labor Economics*, Amsterdam: North-Holland.

Feldstein, M. (1967). 'Specification of the Labor Input in the Aggregate Production Function,' *Review of Economic Studies*, 34.

Fellner, W. (1947). 'Prices and Wages under Bilateral Monopoly,' *Quarterly Journal of Economics*, 61.

Flanagan, R.J. (1976). 'Wage Interdependence in Unionized Labor Markets,' *Brookings Papers on Economic Activity*.

—— (1985). 'Wage Concessions and Long-Term Union Wage Flexibility', *Brookings Papers on Economic Activity*, 1.

Forslund, A. (1986). 'Trade Unions, Wages and Employment in Sweden 1963–83: A Preliminary Assesment of the Explanatory Power of a Simple Model of Union Behavior', Institute for International Economic Studies, University of Stockholm (mimeo).

Franz, W., and Konig, H. (1986). 'The Nature and Causes of Unemployment in the Federal Republic of Germany since the 1970s: An Empirical Investigation', *Economica*, 53.

Geary, P.T., and Kennan, J. (1982). 'The Employment–Real Wage Relationship: An International Study', *Journal of Political Economy*, 90.

Goldberg, S. (1958). *Introduction to Difference Equations*, New York: Wiley.

Gottfries, N., and Horn, H. (1987). 'Wage Formation and the Persistence of Unemployment', *Economic Journal*, 97.

Gylfason, T., and Lindbeck, A. (1984). 'Union Rivalry and Wages: An Oligopolistic Approach', *Economica*, 51.

—— (1986). 'Endogenous Unions and Governments: A Game-Theoretic Approach', *European Economic Review*, 30.

Hamermesh, D. (1986). 'The Demand for Labor in the Long Run,' in O. Ashenfelter and R. Layard (eds.), *Handbook of Labor Economics*, Amsterdam: North-Holland.

—— and Wolfe, J.R. (1987). 'Compensating Wage Differentials and the Duration of Wage Loss', FIEF Working Paper No. 28, Stockholm.

Hegelund, S., Jonung, L., Pettersson, E., and Wadensjö, E. (1975). 'The Phillips Curve for Sweden: The Determinants of Wages and Prices in Sweden 1922–1971', Department of Economics, University of Lund, Working Paper No. 1975:13.

Henry, S.G.B., Payne, J.M., and Trinder, C. (1985). 'Unemployment and Real Wages: The Role of Unemployment, Social Security Benefits and Unionization', *Oxford Economic Papers*, 37.

Hersoug, T. (1984). 'Union Wage Responses to Tax Changes', *Oxford Economic Papers*, 36.

—— (1985). 'Workers versus Government: Who Adjusts to Whom?', *Scandinavian Journal of Economics*, 84.

——, Kjaer, K.N., and Rødseth, A. (1987). 'Wages, Taxes, and the Utility-Maximizing Trade Union: A Confrontation with Norwegian Data', *Oxford Economic Papers*, 38.

Hines, A.G. (1964). 'Trade Unions and Wage Inflation in the United Kingdom, 1893–1961', *Review of Economic Studies*, 31.

Hoel, M. (1984). 'Short- and Long-Run Effects of a Reduced Working Time in a Unionized Economy', Memorandum, Department of Economics, University of Oslo.

—— and Nymoen, R. (1986). 'Wage Formation in Norwegian Manufacturing: An Empirical Application of a Theoretical Bargaining Model', Memorandum, Department of Economics, University of Oslo.

Holden, S. (1987). 'Local and Central Wage Bargaining', *Scandinavian Journal of Economics*, 90.

Holly, S., and Smith, P. (1987). 'Wage Inflexibility in Britain', *Oxford Bulletin of Economics and Statistics*, 49.

Holmlund, B. (1983). 'Payroll Taxes and Wage Inflation: The Swedish Experience', *Scandinavian Journal of Economics*, 85.

—— (1986). 'Centralized Wage Setting, Wage Drift, and Stabilization Policies Under Trade Unionism', *Oxford Economic Papers*, 38.

—— and Lundborg, P. (1988). 'The Demand for Unemployment Insurance and Union Wage Setting', *Scandinavian Journal of Economics*, 90.

Horn, H., and Persson, T. (1988). 'Exchange Rate Policy, Wage Formation and Credibility', *European Economic Review*, 32.

—— and Wolinsky, A. (1988). 'Worker Substitutability and Patterns of Unionization', *Economic Journal*, 98.

——, and —— (1987). 'Bilateral Monopolies in a Market for an Input', Institute for International Economic Studies, University of Stockholm.

128   *References for Part I*

Johnson, G. E. (1975). 'Economic Analysis of Trade Unionism', *American Economic Review*, 65.

—— (1977). 'The Determination of Wages in the Union and Non-union Sectors', *British Journal of Industrial Relations*, 15.

—— (1984). 'Changes over Time in the Union–Nonunion Wage Differential in the United States', in J. J. Rosa (ed.), *The Economics of Trade Unions: New Directions*, Boston, Mass.: Kluwer-Nijhoff.

Kennan, J. (1986). 'The Economics of Strikes', in O. Ashenfelter and R. Layard (eds.), *Handbook of Labor Economics*, Amsterdam: North-Holland.

Keynes, J. M. (1936). *The General Theory of Employment, Interest and Money*, London: Macmillan.

Kjellberg, A. (1983). *Facklig organisering i tolv länder* ['Unionism in Twelve Countries'], Lund: Arkiv.

Layard, P. R. G. (1982). 'Is Incomes Policy the Answer to Unemployment?', *Economica*, 49.

——, Metcalf, D., and Nickell, S. (1978). 'The Effects of Collective Bargaining on Relative Wages', *British Journal of Industrial Relations*, 16.

—— and Nickell, S. (1985a). 'The Causes of British Unemployment', *National Institute Economic Review*, 1/85.

—— and —— (1985b). 'Unemployment, Real Wages and Aggregate Demand in Europe, Japan and the U.S.', *Carnegie-Rochester Conference Series on Public Policy*, 23, Amsterdam: North-Holland.

—— and —— (1986). 'Unemployment in Britain', *Economica*, 53, Supplement.

—— and —— (1987). 'Is Unemployment Lower if Unions Bargain Over Employment?', Centre for Labour Economics, London School of Economics, Working Paper No. 955.

Leontief, W. W. (1946). 'The Pure Theory of the Guaranteed Annual Wage Contract', *Journal of Political Economy*, 54.

Lewis, H. G. (1963). *Unionism and Relative Wages in the United States*, Chicago, Ill.: University of Chicago Press.

—— (1986). *Union Relative Wage Effects: A Survey*, Chicago, Ill.: University of Chicago Press.

Lindbeck, A., and Snower, D. J. (1986a). 'Wage Setting, Unemployment and Insider–Outsider Relations', *American Economic Review*, 71.

—— and —— (1986b). 'Wage Rigidity, Union Activity and Unemployment', in W. Beckerman (ed.), *Wage Rigidity and Unemployment*, London: Duckworth.

—— and —— (1987). 'Union Activity, Unemployment Persistence and Wage–Employment Ratchets', *European Economic Review*, 31.

MaCurdy, T. E., and Pencavel, J. H. (1986). 'Testing Between Competing

Models of Wage and Employment Determination in Unionized Markets', *Journal of Political Economy*, 94, Supplement.

McDonald, I. M., and Solow, R. (1981). 'Wage Bargaining and Employment', *American Economic Review*, 71.

—— and —— (1985). 'Wages and Employment in a Segmented Labor Market', *Quarterly Journal of Economics*, C. 41.

Manning, A. (1987). 'An Integration of Trade Union Models in a Sequential Bargaining Framework', *Economic Journal*, 97.

De Menil, G. (1971). *Bargaining: Monopoly Power Versus Union Power*, Cambridge, Mass.: MIT Press.

Minford, P. (1983). 'Labor Market Equilibrium in an Open Economy', *Oxford Economic Papers*, 35, Supplement.

Moore, W. J., and Raisan, J. (1980). 'Cyclical Sensitivity of Union/Nonunion Relative Wage Effects', *Journal of Labor Research*, 1.

Nash, J. F. (1950). 'The Bargaining Problem', *Econometrica*, 18.

—— (1953). 'Two Person Cooperative Games', *Econometrica*, 21.

Neftci, S. N. (1978). 'A Time Series Analysis of the Real Wages–Employment Relationship', *Journal of Political Economy*, 86.

Newell, A., and Symons, J. (1985). 'Wages and Employment in the OECD Countries', Centre for Labour Economics, London School of Economics, Discussion Paper No. 219.

—— and —— (1986). 'The Phillips Curve is a Real Wage Equation', Centre for Labour Economics, London School of Economics, Discussion Paper No. 246.

Nickell, S. (1986). 'Dynamic Models of Labour Demand', in O. Ashenfelter and R. Layard (eds.), *Handbook of Labor Economics*, Amsterdam: North-Holland.

—— (1987). 'Why is Wage Inflation in Britain so High?', *Oxford Bulletin of Economics and Statistics*, 49.

—— and Andrews, M. (1983). 'Trade Unions, Real Wages and Employment in Britain 1951–79', *Oxford Economic Papers*, 35, Supplement.

—— and Symons, J. (1986). 'The Real Wage–Employment Relationship in the United States', Centre for Labour Economics, London School of Economics, Discussion Paper No. 269.

Oswald, A. J. (1984). 'Efficient Contracts are on the Labour Demand Curve: Theory and Facts', Industrial Relations Section, Princeton University, Working Paper No. 178.

—— (1985). 'The Economic Theory of Trade Unions: An Introductory Survey', *Scandinavian Journal of Economics*, 87.

—— (1987). 'New Research on the Economics of Trade Unions and Labor Contracts', *Industrial Relations*, 26.

Pencavel, H. (1977). 'The Distribution and Efficiency Effects of Trade Unions in Britain', *British Journal of Industrial Relations*, 15.

—— (1984*a*). 'The Empirical Performance of a Model of Trade Union Behavior', in J. J. Rosa (ed.), *The Economics of Trade Unions: New Directions*, Boston, Mass.: Kluwer-Nijhoff.

—— (1984*b*). 'The Trade-Off Between Wages and Employment in Trade Union Objectives', *Quarterly Journal of Economics*, 99.

—— (1985). 'Wages and Employment under Trade Unionism: Microeconomic Models and Macroeconomic Applications', *Scandinavian Journal of Economics*, 87.

—— and Hartsog, C. (1984). 'A Reconsideration of the Effects of Unionism on Relative Wages and Employment in the United States, 1920–1980', *Journal of Labor Economics*, 2.

—— and Holmlund, B. (1988). 'The Determination of Wages, Employment, and Work Hours in an Economy with Centralized Wage Setting: Sweden 1950–83', *Economic Journal*, 98.

Phelps Brown, E. H. (1962). 'Wage Drift', *Economica*, 19.

Phillips, A. W. (1958). 'The Relation between Unemployment and the Rate of Change of Money Wage Rates in the United Kingdom, 1861–1957', *Economica*, 25.

Pissarides, C. A. (1986). 'Equilibrium Effects of Tax-Based Incomes Policies', in D. Colander (ed.), *Incentive-Based Income Policies*, Cambridge, Mass.: Ballinger.

Pohjola, M. (1987). 'Profit Sharing, Collective Bargaining and Employment', *Journal of Institutional and Theoretical Economics*, 143.

Rødseth, A. (1985). 'Centralized Unions and Macroeconomic Policy: A Note', Institute of Economics, University of Oslo.

Ross, A. M. (1948). *Trade Union Wage Policy*, Berkeley, Calif.: University of California Press.

Sargent, T. (1978). 'Estimation of Dynamic Labor Demand Schedules under Rational Expectations', *Journal of Political Economy*, 86.

Slichter, S. (1950). 'Notes on the Structure of Wages', *Review of Economics and Statistics*, 32.

Söderström, H. T. (1985). 'Union Militancy, External Shocks and the Accommodation Dilemma', *Scandinavian Journal of Economics*, 84.

Strand, J. (1986). 'Monopoly Unions versus Efficient Bargaining: A Repeated Game Approach', FIEF Working Paper No. 22, Stockholm.

—— (1987). 'Oligopoly with Monopoly Unions', Stockholm: FIEF, (mimeo).

Svejnar, J. (1986). 'Bargaining Power, Fear of Disagreement, and Wage Settlements: Theory and Evidence from U.S. Industry', *Econometrica*, 54.

Symons, J. (1985). 'Relative Prices and the Demand for Labour in British Manufacturing', *Economica*, 52.

—— and Layard, P. R. G. (1984). 'Neoclassical Demand for Labour Functions for Six Major Economies', *Economic Journal*, 94.

Tarshis, L. (1939). 'Changes in Real and Money Wage Rates', *Economic Journal*, 49.

Topel, R. H. (1984). 'Equilibrium Earnings, Turnover, and Unemployment: New Evidence', *Journal of Labor Economics*, 2. 500–522.

Wabe, S., and Leech, D. (1978). 'Relative Earnings in UK Manufacturing: A Reconsideration of the Evidence', *Economic Journal*, 88.

PART II

The Duration of Unemployment: Theory and Evidence

Introductory

One of the most characteristic features of recent economic history is the sharp rise in the rate of unemployment in the industrialized world. Unemployment rates in 1985 exceeded 10 per cent in several OECD countries, e.g. Italy, Belgium, the UK, and Canada. At the lower end of the scale Sweden, Austria, Norway, Japan, and Switzerland were still experiencing open unemployment rates around 3 per cent, indicating that the number of unemployed has doubled. Many aspects of the labour market today are reminiscent of the great depression, although there are few signs of a depression in product markets.

Elaborate explanations have been suggested, including rapid labour force growth with demand lagging behind supply, the oil crisis, and resulting excessive real wages due to wage stickiness. It would be an interesting and worthy task to review all of them. The task of this paper is, however, much more limited. Since the end of the 1960s, labour economics has focused on turnover in the labour force and labour force dynamics. According to this approach, the unemployed are no longer viewed as a stagnant pool of job-seekers awaiting a brighter business outlook. One main theme in this literature has been that, if properly measured, the average duration of completed spells of unemployment is quite short, and that frequent transitions into and out of unemployment characterize the experience of people who typically have high unemployment rates. The turnover view has also taught us how to decompose unemployment into an inflow and a duration component. The secular rise in

The authors acknowledge comments on earlier drafts of this paper, in particular from Anders Björklund, Bertil Holmlund, and Richard Layard. Bo Axell, Bo Ranneby, Andrew Oswald, and the participants of the FIEF seminar have also contributed to the finished product. Special thanks are due to Per-Olov Johansson, who suggested that one of the authors should take on a topic he knew so little about. Per-Olov, like the others, is not responsible for what is still unknown to us. Finally, we thank Barbara Lee, who has not only made the paper readable, but also pointed out sections that contained unclear thinking.

unemployment combined with the 'equilibrium view'[1] of unemployment do indicate that the influence of the inflow component has increased over time, i.e. that today more people become unemployed per unit of time.

The equilibrium view has, of course, been challenged, the major work being Clark and Summers (1979). More important, however, the turnover view and the debate surrounding it have launched a string of empirical and theoretical research papers on labour force turnover and unemployment durations, which have transformed labour economics from a sparsely populated research field into one attracting some of the best minds in the business. In particular, we have learned a lot about unemployment durations and the incidence of unemployment, and the unemployment duration literature has contributed considerably to our understanding of the causes and structure of the rise in unemployment. The present paper is an attempt to review the unemployment duration literature. The focus is on the empirical results; but the technical problems connected with measurement cannot be neglected: in order to assess the empirical evidence it is necessary to know the nature of unemployment.

In Chapter 7 we begin by introducing the relevant duration concepts, and discuss their meaning by relating them to corresponding concepts in demography and reliability theory. We also derive the distribution functions of the duration measures, and we show how the probability of leaving the stock of unemployed can be related to search theory.

In Chapter 8 we introduce empirical evidence on how the burden of unemployment (duration) is distributed among different categories—young, old, male, female—and how the structure of unemployment differs among countries. In particular we ask what has happened over time, to what extent the steep secular rise in unemployment can be explained by inflow and duration trends, and whether and to what extent the trends in turn can be explained by demographic or economic factors. Welfare consequences and policy implications are also illuminated.

In Chapter 9 we report evidence on a much-debated issue in the

---

[1] Some of the notable contributions are Friedman's presidential address—see Friedman (1968)—and two influential papers by Robert Hall (1970, 1972). Other contributions belonging to the same stream include Perry (1972), Feldstein (1975), and Salant (1977).

duration literature concerning the effects of unemployment benefits on incentives to work. According to standard search theory, the subsidized benefits of a general unemployment insurance system will create substitution effects in favour of greater frequency and longer duration of periods of unemployment. The magnitude of these substitution effects is a controversial issue, and we show that, in spite of much theoretical and empirical work, certain aspects of the controversy remain essentially unresolved.

In Chapter 10 we report empirical evidence on another major issue in the duration literature, namely whether the probability of leaving unemployment falls, is constant, or rises with the duration of unemployment. Standard partial-equilibrium search theory tells us that the reservation wage is constant or falls over time, implying that the probability of finding an acceptable wage offer increases with time. If this partial-equilibrium effect dominates other counteracting influences, one would expect the probability of leaving unemployment to be constant or to increase with duration. One conteracting effect could be that the wage offer distribution deteriorates because employers, rightly or wrongly, feel that the skills of the unemployed depreciate with the unemployment duration. This effect can be reinforced if long-term unemployment induces attitudes less likely to be consistent with finding employment. For example, unsuccessful job search can lead to an attitude of fatalism or loss of initiative. Duration, however, affects not only mental well-being but also wages. 'Search' may be productive in the wage sense, but also very unproductive after a certain stage.

There is a difficult theoretical problem involved in attempting to estimate this duration effect with empirical data. Loosely speaking, the individuals with the highest probability of leaving unemployment will, on average, leave the stock of unemployed first. Hence, the 'low-probability people' will dominate the stock of long-term unemployed. If the characteristics determining the differences in the probability of leaving unemployment are not appropriately controlled for in the regression equation, the duration coefficient will catch these differences and show an employment probability decreasing with time.[2] The technical estimation problems, the

---

[2] This is not, however, the only problem. Even if the omitted variables are correlated with those which are included, the ML estimates of the coefficients may still be biased toward zero: see Lancaster (1985). The reason is analogous to the reason why errors in variables bias least squares estimates.

existing empirical evidence, and some new empirical evidence on the duration dependence of the probability of leaving unemployment are discussed at some length in this chapter.

Section 10.1 is devoted to two duration dependence studies conducted by the authors on a sample of both open and disguised unemployed white- and blue-collar workers in the north of Sweden. Since this region has the most severe unemployment problems in the country, the idea is that if true negative duration dependence can be detected, it should be revealed in this sample. This chapter also serves to illustrate the standard technique that so far has been used to estimate hazard functions.

Chapter 11 is devoted to an account of the impact on the re-employment probability of more robust independent variables such as age, education, and labour demand. In particular we consider whether personal characteristics of the unemployed or labour demand has the greatest impact on the length of unemployment durations.

Finally, in Chapter 12 we sum up the existing knowledge on the structure and causes of the existing unemployment duration patterns. To what extent can unemployment duration account for the world-wide secular rise in unemployment? What factors determine unemployment duration? How severe are the technical estimation problems? What are the welfare consequences of different duration patterns? What policy lessons does the evidence teach us?

Some of the technical derivations are included in the main text, but most are relegated to the Appendix.

7

The Duration Concepts

It is reasonable to believe that the average time spent in unemployment is an important index of economic welfare, and therefore also an interesting variable from an economic-political standpoint. There are, however, different unemployment duration concepts that have been measured, and there is no general agreement on which is the definitive measure. The duration information which is available in the Swedish AKU[3] statistics or that which is compiled in the US Bureau of Labor Statistics (BLS) is one candidate. There are others. Consider Fig. 7.1, where calendar time is measured along the horizontal axis and the broken line denotes the date of the survey.

At the date of the survey there are three spells of unemployment in progress. What the AKU would observe of these spells, if sampled, is only part of their length. This partial length is often referred to as the length of an uncompleted spell ($\tilde{T}_\mu$), while the duration concept used e.g. in search theory is the length of a completed spell (T_μ). In demography or life statistics these two variables would be called respectively 'age' and 'life-span'. (In reliability theory T_μ is called the mean life length of a unit.) The average uncompleted-spell length, i.e. the average length of spells in progress at the time of the interview, is[4]

$$\tilde{T}_\mu = \frac{\tilde{T}_2 + \tilde{T}_3 + \tilde{T}_5}{3} \qquad (1)$$

This statistic, $\tilde{T}_\mu$, corresponds to the official statistics on uncompleted durations reported by the AKU and the BLS. In terms of Fig. 7.1, the average completed-spell length, i.e. the average complete length of all unemployment spells observed during a given period of time, is

$$T_\mu = \frac{(T_1 + T_2 + T_3 + T_4 + T_5)}{5} \qquad (2)$$

[3] *Arbetskraftsundersökningen* (labour force surveys).

[4] For equation (1) to be an unbiased estimate of E($\tilde{T}$) entrance and exit must be independent of calendar time.

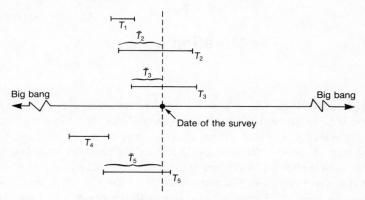

Fig. 7.1. Unemployment spells over time

We can, however, also ask for the average completed-spell length of current spells, e.g. the average complete length of spells in progress at the time of the interview. This measure of unemployment duration, suggested by Akerlof and Main (1980, 1981), is often referred to as the experience-weighted average spell length. According to Fig. 7.1 it can be measured as

$$T_\mu^e = \frac{T_2 + T_3 + T_5}{3} \tag{3}$$

7.1. The Hazard Function

A concept closely related to duration is the re-employment probability. To think in terms of probabilities makes it easier to understand why two identical individuals can have different lengths of unemployment spells. If two individuals are identical and thus have the same re-employment probability, it is still in accordance with the laws of probability that one of them may find a job much earlier than the other one. The person finding a job sooner simply has more luck.

The average duration of unemployment should, however, be the same in two identical groups of individuals, since luck may influence individuals but hardly the average of a larger group. In the same way, a group of individuals with high probabilities of re-employment should have a shorter average duration than a group with low re-employment probabilities. Consequently there is a logical connection between the re-employment probability and the average duration of unemployment.

The fact that luck, or random variations, a more precise statistical concept, have a significant influence on individuals makes it impossible to state the same logical connection between the re-employment probability and the duration for individuals. But a weaker statement can be made. Of two individuals, the one with the higher re-employment probability has a shorter expected duration of unemployment: if we could study many repeated spells of unemployment, the person with the higher re-employment probability would on average have shorter durations.

During the 1980's there has been much effort expended on studying the re-employment probability. Much research has concerned the estimation of so-called hazard functions. In a hazard function, the re-employment probability is a function of different exogenous variables. The exogenous variables have usually included different personal characteristics of those studied, characteristics of the labour markets where the persons are unemployed, and a variable measuring the length of the spell at the time of the survey. A further discussion of conceivable exogenous variables can be found in section 7.2.

The aim of the rest of this chapter is to give a description of the exact relation between the hazard function, duration, and other statistical concepts. Readers who are not familiar with the subject of statistics may find the rest of this chapter rather difficult. We believe, however, that it is possible to understand the reasoning behind the main conclusions in the following chapters without reading the rest of this chapter. The important thing to remember when reading later chapters is the logical connection between the re-employment probability and the expected duration of unemployment. A higher re-employment probability implies a shorter expected duration of unemployment in the same way that those living in a region with a higher probability of rain will on average have shorter periods of sunshine although on account simply of luck there might now and then be a very long period of sunshine.

To leave unemployment in the short interval $(t, t + dt)$ you have to be in the stock of unemployed at time t and leave for employment during the interval.[5] The conditional probability of this event is

$$P(t < T < t + dt \,|\, T > t) = \frac{f(t)dt}{1 - F(t)} = h(t)dt \qquad (4)$$

where $F(t)$ is the distribution function of completed spells, and $f(t)$ is the corresponding density function. The function $h(t)$, which measures the conditional probability of completing the unemployment spell in the interval, is referred to as the hazard function. If we put $G(t) = 1 - F(t)$, equation (4) can be written as

$$\frac{G'(t)dt}{G(t)} = -h(t)dt. \qquad (5)$$

By integrating both members we obtain

$$\ell n \, G(t) = -\int_0^t h(s)ds + C. \qquad (6)$$

To determine C we use the information that $F(0) = 0$ and therefore that $\ell n \, G(0) = 0$, which yields $C = 0$. If we require that $F(\infty) = 1$, and hence that

$$\ell n \, G(\infty) = -\int_0^\infty h(s)ds \qquad (7)$$

then this proves impossible if the integral on the right-hand side of (7) converges. If it converges $F(\infty) < 1$, and consequently there are unemployed who never get a job. The probability of this event is $1 - F(\infty) > 0$. It would also mean that no finite mathematical expectation of a completed unemployment spell would exist (see equation (9) below), which is inconsistent with the ideas behind this paper. Hence we have to require that the integral of the hazard function diverges. From (6) we obtain

$$G(t) = \exp\left(-\int_0^t h(s)ds\right). \qquad (8)$$

---

[5] The rest of the chapter, and parts of the Appendix, rely on Löfgren (1976).

Moreover, it holds that

$$\int\limits_0^\infty G(t)dt = \int\limits_0^\infty [1 - F(t)]dt = \int\limits_0^\infty \int\limits_t^\infty f(s)ds \, dt$$

$$= \int\limits_0^\infty \int\limits_0^s f(s)dt \, ds$$

$$= \int\limits_0^\infty sf(s)ds$$

$$= E(T) \tag{9}$$

i.e. the mathematical expectation of a completed spell of unemployment is obtained by integrating the upper tail of the distribution over the interval $[0, \infty)$.

From (8) it is obvious that the distribution function for completed spells of unemployment is determined as soon as the hazard function is known. A particular interesting case, which is implicit in Kaitz (1970), one of the seminal papers on unemployment durations,[6] is when $h(t)$ is equal to a constant λ. This means that one assumes that the probability of leaving the stock of unemployed is independent of the unemployment duration. As we shall see below, this is an empirically meaningful theorem that can be derived from a standard search model. The constant can of course differ between individuals, and is often specified in the duration literature as a function of individual characteristics such as age, education, or sex.

For $h(t) = \lambda$ we obtain

$$E(T) = \int\limits_0^\infty (1 - F(s))ds = \int\limits_0^\infty e^{-\lambda s} \, ds = \frac{1}{\lambda} \tag{10}$$

i.e. the expected duration of unemployment is obtained by inverting the constant hazard. The resulting distribution is called the exponential distribution.

Let us now turn to a corresponding derivation of the expected duration of an uncompleted unemployment spell. To avoid too

[6] See also Fowler (1968).

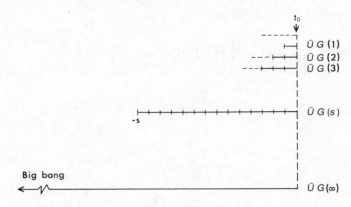

Fig. 7.2. The structure of unemployment at t_0

much mathematical cosmetics we will present this in an intuitive manner. The formal derivation is found in the Appendix. Consider Fig. 7.2, where it is assumed that we investigate the distribution of unemployment durations at time t_0. Assume further that at each point in time $t_0 - s$ exactly $\bar{u}$ persons become unemployed.[7] The share of those people remaining unemployed at t_0 is $1 - F(s) = G(s)$ and their number is $\bar{u}G(s)$. Hence, as can be seen from the figure, the number of people who have been unemployed one and two weeks are $\bar{u}G(1)$ and $\bar{u}G(2)$, respectively. The total number of unemployed is obtained by integrating (summing) s over the interval $[0, \infty)$ to obtain:

$$U = \bar{u}\cdot \int_0^\infty G(s)ds = \bar{u}\cdot E(T) \tag{11}$$

i.e. under these stationary conditions (a constant inflow) unemployment decomposes into an inflow and a duration component. The probability of finding an individual who has been employed $s + ds$ periods[8] can be estimated by its expected share in the total population

---

[7] In a formal derivation this assumption corresponds to an assumption that the inflow distribution is independent of time (stationarity).

[8] For more details, see Appendix.

$$g(s)ds = \frac{\bar{u} \cdot G(s)}{\bar{u} \cdot E(T)} ds = \frac{1 - F(s)}{E(T)} ds \qquad (12)$$

which is the density function for an uncompleted spell of unemployment. Its expected duration is

$$\int_0^\infty s \, g(s)ds = \frac{1}{E(T)} \int_0^\infty s(1 - F(s))ds = E(\tilde{T}). \qquad (13)$$

For the special case when $F(s)$ is exponential we have the surprising equality

$$E(T) = E(\tilde{T}) = \frac{1}{\lambda}. \qquad (14)$$

The intuitive explanation is the following. The uncompleted-spell length observed in this or any other survey contains two sources of biases when used as a measure of the completed length: (1) long spells tend to be over-represented in the sample and (2) uncompleted spells are necessarily shorter than their corresponding complete spells. When the individuals in the population share a common and constant exit probability, there is effectively no sorting process taking place and the two sources of biases exactly offset one another.

Suppose on the contrary that the exit probability depends on duration. If it decreases with duration this will aggravate the over-representation of long spells to such an extent that $E(T) < E(\tilde{T})$, and if the opposite holds $E(T) > E(\tilde{T})$.[9] The latter case is analogous to the fact that the average age of the living population is less than the expected lifetime of the population. The reason is that the death risk (the exit probability) increases with age.

Here it may, however, be interesting to relate more explicitly the expected length of uncompleted and completed spells of unemployment. From equation (13) we obtain[10]

---

[9] The formal proof is somewhat bulky. The interested reader is referred to Barlow and Proschan (1975).

[10]
$$E(\tilde{T}) = \frac{1}{E(T)} \int_0^\infty s[1 - F(s)]ds = \frac{1}{E(T)} \int_0^\infty \int_s^\infty s f(t)dt \, ds = \frac{1}{E(T)} \int_0^\infty \int_0^t s f(t)ds \, dt$$

$$= \frac{1}{2E(T)} \int_0^\infty \psi t^2 f(t)dt = \frac{1}{2E(T)} E[T^2]$$

See also Löfgren (1976) and Salant (1977).

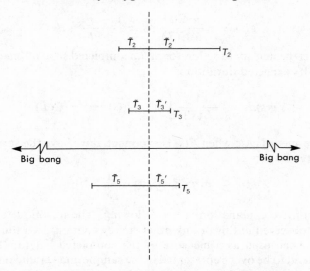

Fig. 7.3. The symmetry in the distribution of the length of uncompleted spells and the remaining length of uncompleted spells

$$E(\tilde{T}) = \frac{E(T^2)}{2E(T)} \text{ or}$$

$$\frac{E(\tilde{T})}{E(T)} = \frac{1}{2}\left[\frac{\text{Var}(T)}{[E(T)]^2} + 1\right] \tag{13a}$$

From this formula it is seen that if the variance of the completed spell length is small in relation to its mean, the expected length of an uncompleted spell will be approximately half the completed spell length. As Salant (1977) points out, this explains why the age of the living population is approximately half of life expectancy. Moreover, if T is exponentially distributed, then $\text{Var}(T) = 1/\lambda^2 = [E(T)]^2$, and (14) follows.

It remains to be shown how the experience-weighted duration measure is related to the completed and uncompleted unemployment spells.

Consider the variation in Fig. 7.3. The experience-weighted duration measure is a measure of the total length of an observed uncompleted unemployment spell. However, if one drops needles of different lengths parallel to the time axis one should expect that the needles, which are hit by the beam of the observer, are on the average hit in the middle. In other words, a symmetry argument (it does not matter which big bang you choose as the end of time) shows that the distributions of $\tilde{T}_i$ and $\tilde{T}'_i$ are identical.[11]

$$E(T^e) = E(\tilde{T}) + E(\tilde{T}') = 2E(\tilde{T}). \tag{15}$$

In Chapter 8 we will discuss more thoroughly why and when the experience-weighted measure is relevant. For a more detailed presentation of duration concepts, the reader is referred to the Appendix and to Salant (1977), Frank (1978), and Heckman and Singer (1984a). For a comprehensive and excellent survey of the econometrics of hazard functions and duration data, the reader is referred to a recent survey by Kiefer (1988).

7.2. The Specification of the Hazard Function

A reader more interested in economics than statistics would at this stage ask what kind of economic model and what kinds of economic factor determine the magnitude of the re-employment probability. There are many potential candidates,[12] but search theory is a coherent theoretical body that has frequently been employed. This tradition stems from e.g. Lancaster (1979), Nickell (1979), Kiefer and Neuman (1979, 1981), Narendranathan *et al.* (1985), and Albrecht *et al.* (1986). There are many refinements of search theory, but a standard version of the original theory is built on the following rather restrictive assumptions. The agent maximizes the expected present value of income over an infinite planning horizon at a given discount rate r. While unemployed the job-seeker receives unemployment benefits, b, and other income, y. The job offers arrive randomly at a constant[13] rate, and an offer is described by a given wage w, with a stationary distribution function $H(w)$, which has mean $\bar{w}$. The job lasts forever, and gives total work income of $(\bar{w} + y)$/period, as compared to the total periodical income as unemployed, $b + y$. The person is free to accept or reject job offers,

[11] For the same reason, if you observe a taxi with number 50 in Umeå, you should estimate the total number of taxis in Umeå to be twice as large.

[12] Another possibility is the continuous-time labour supply model. For details, see Heckman and Singer (1984a).

[13] A frequently used modification of the theory is to assume that the searcher can affect the intensity with which job offers arrive.

and rejecting a job offer does not mean that he is no longer entitled to unemployment benefits.

Rational individual behaviour can under these circumstances be shown to imply that the searcher chooses a reservation wage $w^* = w^*(b, y, \bar{w})$, such that he accepts the job offer iff $w \geq w^*$. The re-employment probability over a short interval dt is hence

$$h[w^*(b, y, \bar{w})]dt = \theta[1 - H(w^*)]dt \qquad (16)$$

where θ is the rate at which job offers arrive. As indicated above, the reservation wage will be a function of the parameters of the wage distribution (e.g. its mean), the unemployment benefit, and the non-labour income[14] y. It is fairly easy to show that the reservation wage in this setting is an increasing function of the magnitude of the unemployment benefits and thus $h(\cdot)$ is decreasing in benefits. Loosely speaking, we would also expect w^* to be an increasing function of the mean, $\bar{w}$. This is, however, not generally true, but follows if we assume that $\bar{w}$ is moved by translations of the distribution. Moreover, if the planning horizon is finite the reservation wage will be time-dependent and falling as a function of time. The key problem is that, as Atkinson *et al.* (1984) put it: 'There is no apparent analogue of the Cobb–Douglas.' In other words, even if one chooses a simple wage offer distribution, there is no simple and/or explicit functional form of the hazard function that follows from the optimization problem. The role of the theory has therefore been to indicate which proxy variables to use for the reservation wage, while the form of the hazard function has been borrowed from existing knowledge within reliability theory (e.g. the Weibull hazard function). This is unfortunate, since the estimation results have been shown to be rather sensitive for the specification of the model.

Finally, the search-theoretical underpinning has long been a 'partial-partial' equilibrium approach treating only the behaviour of the 'voluntarily unemployed'.[15] The behaviour of the firms is likely to affect the wage offer distribution, and the specification of the hazard function should therefore also contain demand factors.

---

[14] If the income y is obtained irrespective of employment status, it will not be an argument in the reservation wage equation of 'the income maximizer'. For an early but fairly complete survey of search theory, see Lippman and McCall (1976).

[15] The availability effect—to be discussed below—introduces an 'involuntary element': chance in addition to choice.

It is difficult to say whether this specification problem has hampered empirical research. Empirical data are and have been scarce, and it is the feeling of the authors that the researchers have been restricted by data availability.

The lack of a general-equilibrium search model has recently been partially remedied (see e.g. Albrecht and Axell (1984), Albrecht *et al.* (1986), Axell and Lang (1986), and Mavromaras (1987)) and these analyses show that the general-equilibrium answer to the effects of parameter changes may look very different from the partial-equilibrium effects.

8

Analysing the Length of Spells of Unemployment

In the preceding chapter we have introduced three possible measures of the length of an unemployment spell, with the implication that a choice must be made as to which measure should be used. As always, questions like these tend to have no simple answer. In an analysis of unemployment and unemployment duration many different questions can be asked. From equation (11) we have seen that unemployment can be decomposed into a duration and an inflow component. If we want to know whether changes in the inflow or duration component account for the recent secular rise in unemployment, it is obvious that we need the expected duration of a completed unemployment spell. Also, if we want to compare the unemployment durations of different groups in the population, it may seem natural to choose the completed-spell concept. However, if we want to inquire about the normative aspects of unemployment it has been argued[1] that the cost of unemployment is best measured by the uncompleted-spell concept, which is readily available in the labour statistics of many countries (e.g. the USA, the UK, and Sweden). It is reasonable to assume that the total cost of unemployment in any current week is a function of the stock of unemployment times the average weekly cost of an uncompleted spell, where the latter in turn depends on the duration distribution of the existing unemployment.[2] More precisely, let U_t be the number of people who have been out of work for t weeks, and C_t be the weekly cost of a person who has been out of unemployment for t weeks. The total weekly cost, TC_w, is then

---

[1] See Layard (1981).

[2] Under steady-state conditions, inflow into unemployment equals outflow from unemployment; the weekly cost can of course be expressed in terms of the weekly flow into unemployment. For details, see Layard (1981). The measure in equation (20) has the advantage of always being 'correct'; it also demands more readily available information.

$$TC_w = \sum_{t=1}^{\infty} U_t C_t = U \left(\sum_{t=1}^{\infty} \frac{U_t}{U} C_t \right). \tag{17}$$

Now U_t/U measures the proportion of total unemployment which consists of people who have been unemployed for t periods, i.e., U_t/U corresponds to $\bar{u}G(s)/\bar{u}E(T)$ in equation (12) and is available from a survey of uncompleted spells at time t_0, as is suggested by Fig. 7.2.

The cost component C_t is essentially the value of the weekly output which is lost minus the value of one week's leisure time.[3] Say that the compensated supply curve for annual hours is linear and increasing. We can then measure the weekly value of leisure for a person who has been unemployed for t weeks as the difference between the wage-rate and the wage-rate that would induce him to supply $52H - Ht$ hours annually, where H is the weekly hours as employed.[4] Since the supply curve is linear, this shadow wage can be easily computed, and one obtains

$$\text{Value of a week's leisure time} = (w - aHt)H$$
$$\text{where } a = \text{slope of supply curve} \tag{18}$$

The value of the loss in weekly output is wH, and the cost of one man's unemployment, under the condition that he has been unemployed for t weeks, is

$$C_t = [w - (w - aHt)]H = aH^2 t. \tag{19}$$

If this expression is inserted into the formula for the total weekly cost one obtains

$$TC_w = U \sum_{t=1}^{\infty} \frac{U_t}{U} tA = U\tilde{T}_\mu A \tag{20}$$

where $A = aH^2$, and where $\tilde{T}_\mu$ is the average duration of an uncompleted spell of unemployment. In other words, the costs of unemployment during a week are directly proportional to the average length of an uncompleted spell times the total number of unemployed. If one is willing to assume that the A component does

[3] Ideally one would also like to include the net yield from one additional week of search.

[4] This presupposes that there are no repeated spells of unemployment, and that the unemployed is willing to work more at the going wage (involuntary unemployment). The reasoning is Layard's in his 1981 paper.

not differ among countries, one can estimate and compare the weekly average costs of being unemployed in different countries simply by comparing the length of an average uncompleted unemployment spell.

It has also been argued that even a positive analysis of unemployment should focus upon the uncompleted-spell length. The argument runs like this. Even if most spells of unemployment are rather short,[5] the short spells contribute little to total unemployment.[6] To understand unemployment one must focus on the prospects facing the existing stock of the unemployed. One should therefore ask how long the existing stock will on averge be unemployed from now on.[7] Since the latter statistics, under steady-state conditions, are exactly one-half of the former[8] and equal to the unemployment spell length, which is readily available, the choice is obvious.

On the whole, however, the discussion of which duration concept provides the best measure seems unnecessary. It should be obvious from the theoretical discussion in Chapter 7 that all three measures are computable as soon as the hazard function is known, which explains why so much research effort has been devoted to the estimation of the hazard function. As will become clear from Chapters 9 and 10, the parameters of the hazard function can (in theory) be estimated from data on both completed and uncompleted unemployment spells. From a positive standpoint it is also obvious that if we can identify the shape of the hazard function we can understand some of the reasons behind short as well as long unemployment spells.[9] And the shape of the hazard as a function of explanatory variables such as duration should be able to tell us something about the reasonableness of different theoretical explanations of unemployment.

On the other hand, it is understandable that labour policy makers want simple statistics which tell a lot about both the situation in the labour market and the welfare consequences of unemployment. The

---

[5] Noted e.g. by Hall (1972).

[6] See also below.

[7] This measure was first suggested by Akerlof and Main (1981), Main (1981), and Main (1982). It is challenged by among others Carlsson and Horrigan (1983), and to some extent by Björklund (1983).

[8] See ch. 7 above.

[9] Since the hazard function is only a small piece of a general-equilibrium framework, its information content is obviously not enough to tell us the full story of the causes of unemployment durations.

uncompleted-spell length may, as we have seen, provide much of the desired information.

8.1. The Structure of Unemployment Durations

Early empirical work on unemployment durations did create some confusion. It was claimed that the typical labour market behaviour was characterized by large flows into and out of unemployment, short unemployment spells, and instability of employment. This view, which may be termed the turnover view, was emphasized both in theoretical and empirical work. One reason for this may be that job search theory happened (?) to be developed together with empirical work on unemployment duration. However, as early as 1970, Kaitz, in his seminal work of how to analyse unemployment durations in the USA, noted (without referring to job search theory) that under normal business conditions one-fifth of the unemployed are in their first week of unemployment. The bottom line of his paper was that 'average jobless spells are shorter than previously believed, but that there are more of them'. The reason behind his observation was, however, essentially that the completed spell length (T_μ) is shorter than the uncompleted spell length $(\tilde{T}_\mu)$, and that the unemployment rate can be decomposed into a duration and inflow component. The conclusion then follows by a direct application of formula (11).

The following quotation from Feldstein (1975) is more typical for the turnover view.

The traditional view, based on the experience of the depression, pictured the unemployed as an inactive pool of job losers who had to wait for a general business upturn before they could find new jobs. Modern research has shown that this picture is distorted. The majority of the unemployed do not become unemployed by losing their previous jobs, they quit voluntarily or are new entrants or reentrants into the labour force. Moreover, the typical duration of unemployment is very short; more than half of the unemployment spells end in four weeks or less.[10]

Although the statement about voluntary quits is perhaps not generally valid, the content of the last sentence is.[11] A lot of studies

---

[10] Feldstein (1975, pp. 725-6).

[11] Since 1975 there has been information available in Sweden about the causes of

in different countries have shown that a large (although sometimes decreasing) proportion of spells ends within one month.[12] For example, the proportion of the unemployment spells that end within one mouth in the USA and Canada has stayed fairly constant, and close to the figure suggested by Feldstein.[13] On the other hand, it is also almost universally true that those in short-term unemployment account for only a small share of the existing unemployment. In other words, most unemployment is characterized by relatively few persons who are out of work a long period of time. In Canada, during the period 1976–80, people who were unemployed more than one month accounted for approximately 75 per cent of the existing unemployment.[14] The corresponding figure for the USA in 1975 was almost exactly the same. Fig. 8.1, which is borrowed from Björklund (1981), shows that a considerable share of the Swedish unemployed stay unemployed for more than three months.[15]

The answer to this apparent paradox is that in the duration concept, T_μ all spells of unemployment are given the same weighting, irrespective of the amount of unemployment for which they account. Hence T_μ does not reflect the length of a spell in which a typical week of unemployment is spent.[16]

Another important feature of the structure of unemployment is that a large proportion of unemployment spells end with withdrawals from the labour force. The proportion varies considerably, however, between demographic groups. It is approximately 0.25 for men over twenty, while it is 0.6 for young women. Similarly, almost three-quarters of the newly employed during a month enter from

---

unemployment in the sense that the unemployed are asked how they become unemployed. The category 'other causes' was in 1983 approximately 17% of the total unemployment and may contain, among other things, voluntary quits. The experience-weighted measure of unemployment duration for this category is close to 48 weeks, which suggests that there are also other causes involved.

[12] The evidence is overwhelming. See e.g. Hall (1972), Feldstein (1975) Clark and Summers (1979), Hasan and De Broucker (1982), and SOU 1984:31, ch. 9.

[13] The following series for the period 1976–80, borrowed from Hasan and De Broucker (1982), makes this point: 0.57, 0.53, 0.52, 0.55, 0.55. The figure for 1975 in Clark and Summers (1979) is 0.55 and the corresponding figure for 1969 is considerably higher, 0.71.

[14] Hasan and De Broucker (1982) and Clark and Summers (1979).

[15] Note, however, that Björklund's figures include repeated spells of unemployment and represent the experience-weighted spell measure.

[16] This fact induced Akerlof and Main (1981) to introduce the experienced-weighted duration measure T_μ^e.

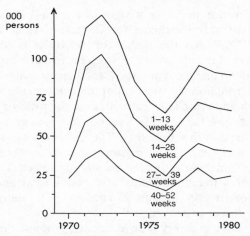

Fig. 8.1. The stock of unemployed 1970–1980, 16–74 years, categorized according to unemployment weeks during a year

Source: Björklund (1981): the experience-weighted spell measure.

outside the labour force, and an equally large proportion withdraw from the labour force without ever being measured as unemployed.

The concentration of unemployment towards long-term unemployment will stand out even more clearly if one considers that many unemployed individuals experience more than one unemployment spell. The distribution by number of unemployment spells can be found out through the annual retrospective surveys in e.g. the USA, Canada, and Sweden.[17] These estimates suffer from two kinds of bias, namely recall bias and interruption bias. The recall bias tends to overlook brief periods of unemployment, and there is therefore a tendency to underestimate the number of spells per person. The interruption bias works in the opposite direction, since, for example, spells that are in progress at the beginning and at the end of the year are counted as completed spells.[18]

'Conservative' measures[19] of the average number of spells per

---

[17] In Sweden this survey is called *Februariundersökningen*.

[18] Whether there is an over- or underestimation is in the end an empirical question.

[19] See Axelsson *et al*. (1977). The measures are conservative in the sense that they assume that the individuals belonging to the category '3 spells' experience exactly 3 spells. Neither recall nor interruption biases are accounted for. However, since 1976 the information in this respect has been more complete.

person in Sweden indicates a figure between 1.30 and 1.54. A similarly conservative estimate for Canada gives a slightly lower estimate (1.22),[20] and the figure for Australia is somewhere in between. Part of the difference between the Swedish and Australian estimates on the one hand and the Canadian estimates on the other hand stems from how the problem of interruption is accounted for. The Swedish and Australian estimates are the ratio of spells which take place at some time during a year to the number of people who are unemployed during that year. The Canadian estimates, on the other hand, account for interruption bias; it is therefore not surprising that the Canadian estimates are slightly lower. The Canadian data also show that individuals who had a total unemployment experience longer than three months accounted for more than 73 per cent of the total unemployment.[21]

So far we have said very little about exit probabilities, the length of unemployment durations, and to what extent the unemployment is involuntary. Nor have we shown the duration and inflow components of the secular rise in unemployment. We now turn to these problems.

In Table 8.1 the unemployment rates in all OECD countries are listed.[22] Between 1975 and 1985 the rate of unemployment increased in all countries except the USA and Norway. Is this increase due to an increased inflow into unemployment or has the duration component increased?

In Table 8.2 the unemployment rates in USA and Britain are decomposed into a flow and a duration component. During the period 1962–78 the rate of unemployment was fairly constant in the USA but increased substantially in Britain. The increase was clearly caused by longer spells of unemployment. In the USA there was no significant change in either inflow or duration.

After 1978 the rate of unemployment has continued to increase in Britain, and the increase is still due to longer durations. There are no data in Table 8.2 on inflow and completed spells after 1978 in the

[20] See Hasan and De Broucker (1982) and Trivedi and Baker (1983).

[21] Note that the merger of adjacent spells tends to 'overestimate' long-term unemployment.

[22] The reader interested in more details is referred to Clark and Summers (1979) and Akerlof and Main (1981) for the USA, Björklund (1981) for Sweden, Main (1981) and Nickell (1979) for the UK, Hasan and De Broucker (1982) for Canada, and Trivedi and Baker (1983) for Australia.

TABLE 8.1. *Unemployment in the OECD*

	Unemployment rates[a] (% total labour force)					
	1975	1979	1982	1983	1984	1985
Australia	4.8	6.2	7.1	9.9	8.9	8.2
Austria	1.7	2.1	3.5	4.1	3.8	3.5
Belgium	5.0	8.2	12.6	13.9	14.0	13.2
Canada	6.9	7.4	10.9	11.8	11.2	10.4
Denmark[b]	4.9	6.0	11.0	11.4	8.5	7.6[d]
Finland	2.2	5.9	5.8	6.1	6.1	6.2
France	4.0	5.9	8.1	8.3	9.7	10.1
Germany	3.6	3.2	6.1	8.0	8.5	8.6
Greece[b]	2.3	1.9	5.8	7.9	8.1	8.4[d]
Iceland[b]	0.6	0.4	0.7	1.0	1.3	1.7[d]
Ireland[b]	7.3	7.1	11.4	14.1	15.5	16.8[d]
Italy	5.0	6.5	7.9	8.5	8.7	9.0
Japan	1.9	2.1	2.4	2.6	2.7	2.6
Luxembourg[b]	0.2	0.7	1.2	1.6	1.7	1.8[d]
Netherlands	5.2	5.4	11.4	13.7	14.0	13.0
New Zealand[b]	0.2	1.9	3.5	5.6	5.7	6.3[d]
Norway	2.3	2.0	2.6	3.3	3.0	2.5
Portugal[b]	4.4	8.0	7.3	8.2	8.9	8.6[d]
Spain	3.7	8.5	15.9	17.4	20.1	21.6
Sweden	1.6	2.1	3.1	3.5	3.1	2.8
Switzerland	0.4	0.3	0.4	0.9	1.1	0.9
Turkey[b]	12.9	13.2	15.1	15.7	15.7	16.5[d]
UK	4.3	5.1	11.4	12.6	13.0	13.2
USA	8.3	5.8	9.5	9.5	7.4	7.1
North America	8.2	5.9	9.7	9.7	7.8	7.4
OECD Europe[c]	4.1	5.4	8.9	10.0	10.8	11.0[d]
Total OECD[c]	5.1	4.9	7.9	8.5	8.1	8.0[d]

a. Data for all countries except Denmark, Iceland, Ireland, Luxembourg, New Zealand, Portugal, and Turkey are standardized unemployment rates which are more comparable between countries than the unemployment rates published in national sources. For a detailed description of the sources and methods used, see OECD, Standardized Unemployment Rates, Sources and Methods.
b. National data based on national definitions.
c. Based on countries with standardized unemployment rates. These countries represent 90% of the total OECD labour force.
d. Secretariat estimates.
Source: OECD, *Employment Outlook*, Sept. 1986, table *h*.

TABLE 8.2. *Unemployment flow and duration*

	USA				UK (males)[d]			
	Unemployment rate (%)	Flow per month (%)	Average completed spell length (months) (T_μ)	Experience-weighted average spell length (months) (T_μ^e)	Unemployment rate (%)	Flow per month (%)	Average completed spell length (months) (T_μ)	Experience-weighted average spell length (months) (T_μ^e)
	(1)	(2)[a]	(3)[b]	(4)[c]	(5)	(6)	(7)	(8)
1962	5.5	3.8	1.4	6.9	2.3	1.3	1.8	12.6
1963	5.7	3.8	1.5	6.5	3.1	2.0	1.5	13.5
1964	5.2	3.9	1.4	6.2	2.0	1.6	1.3	14.1
1965	4.5	3.7	1.2	5.5	1.8	1.5	1.2	13.8
1966	3.8	3.9	1.0	4.8	1.8	1.1	1.6	12.9
1967	3.8	3.3	1.2	4.1	3.1	1.5	2.0	12.7
1968	3.6	3.4	1.1	3.9	3.2	1.5	2.1	13.2
1969	3.5	3.3	1.1	3.7	3.2	1.6	2.0	19.9
1970	4.9	3.9	1.3	4.1	3.5	1.5	2.3	14.2
1971	5.9	3.7	1.6	5.3	4.5	1.7	2.6	14.2
1972	5.6	3.9	1.4	5.6	5.1	1.7	3.0	16.5
1973	4.9	3.0	1.6	4.7	3.7	1.6	2.3	17.9

	(1)	(2)	(3)	(4)	(5)	(6)	(7)	(8)
1974	5.6	4.3	1.3	4.5	3.6	1.7	2.1	16.7
1975	8.5	4.0	2.1	6.6	5.2	1.6	3.3	14.5
1976	7.7	4.1	1.9	7.4	7.0	1.9	3.6	16.3
1977	7.0	4.2	1.7	6.7	7.2	1.8	3.9	18.1
1978	6.0	4.1	1.5	5.5	7.1	1.8	4.0	18.9
1979	5.8	—	—	5.0	6.5	1.4	4.8	21.3
1980	7.0	—	—	5.5	8.3	1.5	5.5	19.2
1981	7.5	—	—	6.3	13.0	1.5	8.6	18.8
1982	9.5	—	—	7.3	15.2	1.6	9.4	23.1
1983	9.5	—	—	9.2	16.0	1.7	9.4	26.5

a. An estimate of inflow per month.
b. An estimate of the duration of spells beginning in the period. Columns (2) and (3) are based on estimates of cohort survival rates in unemployment.
c. The average uncompleted spell length × 2 = the experience-weighted measure.
d. Up to 1970 the methodology is the same as that used for the USA. From 1971 it is as follows: column (6): average of inflow and outflow per month; column (7): column (5)/column (6); column (8): average uncompleted spell length × 2.

Source: Johnson and Layard (1986).

TABLE 8.3. *Youth unemployment in selected OECD countries: % of total youth labour force*

	1980	1981	1982	1983	1984	1985	1986	1987
Youth unemployment rates[a]								
USA	13.3	14.3	17.0	16.4	13.3	13.0	12.5	12.0
Japan	3.4	4.0	4.3	4.5	4.9	4.8	5.5	6.0
Germany[b]	3.9	6.5	9.5	10.7	9.9	9.5	8.25	7.0
France[c]	15.0	17.0	19.0	19.7	24.4	25.6	25.75	26.5
UK[d]	14.1	18.1	23.1	23.2	21.8	21.7	21.75	20.75
Italy	25.2	27.4	29.7	32.0	33.4	33.7	35.5	37.0
Canada	13.2	13.3	18.7	19.9	17.9	16.5	14.75	14.25
Total	12.2	13.7	16.4	16.6	15.4	15.3	15.0	14.75
Four major European countries	13.6	16.5	19.7	20.9	21.6	21.7	21.5	21.25
Australia[e]	12.3	10.8	12.9	17.9	16.1	14.3	12.75	12.5
Finland	9.0	9.7	10.5	11.3	10.4	9.1	9.5	9.5
Norway	5.4	5.8	8.1	9.7	7.6	6.8	5.0	5.75
Spain[f]	28.5	33.7	36.9	38.9	44.5	43.6	43.25	42.25
Sweden	5.1	6.3	7.6	8.0	6.0	5.8	6.0	6.25
Total of the 12 countries above[g]	12.9	14.5	17.2	17.7	16.8	16.6	16.25	16.0
Youth unemployment levels (m.)								
7 major countries	6.8	7.7	9.2	9.2	8.5	8.4	8.25	8.0
4 major European countries	2.7	3.3	4.0	4.2	4.3	4.4	4.25	4.25
12 countries	8.0	9.1	10.7	10.9	10.4	10.2	10.0	9.75

a. The term 'youth' refers to the 15–24 age group, with a few exceptions: the age group is 14–24 in Italy and 16–24 in USA, UK, Norway, Spain, and Sweden. Data refer to the total youth labour force in all countries except Canada and Autralia, where the armed forces are excluded from the youth labour force. Data for the USA, Japan, Canada, Finland, and Sweden are averages of monthly figures, while data for Italy and Norway are averages of quarterly data.

b. Unemployment figures refer to the registered unemployed at the end of Sept. each year. Labour force figures are annual averages based on various national sources including the micro-census.

USA, but the experience-weighted unemployment duration measure shows a slight increase after 1978. Moreover, data in Sidder (1985) indicate that completed unemployment spell lengths increased in the USA after 1978. Sidder also shows that measures of durations based on steady-state conditions tend to dampen actual fluctuations in the duration component over the business cycle. This is so because when unemployment rises, exit probabilities are over-estimated by the heavy weights given to shorter spells, while they are underestimated when business conditions improve. Sidder's data refer to the period 1968–82 and it is fair to say that the rise in the US duration component is more pronounced than in Table 8.2.

Data from Australia[23] and Sweden (see below) also show that the duration component's contributions to the rising unemployment rates outweigh the contributions of the flow component.

The youth unemployment rate is generally higher than the unemployment rate for other groups in the population. According to Tables 8.1 and 8.3 Germany was the only country with a youth unemployment rate equal to the aggregate rate of unemployment.

There is, however, empirical evidence indicating a shorter duration of youth unemployment. In Table 8.4 evidence from Canada, Germany, the UK, and the USA is shown. A higher rate of unemployment than other groups in the population, combined with shorter unemployment spells, implies that the turnover in the youth labour market is clearly above average.

---

[23] See Trivedi and Baker (1983).

---

c. Data refer to Mar. each year, except for 1982 when data refer to Apr.–May. Conscripts are included in the labour force aged 15–24.

d. Unemployment figures relate to July each year and are based on registrations up to 1982 and claimants from 1983 on. The figures for 1983 and later include non-claimant school leavers registered at careers offices. Labour force data are estimated from several sources including the EEC Labour Force Sample Survey, and refer to June each year.

e. Data refer to Aug. each year.

f. Data refer to the last quarter of each year.

g. These countries accounted for about 85% of the youth labour force in the OECD area in 1979.

Source: OECD, *Employment Outlook*, Sept. 1986, table 10. Youth unemployment data for all countries except Germany and the UK are from household surveys. The German and UK youth rates represent registered unemployment as a percentage of the labour force as measured by household surveys. For more details see OECD, *Labour Force Statistics*, pt. iii.

TABLE 8.4.   *Average completed-spell lengths* (T$_\mu$) *of youth unemployment (months)*

		Teenagers[a]		Young adults[b]		Prime-age adults[c]	
	Year	Male	Female	Male	Female	Male	Female
Canada	1980	2.0	1.9	2.5	2.3	2.7	2.1
Germany	1977	2.1	2.3	2.4	3.3	3.3	4.1
UK	1973	0.8	0.7	1.1	1.0	2.2	1.8
	1976	2.0	1.9	3.0	2.6	4.8	4.3
	1979	3.7	3.4	3.6	3.8	5.3	5.6
	1981	4.7	4.0	7.8	6.3	10.1	8.4
USA	1973	1.6(1.8)	1.5(1.6)	1.7(3.1)	1.6(1.8)	2.0(2.1)	1.7(2.4)
	1975	1.9(1.8)	1.7(1.8)	2.6(2.7)	2.1(2.2)	2.9(2.7)	2.3(2.0)
	1979	1.7(1.8)	1.6(1.8)	2.0(2.3)	1.8(2.0)	2.3(2.5)	1.9(2.0)
	1981	1.9(1.9)	1.8(1.8)	2.5(2.8)	1.9(2.3)	2.6(2.8)	2.1(2.3)

a. Teenagers in the UK are the 16–18 age group, in Canada and Germany the 15–19 age group, and in the USA the 16–19 age group.
b. Young adults are 20–4-year-olds except in the UK, where the age group is 18–24.
c. Prime-age adults are 25–44-year-olds except in the USA where the age group is 25–59.
d. Data refer to Great Britain only and are for July each year.
e. Data refer to whites only. Data in parentheses refer to non-whites.
Source: OECD Employment Outlook, Sept. 1983, table 34.

When comparing Tables 8.3 and 8.4 it is natural to conclude that the situation for youth is not as bleak as Table 8.3 alone indicates. There are, however, some valid reservations made by the OECD in connection with the presentation of Table 8.4.

The dividing line between unemployment and non-participation in the labour market is 'often fuzzy'. Many unemployed people stop searching for a job only because they become discouraged, and are not counted in official labour force statistics even though they could very reasonably be classed as unemployed. Hasan and De Broucker present evidence which implies that youths are more prone to discouragement than adult workers.[24] They show that, if part of withdrawals out of the labour force from unemployment are ignored (those occurring after unemployment has already continued for a certain number of months), then the average unemployment duration of teenagers would increase by significantly more than prime-age adults.

[24] See Hasan and De Broucker (1982).

A final descriptive characteristic worth mentioning is that the average completed-spell length of all unemployment spells, almost without exception, is shorter than the average uncompleted-spell length $(T_\mu < \bar{T}_\mu)$.[25] This is seen, for example, by noting that the numbers in columns (4) and (8) of Table 8.2 are more than twice the numbers in columns (3) and (7).

We now develop the question whether all this structural evidence —i.e. long-term unemployment explaining a larger share of the unemployment, a large share of unemployment spells ending in withdrawals, and a mixed international picture of the flow duration composition as well as the level of youth unemployment—is consistent with the turnover view and/or job search theories.

What Clark and Summers, Akerlof and Main, Hasan and De Broucker, and Trivedi and Baker all claim is that the phenomena of long-term unemployment, higher exit rates from the labour force, etc., are an indication of a market failure or a disequilibrium situation, in the sense that people are either involuntarily unemployed or are rationed out of the market. Considering the analysis in connection with the introduction of the duration measures in section 7.1, $T_\mu < \bar{T}_\mu$ can be taken as an indication that the exit probability decreases over time (see the discussion following equation (14)). From the job search theory in section 7.2 we know that the exit probability should be constant or increase with the duration. Hence job search theory cannot explain existing unemployment patterns.

The counter-argument runs like this. Unemployed persons are heterogeneous: age, sex, education, and the parameters in the economic environment vary. Those with relatively low reservation wages, and hence with higher probabilities of leaving unemployment, tend to get sorted out more quickly. Over time, out of an original cohort, those with higher probabilities of staying unemployed make up a larger proportion of the remaining unemployed. The duration dependence that we observe is therefore a natural reflection of a sorting process, and not a scar from the length of the unemployment duration as such.

Obviously, as soon as the stock of unemployed is heterogeneous there will be sorting, and there is no simple way in which a negative

---

[25] Strangely enough the two measures seem to have converged in Sweden recently: see Holmlund (1986).

'time dependence' can be separated from sorting. In other words, it is difficult to reject the hypothesis that job search theory is a possible candidate as a micro-foundation for unemployment–employment behaviour. On the other hand, if data indicate a non-negative 'time' dependence, i.e. exit probability, which increases with, or is independent of the duration of the unemployment, then it would be safe to conclude that there are no 'scars' from duration as such, since the time dependence coefficient is biased towards a negative duration dependence. We will return to attempts to deal with the sorting versus time dependence problem in Chapter 10 below.

8.2. Duration and Inflow Behaviour over the Business Cycle

In this section we will say a few words about the typical behaviour of the duration and inflow components of unemployment over the business cycle. The reasoning in connection with the derivation of the reservation wage in section 7.2 presupposes a given wage distribution and a given number of job offers per unit of time.[26] Over the business cycle, however, both the wage offer distribution and the number of vacancies change. Hence one would expect the transition probability, which is the product of the job offer probability and the job-searcher's acceptance probability, to change over the business cycle. The direction in which the duration component changes is, however, not in general derivable from theory. An increase in aggregate demand will have the following three effects on the transition probability.[27]

1. *The availability effect.* An increased number of winning tickets in terms of job offers tends to reduce the average time it takes for locating a vacancy, and will mean—at a constant reservation wage—shorter spells of unemployment.

2. *The detection lag effect.* Changes in aggregate demand will

[26] A frequently used assumption in standard search theory is that the number of job offers received per period is constant (equals one), thus the constant θ in equation (16).

[27] Note that although the discussion in this section is related to the one in Sidder (1985), the questions here are different. The answers may, however, be biased by a decomposition of unemployment into flow and duration which is based on steady-state assumptions.

affect the location of the wage offer distribution. Since it will very likely take time to discover that a rise in aggregate demand has improved the wage offer distribution, reservation wages will be unaffected in the short run, and this will cause unemployment durations to decline.

3. *The suply effect.*   A recognized increase in the number of job offers increases the yield from search, and, at a given wage distribution, this will increase the reservation wage and the probability of accepting a wage offer will decrease.

Feinberg (1977) demonstrates under what assumptions the availability effect will dominate the supply effect.[28] Hence since a detection lag effect, if it exists, works in the same direction as the availability effect, one would expect unemployment durations to show a countercyclical pattern. This is indeed the case, although the upward trend in unemployment durations has been the dominating pattern lately. The inflow pattern is more neutral with respect to the business cycle. Fig. 8.2 shows unemployment inflow and unemployment durations for men and women in Sweden between 1965 and 1986.

One can also ask how important the detection lag effect is for the cyclical behaviour of the unemployment rate. In other words, is there a detection lag effect or is the dominance of the availability effect over the supply effect the main cause of the cyclical variation in the unemployment rate? The answer to this question has a bearing on the validity of the modern neo-classical schools of inflation and unemployment. Friedman, Phelps, and Mortensen[29] emphasize the role of inflation surprises as a major mechanism behind the short-run Phillips curve, while a Muth–Lucas rational expectation[30] approach, as well as (to some extent), a neo-Keynesian approach, would gain in credibility if the detection lag effect is weak or non-existent. This is because rational expectations presuppose that agents, even the unemployed, know how the economy works and are able to forecast the effects of aggregate demand on the wage

---

[28] Feinberg showed that this is true when the wage offer distribution is normal or uniform. As always in matters like this, there is an elasticity involved. The availability effect will outweigh the supply effect if the elasticity of accepting a wage offer with respect to vacancies be less than one in absolute value. A slightly more general condition is derived by Burdett (1981).

[29] Friedman (1968), Phelps (1967), and Mortensen (1970).

[30] See Muth (1961) and Lucas (1972).

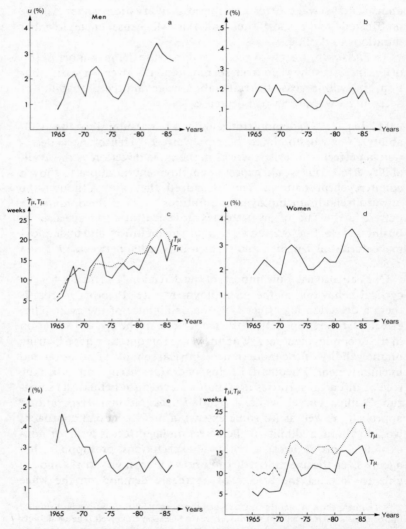

Fig. 8.2. Unemployment rates (u), flow into unemployment each week (f), average uncompleted-spell lengths $(\bar{T}_\mu)$, and average completed-spell lengths (T_μ) for men and women in Sweden 1965–1986

Source: Axelsson *et al.* (1987).

distribution, and to be right on average. The neo-Keynesian interpretation would rely on a transition probability that rises through the relaxation of a job-rationing constraint that is caused by an increasing number of vacancies. (Note also that rational expectations and rationing constraints are not mutually exclusive.)

There is some empirical evidence concerning this matter. Early empirical evidence produced by Barron (1975) and Axelsson and Löfgren (1977) indicates that the supply effects dominate the detection lag effect, while more recent evidence produced by much more elaborate methods—see Björklund and Holmlund (1981)—shows a significant detection lag effect for short-term unemployment in Sweden. The corresponding effect in the USA is insignificant.[31] This is a somewhat puzzling result. As the authors point out, the case for a detection lag would appear to have more support in the US decentralized labour market than in the highly unionized and centralized Swedish labour market. The latter should give rise to relatively uniform, long-term, and well-advertised wage contracts. The authors' attempted explanation relies on the much larger share of temporary lay-offs in the USA than in Sweden.[32] This category is waiting rather than searching, and is also fairly well informed about the wage offer distribution in their particular branch of industry. Hence, the search behaviour of those truly unemployed will be blurred by the behaviour of a category which is either not searching or searching but well informed.

The explanation has some appeal, but there are of course alternative reasons for the observed correlations. As the authors point out, they are really testing a joint hypothesis of the job search model coupled with different hypotheses on how wage expectations are formed. If the joint hypotheses are refuted, it is impossible to determine whether it is the hypothesis of rationality, or the job search model, or perhaps both, which should be rejected.

The rational expectation hypothesis and the job search model are only tested indirectly by the authors through a comparison between the predicted transition probability with and without a detection lag variable; in the latter case it is assumed that inflation is perfectly

[31] Dominance of Swedish studies may be partly explained by the excellent Swedish vacancy statistics. Vacancy statistics for the USA are available only for 1969–73. Björklund and Holmlund (1981) used the Help-Wanted Advertising Index as a proxy.

[32] The lay-off shares are 2–3% in Sweden and 10–20% in the USA, and the major part of lay-offs in the USA are temporary.

foreseen, so a vacancy variable alone takes care of the prediction.[33] Not surprisingly, the two forecasts almost coincide for the USA—a possible interpretation being that US data cannot refute a hypothesis of rational expectations coupled with a neo-Keynesian hypothesis that the transition probability falls or rises with a more or less biting job-rationing constraint.[34]

[33] The specification of the regression equation is

$$\mu_t = \alpha_1 \cdot v_t^a \left(\frac{w_t}{w_t^*} \right)^{\alpha_3}$$

where μ_t is the transition or exit probability. v_t is vacancies and w_t and w_t^* are the true and expected wages, respectively.

[34] It would have been preferable, however, if the detection lag hypothesis had been formulated in terms of a difference between the true real-wage rate and the expected real-wage rate. In search theory, as in the traditional neo-classical labour supply model, it is the real and not the nominal wage-rate that matters.

9

Unemployment Benefits and Unemployment Duration

One of the more challenging problems in labour economics is to determine the extent to which an improved job security, and the unemployment benefit in particular, have contributed to the rise in unemployment. The evidence has been discussed several times,[1] and a new investigation may seem superfluous. However, since this problem corresponds to the core of duration research, and since we feel that there are a few new considerations—both theoretical and empirical—to add, we will reconsider the evidence rather thoroughly.

Let us start by considering what potential effects can be expected from an increased unemployment benefit (UB). The following effects have been analysed: Unemployment can increase through an increased number of quits and lay-offs. The duration of unemployment may increase, since an increase in the UB raises the reservation wage. Finally, 'entitlement effects' may induce some persons to enter the work-force to qualify for future benefits, or to work more hours to raise the benefits to which they are entitled.

The quits and entitlement effects have not been devoted much attention in empirical research. The few studies that exist show that the effects, on the whole, are negligible.[2] No further evidence will be introduced here.[3]

As was indicated above, the effect of UB on duration of unemployment has been assessed in several papers[4] during the last fifteen years, and the following conventional wisdom has been distilled:

---

[1] See Atkinson *et al.* (1984) for a review.

[2] See Danziger *et al.* (1981) for a survey.

[3] There is, however, evidence that lay-off effects may be important in the USA: see Feldstein (1976), Topel (1983).

[4] One reason behind the interest for studies on UB is that improvements of the benefit system in many OECD countries have paralleled the growth of unemployment.

Despite the problems [data and estimation problems] a positive relation between UI and duration of unemployment appears robust.   (Danziger *et al.* (1981, p. 982))

The theory of job search suggests that subsidized benefits of a general insurance system . . . create substitution effects in favour of greater frequency and longer duration periods of unemployment. . . . Indeed, empirical studies do indicate a statistically significant effect of this type.   (Lindbeck (1981, p. 38))

The above quotations should be balanced by the following more humble attitude:

There may be a significant link between benefits and duration, but it does not stand out strongly from the—quite large and extensive—microdata set that we have been using. In order to establish any relationship, we are going to need a combination of richer data, a more fully specified theoretical framework, and the development of the statistical treatment.   (Atkinson *et al.* (1984, p. 25))

If we start with a few additional theoretical considerations, job search models have been used to analyse the labour supply reactions to changes in UB payments when the demand for labour is held constant.[5] The standard result is that the introduction of an UB payment makes the unemployed more selective in evaluating job offers. This implies an increase in the expected duration of unemployment, and if we can neglect the UB effect on quits, (inflow) unemployment should increase. As always, however, empirically meaningful theorems are consequences of the underlying assumptions. Two key assumptions seem crucial for the standard prediction to hold true: (*a*) that UB payments are received by all unemployed workers, independently of their duration of unemployment, and (*b*) that employed workers are not laid off. It is fair to say that most existing unemployment insurance schemes and labour markets do not have these properties.

Burdett (1979) shows that if these assumptions are relaxed, so that UB payments have finite duration and the lay-off probability is positive, significantly different predictions are obtained. For example, an increase in the UB payments will have less adverse incentive effect on those unemployed whose UB payments have

---

[5] Mortensen (1970) is the seminal work in the field, although the problem was touched upon by Stigler (1962).

expired.[6] Loosely speaking, this category cannot gain anything from an increased benefit if the unemployment duration exceeds the duration of the benefit payment. On the other hand, the return from accepting a wage offer increases, due to a positive lay-off probability, combined with the increased benefit payment during a potential future spell of unemployment.

Burdett's scenario also implies that an increase in the UB payment will change the composition of the stock of unemployed towards a larger share of short-term unemployment.

9.1. The Empirical Evidence

The 'heavy' empirical evidence on the impacts of UB on unemployment have mainly been produced in the USA and the UK. One reason for the massive research effort in the USA is that amendments of 1970 and 1976 extended the UB system, while the main factor behind the scientific efforts in the UK is probably the recent historically high unemployment rate combined with the long duration of the UB payments.

Three kinds of analysis have been done. First is the aggregate time-series approach, where one obtains direct estimates of the elasticity of unemployment with respect to benefits. In the UK such studies include Maki and Spindler (1975), Cubbin and Foley (1977), and Taylor (1977). The technique is to regress the (log) male unemployment or unemployment duration on a measure of the ratio of benefits to income (the replacement ratio) for the unemployed population, a measure of aggregate demand and other variables. The US studies are surveyed by Danziger *et al.* (1981), and to some extent by Kiefer (1988).

Second is the cross-section approach, where the coefficients for the independent variables in the hazard function are estimated by the maximization of the likelihood of the sample. The data include either uncompleted or completed spells or both. Independent variables in addition to the replacement ratio[7] include age,

[6] A person is long-run unemployed if the length of the unemployment spell exceeds the duration of the UB.

[7] The replacement ratio—defined as disposable income (excluding housing costs) when unemployed relative to spendable income in work—has been stable in the UK since the 1960s. This means that the UB payments have increased in real terms.

education, other personal characteristics, labour demand indicators, and the length of time unemployed.[8]

Finally, the third category includes general equilibrium models estimated with time-series data. Examples of this category are Minford (1983),[9] Axell and Lang (1986), Albrecht *et al.* (1986), and Lang (1985), the latter three containing major theoretical contributions.

Below, we will concentrate on the cross-section studies, but will begin by saying a little about the results of the two other approaches. A difficult problem in connection with time-series data is that the secular rise in the unemployment rates has come together with a rise in the replacement ratio (the ratio of unemployment benefits to income). This means that introducing any variable with a time trend or a time trend variable will tend to reduce the impact of the replacement rate variable. The theoretical foundation for the specification of the regression equation is weak, so there are no good criteria for choosing between different specifications. Also, as Nickell (1979*b*) has pointed out, only Taylor (1977) uses a benefit variable which reflects the actual benefits paid out. Both Maki and Spindler and Cubbin and Foley impute the benefits of a typical man. However, the Earnings Related Supplement (ERS),[10] which was introduced back in 1966, corresponds solely to 'a tiny bump' in the series of actual benefits paid out, while the bump in Maki and Spindler's data is 40 per cent. Because of this, Nickell suspects that ERS may have been over-imputed by Maki and Spindler, who claim that it has increased male unemployment rates by one-third.

On the whole, the time-series estimates are non-robust. The elasticity estimates of Taylor range between 2 and 0.9 depending on the specification of the model. Cubbin and Foley obtain estimates of the corresponding elasticity ranging between 0.8 and zero, while Maki and Spindler's estimate is 0.7, and their estimate of the effect of

[8] Studies of this kind include MacKay and Reid (1972), Lancaster (1979), Nickell (1979*b*), Atkinson *et al.* (1984), Narendranathan *et al.* (1985).

[9] The Maki and Spindler paper also contains a simultaneous system, where the unemployment rate and the replacement ratio are the endogenous variables. Minford's model is, however, slightly more 'elaborated', and in particular built on a kind of macro-economic foundation.

[10] For further information about the British unemployment benefits, see Layard (1986).

ERS[11] imputes one-third of the increase in the unemployment rate to its introduction.[12]

The Minford 'general-equilibrium'[13] approach to the problem of how unemployment benefits affect unemployment and unemployment durations is sound, since it catches not only the impact effect but also the indirect or induced effects. Minford finds that there is a significant and powerful total elasticity of real benefits on unemployment (operating through higher real wages) of nearly 3. To use his own words, 'This is substantially higher than other post war estimates as far as these are comparable.'

Minford's model of the labour market is based on the dynamic theory of the firm outlined by Sargent (1979). The economy is divided into a unionized and a competitive sector. Non-market clearing wages and excess supply in the unionized sector spill over to the competitive sector. Since the competitive real wage clears the labour market, there is no involuntary unemployment in the model.

A real-wage equation representing the supply side of the economy is derived by aggregating over sectors,[14] and substituting for the parameters determining the competitive real wage. The exogenous parameters are union density, working population, the average income tax rate, average real benefits, and lagged real wages. The unemployment rate is an endogenous variable in the equation. The demand side is represented by an unemployment equation, with real output, lagged unemployment, and the employers' contribution to National Income as exogenous parameters. The unemployment equation contains the competitive real wage as an endogenous variable.

The immediate reaction to the specification of the model is that many endogenous and exogenous variables are missing, and that there are some serious problems in measuring the degree of

[11] Similar elasticity estimates for Canada and the USA yield similar results. See Grubel *et al.* (1975), and Grubel and Maki (1974).

[12] This estimate is obtained through a shift dummy which takes on the value starting in 1966 when ERS was introduced. Estimates of the elasticity of unemployment with respect to benefits within a similar framework on data for the USA and Canada show similar results. See Grubel *et al.* (1975) and Grubel and Maki (1974).

[13] The model contains only two equations, one for the real wage-rate and one for the unemployment rate.

[14] Minford's paper also contains extensive disaggregated general-equilibrium studies.

unionization. The main reason for taking the model seriously is that it seems to work according to traditional econometric criteria.

Like other models estimated with time-series data, this model is sensitive to both specification and new data. Henry *et al.* (1985) have tested the robustness of the model by using revised data for unionization, by exploring the role of certain restrictions in the estimated equations, and by extending the data set from the second quarter of 1979 up to the end of 1982. Without going into details, it is nevertheless safe to say that much of the empirical support for Minford's model disappears. Certain theoretically important relations between variables no longer hold, and the impact of UB on unemployment turns out to be sensitive to the specification of the model, but not extremely so, which is stressed in Minford's (1985) answer to the criticism. On the other hand, since the degree of unionization and real benefits are the only trended variables one should not, as has been pointed out by Nickell (1984), be surprised if they pick up the upward trend in the unemployment rate.

The two Swedish time-series studies on the effect of unemployment benefits on duration we know of are Ståhl (1978) and Björklund (1978). Using a logit model Björklund regresses survival rates (1 − exit rate) on the vacancy unemployment ratio, a time trend, and a dummy variable taking care of the extension of the unemployment benefit system in Sweden in 1974. He allows for the 'benefit effect' to vary with both the age of the unemployed and the duration of unemployment. He does not obtain any systematic effect on durations of the extended unemployment system. The only exception is found in the oldest age class, 55–66 years, where the results are entirely consistent with the theoretical results in Burdett (1979). In a later Swedish cross-section study of youth unemployment, Holmlund (1986) obtains a negative and significant unemployment insurance dummy coefficient.

A straightforward method of estimating the impact of UB on the duration of unemployment from cross-section data would be to regress duration on UB and variables picking up other personal characteristics of the unemployed, and to estimate the equation by ordinary least squares. This was done by MacKay and Reid (1972). They found that the unemployment benefit had a weak disincentive effect.[15]

---

[15] An increase in unemployment benefit of £1 per week would increase the length of unemployment by almost half a week.

There is, however, a severe statistical problem involved in this approach. The authors themselves comment on the low value of the coefficient of determination, R^2. As Lancaster (1976) points out, if each duration is an observation on an exponential variate with mean $1/\lambda$, then a low value of R^2 is an inherent property of the model. According to the discussion in connection with equation (13a), the variance of the exponential distribution is equal to the square of the mean $1/\lambda^2$, which means that the specification of the regression model implies that the error variance is at least equal to the square of the mean of the regression function. In other words, in contrast to the standard regression model there is no independent error variance parameter.[16] Lancaster shows that if durations are generated by an exponential process, then the coefficient of variation will be bounded from above by one half. Also, all the standard errors of an OLS regression will be inconsistent estimates. Moreover, even if you know the value of all independent variables that determine the probability of an individual obtaining a job in any period, you would still be unable to predict his unemployment duration.

These problems have induced Lancaster and others[17] to estimate the parameters of a hazard function by Maximum Likelihood Estimation. The particular functional form used varies, but the proportional Weibull hazard function[18]

$$\lambda(t) = \alpha t^{\alpha - 1} e^{x\beta} \cdot \nu \tag{21}$$

is without doubt the most frequently used specification.

The vector x contains variables like individual characteristics, labour market conditions, and the replacement ratio, while t denotes the duration of the experienced unemployment. Hence, the parameter α picks up the effect of possible duration dependence. Finally, ν is a stochastic error component which is there to pick up heterogeneity resulting from omitted variables.[19]

As was pointed out in section 7.2, search theory is not very helpful in guiding the specification of the hazard function. The Swedish

[16] For a discussion of how to solve this problem see Brännäs (1986). The idea is essentially to use log duration as the dependent variable.

[17] The main references are Lancaster (1979), Nickell (1979a, 1979b), Heckman and Borjas (1980), Atkinson et al. (1984), and Narendranathan et al. (1985).

[18] Another possibility is to use the Gompertz distribution with hazard function $\lambda(t) = \exp(\beta x + \alpha t)$. Both functions belong to the same 'family' of hazards, $\lambda(t) = \exp(\beta x + z(t))$. $z(t) = \alpha \ln t$ generates the Weibull hazard, while $z(t) = \alpha t$ produces the Gompertz hazard function.

[19] The nature of this problem will be further discussed in the next chapter.

engineer Weibull found the distribution implicit in (21) convenient to describe experimentally observed variations in the fatigue resistance of steel, its elastic limits, the dimensions of particles of soot, etc.[20] Later it was used to study the variations in the length of service of radio electronic equipment. Recently it has been found convenient to use as a hazard function in unemployment duration models. Apart from its convenience, there are also tests designed to determine whether the Weibull distribution fits the data. These tests, although fairly simple, have not been very frequently applied.[21]

The spell data used are of two kinds (or mixes of the two): completed and uncompleted unemployment spells. The latter is naturally the most common type of available cross-section data. Using the derivation in the Appendix, the likelihood of a sample of uncompleted spells can be written

$$L_u = \prod_{i=1}^{N} g(\widetilde{T}_i) \tag{22}$$

where

$$g(\widetilde{T}\cdot) = \frac{1 - F(\widetilde{T}_i)}{E(T_i)} \tag{23}$$

is the probability density function for the distribution of uncompleted unemployment spells and N is the number of observations. The likelihood of the completed unemployment spell sample is (using equation (4))

$$L_c = \prod_{i=1}^{N} f(T_i) = \prod_{i=1}^{N} \{h(T_i)[1 - F(T_i)]\} \tag{24}$$

where

$$1 - F(T_i) = \exp\left\{ -E\left[\int_{0}^{T_i} h(t)dt \right] \right\}. \tag{25}$$

---

[20] See Weibull (1951). The Weibull distribution was known earlier in probability theory as the limiting distribution (as $n \to \infty$) of the smallest of n independent random variables with the same distribution.

[21] One exception is Brännäs (1986). For details about the test the reader is referred to Kalbfleisch and Prentice (1980).

The expectation operator in (25) is there to indicate that the hetero-geneity component v has to be integrated away. See also the Appendix for a more detailed specification of the completed-spell model.

The results with respect to the unemployment benefit effect from the most important UK studies are summed up in Table 9.1 below.

The study by MacKay and Reid has already been commented upon. There is another study using a similar estimation technique on US data executed by Ehrenberg and Oaxaca[22] (1976). They estimate the reduced-form equation for the unemployment duration as well as the post-unemployment wage as functions of, among other things, the replacement ratio. Their findings that an increase in this ratio from 0.4 to 0.5 (i.e. by 25 per cent) would increase the expected duration of unemployment by 1.5 weeks (say 10 per cent) and raise the post-unemployment wage by 7 per cent (search is productive) may appear to deserve criticism similar to that applied to MacKay and Reid. However, Ehrenberg and Oaxaca regress the natural logarithm of completed unemployment spells on the independent variables. If the underlying duration distribution is Weibull, it can be shown that the stochastic component in the Ehrenberg and Oaxaca equation is distributed as log-generalized[23] F, and hence that OLS yields unbiased estimates of the coefficients.[24]

The fact that search as such can be productive is interesting, since it indicates a trade-off problem. Any discussion of the appropriate level of the unemployment benefit must consider whether the cost to society from the increased durations of spells of unemployment when benefits are raised is more than offset by the increase in expected post-unemployment wages.[25] For a comprehensive and recent discussion on the economics of unemployment insurance, the reader is referred to Björklund and Holmlund (1986).

The study by Lancaster listed in Table 9.1 is a mainly theoretical investigation of the econometric problems arising when search theories are confronted by empirical data. In particular, he draws

[22] This study is not commented upon in the review by Danziger *et al.* (1981), although it is in their reference list.

[23] For more details see Brännäs (1986).

[24] However, their statistical inference is incorrect.

[25] Ehrenberg and Oaxaca use data from the National Longitudinal Survey, which was conducted by the US Bureau of the Census for the Manpower Administration. The data used in this particular study comes from the period 1966–9.

TABLE 9.1. *The effect on unemployment duration of unemployment benefits: results from some major cross-section studies*

Study	Population analysed	Data used	Dependent variable	Program variables	Specification	Results
MacKay and Reid (1972)	Redundancy unemployed in 23 plants in the UK metal manufacturing, engineering, and electrical goods industry	Male employees redundant during unemployment 1966–8	Duration of unemployment	Unemployment benefit and redundancy pay (£s)	Ordinary least squares $\epsilon \sim N(0, \sigma^2)$	Unemployment benefit significant, redundancy pay insignificant. A £1 increase in UB increases the duration of unemployment by half a week
Lancaster (1979)	A sample of 479 British unskilled unemployed	Interviews with unemployed performed for political and economic planning (1973)	Hazard function approach (completed and uncompleted spells)	Replacement ratio	Maximum likelihood	Elasticity of duration with respect to the replacement ratio = 0.6
Nickell (1979b)	Unemployed males in UK	Interviews in the General Household Survey of 1972	Hazard function approach (uncompleted spells)	Replacement[a] ratio defined in four different ways	Maximum likelihood	Elasticity of duration with respect to the replacement ratio in range 0.61–1.82
Atkinson et al. (1984)	Job-seeking and unemployed males 16–64	Family Expenditure Survey 1972–7	Hazard function approach (uncompleted spells)	Replacement[a] ratio and log (replacement ratio) average and marginal	Maximum likelihood	Elasticity of duration with respect to the replacement ratio in range 0–0.6
Narendranathan et al. (1985)	Unemployed males 16–64	DHSS cohort study of the unemployed in 1978	Hazard function approach (completed-spell data specified with and without stochastic components)	Log income (while unemployed)	Maximum likelihood	Elasticity of duration with respect to unemployment income varies with age. On the 'average' it is 0.28–0.36 Teenage men = 0.65 > 45 = 0.08 No effect on long-term unemployed

The numerator is the replacement variable...

attention to the importance of making appropriate allowance for regression error.[26] He is also the first to suggest and empirically use the Weibull hazard function. The empirical material employed to illustrate his models are interviews with a sample of 479 British unskilled, unemployed people. The denominator of the replacement ratio is critical in studies like this. Lancaster uses the actual income before the spell of unemployment. This can be criticized—as Nickell (1979a) points out—since there may be a spurious correlation between this and unemployment duration arising from the negative correlation of both of these with omitted quality variables. Lancaster's estimate of the elasticity under consideration seems, however, fairly reasonable in comparison with the other estimates presented in the table.

Nickell (1979b) uses a logit specification of the probability of leaving unemployment (the hazard)

$$h(s) = [1 + e^{-z(s)}]^{-1} \tag{26}$$

and he experiments with a number of different specifications of $z(s)$. In particular, he tests the hypothesis that follows from the theoretical work by Burdett (1979), that an unemployment benefit variable has a smaller impact for the long-term unemployed. Moreover, he investigates whether the income variables, the unemployment benefit, and the potential family income variable can be entered in the regression equation as a replacement ratio. He does not correct for the effect from omitted variables by allowing for a stochastic component in the hazard function.

Apart from the range of the replacement elasticity reported in Table 9.1, Nickell's results do not reject the hypothesis that the duration impact of the unemployment benefits decreases with the duration of unemployment. Moreover, he is not able to reject the hypothesis that benefits and potential income effects on duration enter solely via the ratio between these variables. Finally, in contrast to Maki and Spindler's results, he finds that the ERS has had a rather modest effect on unemployment—10 per cent as compared to 33 per cent, according to Maki and Spindler (1975).

The main criticism that can be made against Nickell's results is

---

[26] Since the statistical problems are more severe in connection with the analysis of duration dependence, we will save the discussion of these to the next chapter.

that omitted variables may bias the estimates.[27] However, simulations in Lancaster (1979) show that a sample[28] of 400–500 observations may be too small to estimate both the duration dependence parameter (α) and the variance of the stochastic error component (σ^2). Another limitation of Nickell's analysis is that his data source forced him to calculate benefits by applying the rules for a 'standard case'. This, in combination with the availability of a better data source, inspired Atkinson *et al.* (1984) to redo the analyses of Lancaster (1979) and Nickell (1976*b*). Atkinson *et al.* use data from what is called the Family Expenditure Survey (FES). These data are drawn from surveys conducted over the period 1972–7. The number of observations is twice as high as in Lancaster's and Nickell's studies. In addition, the information on spell length is more precise than in most previous studies, as is the information on benefits, although Atkinson *et al.* (like most other researchers of unemployment benefits) had to calculate the relevant variable for all weeks that the person has been unemployed.

The hazard function in Atkinson *et al.*'s paper includes duration dependence, but also a dependence on calendar time. The latter variable is included to allow for changes in the macro-economic situation over the period under consideration. The state of the labour market is measured by the ratio of unemployment to vacancies, which varies over time and over regions. Omitted variables are not allowed for, which may bias the replacement coefficient.

A standard run, where the replacement variable is introduced in average after tax form,[29] yields the 'conventional-wisdom' estimate of the replacement elasticity, i.e. 0.6. But as Atkinson *et al.* point out, the precision of the replacement coefficient is as weak as those in the standard-case runs of other researchers. They also point out

---

[27] Simulations in Lancaster and Nickell (1980) show that this does not seem to be a serious problem in this context, since the replacement coefficient has the same magnitude with and without allowance for omitted variables.

[28] Nickell's sample consists of 426 observations.

[29] $R_A = \dfrac{b + y}{(1 - u)(w + y) + uv}$ where b = benefit, y = other family income, u = the marginal tax-rate, w = earnings as employed, and v = the exemption level. This is to be contrasted with the marginal after-tax replacement ratio $R_C = \dfrac{b}{(1 - u)w}$.

that extra sample information supports the view that people are not simply getting the benefits hypothesized with the standard assumption. When the standard-benefit variable is replaced by extraneous information in the FES, the replacement coefficient drops to zero. There are a variety of possible interpretations of this result (spurious correlations, etc.), but AGMR are cautious and conclude that the replacement coefficient was poorly determined in the first place.[30]

Narendranathan *et al.* use yet another data set, the DHSS cohort study of the unemployed. This is a sample of 2,300 unemployed men taken in 1978, and hence contains by far the largest number of observations among the studies listed in Table 9.1. The data on benefits[31] are rich and this, in combination with the large sample, enable the authors to allow for variation in the benefit effect with respect to both age and duration.

The study shows that there are considerable differences in both respects. The impact of the benefit for teenagers is considerably greater than that for prime-aged men, and the effect on older men is zero (benefit elasticities range from 0.65 to 0.08). The not too rigorous intuition behind this pattern is that teenage searchers face wage distributions with lower variances than more established job-searchers. If the wage distribution is concentrated in the low-variance sense, an increase in the reservation wage will exclude many potential jobs. Moreover, the impact of the unemployment benefit very clearly diminishes with duration of unemployment. The search theoretical explanation for this should be clear from Burdett (1979). Nickell (1979*b*) suggests an alternative hypothesis, which might be more appropriate in a British context, since unemployment benefits have a very long duration in the UK. A low rate of job offers and the unpleasantness of long-term unemployment might imply low reservation wages, and search rules that imply accepting almost any job offer, independently of the benefit level.

Narendranathan *et al.* also modify the specification of the hazard

---

[30] An imprecisely estimated and non-robust replacement coefficient also results from the introduction of a marginal replacement ratio, i.e. $R_C = \dfrac{b}{(1 - u)w}$.
Note, however, that there is no clear theoretical justification for benefits to enter in the form of a replacement ratio.

[31] Narendranathan *et al.* chose to use the log income (while unemployed) instead of the replacement ratio.

in different directions. They allow for declining wage offer distributions—the possibility that the long-term unemployed may search in lower segments of the labour market than the short-term unemployed. They also allow for heterogeneity by a stochastic hazard function. The latter modification does not change the impact of the benefit coefficient—the elasticity of expected duration with respect to income while unemployed is 0.5[32]—and the coefficient is very precisely estimated[33] because of the large number of observations. The problem is instead that the size of the time dependence coefficient becomes 'absurdly' high ($\alpha = 2.09$).

On the whole, however, Narendranathan *et al.*'s results show a very robust benefit coefficient, resulting in a benefit elasticity in the interval 0.3–0.5, which is close to the cross-section conventional wisdom from Lancaster (1979) and Nickell (1979*b*). Moreover, their data set is one of the first to contain precise information on actual benefit receipts, and their results are therefore more credible than those generated by e.g. Atkinson *et al.*'s consisting of estimated individual benefit receipts.

Most of the empirical evidence reported so far has concerned European conditions. Recent evidence from the USA[34] indicates that there are clearly measurable negative incentive effects. One main finding in Blau and Robins (1986*b*) is that UB payments in particular seem to have a significant effect on unemployment durations. In addition, they show how this effect can be decomposed into a decreased job-offer arrival rate effect and a reservation rate effect. It is unclear, however, from the analysis whether the declining job-offer arrival-rate over time reflects diminishing marginal productivity of job search, or whether it indicates that employers use the length of an unemployment spell as an indication of potential productivity. The introduction of a time trend in the equation makes the influence of the UB variable statistically insignificant.

[32] This is only 'marginally larger' than 0.36, which is obtained in the standard model.

[33] Its asymptotic *t* value is -11.4.

[34] See Blau and Robins (1986*a*, 1986*b*). The data used in both papers are drawn from the Employment Opportunity Pilot Project's (EOPP) household survey, which collected data from predominantly low- and middle-income families in 20 dispersed areas in the USA in Apr.–Oct. 1980. Another recent US study is Meyer (1988), who also finds a relatively pronounced negative incentive effect from the UB payment.

As the authors point out, a negative impact of UB payments on resource investment in search is counter-intuitive, since UB programs frequently impose job search restrictions. To accept a negative impact of the UB program on wage offers they have to claim, likely Keeley and Robins (1985), that the search requirements are not effectively enforced. Combined with the fact that they obtain a significant negative duration dependence, which is inconsistent with standard search theory with constant job-offer arrival rates, the evidence for the negative impact of UB payments on job-offer arrival rates is not completely convincing. It should, however, be mentioned that no attempt to control for heterogeneity seems to have been made, so time dependence may well be spurious. Moreover, reservation wages may be allowed to decrease over time, provided that the job-offer arrival rates decrease over time.

It should be emphasized that a precisely determined positive impact of employment benefits on unemployment durations does not tell us the magnitude nor the sign of the corresponding general-equilibrium effect. From a neo-classical labour supply viewpoint it can be argued that an increased reservation wage, caused by an extended unemployment benefit system, shifts the labour supply curve inwards,[35] and—at a constant real wage—any involuntary unemployment would go down, while employment would stay constant. In a labour market in equilibrium the inward shift of the supply curve—assuming flexible prices—presses up the real wage-rate, which will counteract the initial-impact effect on supply.

On the other hand, a labour supply curve is an alien object in a search theoretical setting, the most of the search theoretical discussion above has been partial-partial or at best partial. There are, however, general-equilibrium search models, and one of them is designed to deal with the impact of the unemployment benefit on search unemployment, namely the one presented in papers by Axell and Lang (1986) and Albrecht *et al.* (1986).[36] Within this model one obtains the seemingly counter-intuitive result that the general equilibrium effect of an increase in the unemployment benefit is to shorten expected unemployment durations (the expected duration of search). The intuition behind this result is not entirely unrelated to the loose discussion of the partial-equilibrium effect of the

---

[35] Fewer people would be willing to work at the going wage-rate.

[36] See also Mavromaras (1987).

decrease in labour supply alluded to above. The following quotation from Axell and Lang (1986) indicates the mechanism.

In equilibrium individuals with high UI-benefits will have high reservation wages, while those with low UI-benefits will have low reservation wages. Firms can exploit this condition. The choice is to set a low wage and attract only low-reservation-wage individuals or set a high wage and attract all searchers. The two strategies yield different firm sizes, resulting in an identical total profit for the large and small firms. If now UI-benefits are increased for those who have low benefits these persons will increase their reservation wages. For this reason, the low-wage firms must increase their wage offers. Then the profit of the low-wage strategy will decrease. The most productive of the low-wage firms will then change to the high-wage strategy, and the least productive will go out of business. The net effect is that the relative frequency of high-wage firms will increase. But the high-wage firms are exactly what the search-unemployed are searching for. With a larger frequency of these firms, it will on average take fewer search steps to find a high-wage firm. Therefore, the duration of unemployment decreases.

The Axell–Lang model has a simple structure in relation to neo-classical general-equilibrium models, and the result is of course conditional on this. The empirical realism of the mechanisms involved can also be doubted. On the other hand, increased reservation wages would, in very general settings, induce firms to increase their wage offers. Since the duration of unemployment at a given wage offer (equal to a reservation wage) is as sensitive to an increased reservation wage as to an increased wage offer, the increased reservation wages have to be large in relation to the induced increase in wage offers in order for the cross-section time-series partial-equilibrium effects to be important. Theoretical considerations in Lang (1985) indicate the opposite to be the case.

The policy conclusions that follow from this survey on the impacts of unemployment benefits on duration are the following. The benefits can certainly not provide a major explanation for the secular rise in unemployment rates. This is so even if their partial and general equilibrium effects on unemployment are positive, simply because the replacement ratios in major OECD countries have remained constant over time.[37] A necessary qualification is that

[37] This does not hold true for Sweden, however: see Björklund and Holmlund (1986).

the real value of the unemployment benefit has increased over time, and if this real value, as such, matters (not its real value relative to the real value of income) then the conclusions have to be modified.

Moreover, even if the replacement elasticity is positive (and equal to 0.6), there are reasons to believe that the general-equilibrium effect is smaller than the partial-equilibrium effect, not to say that indirect effects neutralize the direct impact effect. Finally, since search might be productive there is an unresolved optimization problem concerning the correct design of the unemployment insurance system.

10

Falling Reservation Wages and/or Scars from Unemployment

In this chapter we will introduce empirical evidence on a question which has already been touched upon in Chapter 8: whether the conditional probability of leaving unemployment stays constant (increases) or falls with the duration of the unemployment. In a sense, the answer to this question is a test of whether and/or to what extent unemployment is an equilibrium phenomenon. Search theory tells us that reservation wages should fall or stay constant over time, implying that the exit probability rises or stays constant over time. Hence an exit probability that falls with duration would indicate that there are other factors, such as job rationing, or long-term unemployment leading to a depreciation of skills, which induce the development of attitudes less likely to be consistent with finding employment.[1]

Heckman and Borjas (1980) distinguish between four types of state dependence. The first type is called Markovian state dependence, where, during a short interval of time, the probability that an employed worker will become unemployed differs from the probability that an unemployed worker remains unemployed. A second type is occurrence dependence: the number of previous spells of unemployment affects the probability that a worker will become or remain unemployed. The third type is the one under consideration in this chapter, duration dependence. The probability of remaining unemployed depends on the duration of the unemployment spell in progress. The fourth type is lagged duration dependence, when the re-employment probability depends on the length of previous unemployment spells. As Heckman and Borjas (1980) conclude, the test for duration dependence is the most demanding, since it requires strong prior information that is not usually at the disposal of the researcher.

The information required is detailed information on the personal

---

[1] Negative duration dependence can in job turnover models be associated with matching models: see Jovanovic (1979).

characteristics of the unemployed that enables the test to distinguish a normal sorting process from true duration dependence. Here is an obvious source of so-called omitted-variables bias, from unobserved differences in characteristics such as 'motivation'. Obviously, people with low motivation to work will make up a larger share of the long-term unemployed, and if motivation is not controlled for it will show up as a spurious decline in the exit probability, and the coefficient α in the Weibull hazard function will be biased towards zero. There is, however, a second technical problem, which implies that even if the omitted variables are uncorrelated to those that are included in the x vector in equation (24), the β coefficient may still be biased towards zero.[2]

A natural way to deal with the former problem is to assume that the unobserved variable ν has a certain distribution across the inflow into unemployment, which is independent of the other variables in the hazard function. This has in fact been done, and this procedure was referred to in Chapter 9 as controlling for heterogeneity.[3] The estimation of the hazard model will then include the estimation not only of the coefficients β and α but also of the coefficients characterizing the distribution of the unobserved variable. A standard assumption is that the heterogeneity component in equation (21) is gamma-distributed[4] with mean 1 and variance σ^2. The easiest way to control for heterogeneity is to assume that the variable takes on the value ν_1 with probability p and the value ν_2 with probability $1 - p$.

In Table 10.1 we have listed the results from recent studies that allow for duration dependence in a consistent manner. Most studies which include 'many' regressors in addition to time and control for heterogenity conclude that either there is no time dependence or there is a positive time dependence.

There are three exceptions concerning time dependence: Nickell (1979a), Engström and Löfgren (1987), and Trivedi and Hui (1987). The manner in which Nickell controls for duration dependence—though a two-point distribution—is rather primitive. The Trivedi and Hui study uses aggregated gross-flow data on long-term unemployed in Australia (spells lasting more than twenty-six

---

[2] See Lancaster and Nickell (1980) and Lancaster (1985). Obviously, if the omitted variables are correlated to variables in the x-vector, biases of the usual kind would result.

[3] For more details, see appendix.

[4] A sum of exponentially distributed variables is gamma distributed.

TABLE 10.1. *Results on duration dependence of the conditional re-employment probability*

Study	Data	Estimation technique	Hazard	Other regressors	Control	Results
Nickell (1979*a*)	See Table 8.2	Maximum Likelihood	Logit	Many	Discrete two-point distribution	Negative time dependence, which decreases when controlling for heterogeneity.
Lancaster (1979)	See Table 8.2	Maximum Likelihood	Weibull	Few	ν, gamma-distributed	Negative time dependence with uncontrolled heterogeneity. No time dependence when heterogeneity is controlled for.
Heckman and Borjas (1980)	NLS[a] 1969–71 122 observations	Regression techniques Dept. variable log dur.	—	'Many'	Yes	No lagged duration dependence, no occurrence dependence, and a positive duration dependence. Low precision of estimates.
Kooreman and Ridder (1983)	Aggregate data from the Netherlands	Maximum Likelihood	Weibull	Few	ν, gamma-distributed	No male duration dependence, when heterogeneity is controlled for. Weak duration dependence for females.

Study	Data	Method	Distribution	Regressors	Heterogeneity	Comments
Atkinson et al. (1985)	See Table 8.2	Maximum Likelihood	Weibull	'Many'	No	Negative duration dependence in all runs.
Narendranathan et al. (1985)	See Table 8.2	Maximum Likelihood	Weibull	Many	v, gamma-distributed	No duration dependence with uncontrolled heterogeneity, but very strong positive duration dependence when heterogeneity is controlled for ($\alpha = 2.09$).
Engström and Löfgren (1987)	Laid-off workers and a control group	Maximum Likelihood	Weibull	Many	v, gamma-distributed	Negative duration dependence. The heterogeneity parameter is strongly significant, but has a magnitude that is inconsistent with the model.
Trivedi and Hui (1987)	Aggregate gross-flow data on long-term unemployed in Australia	Least Squares (the log of the transition probability is regressed on standard regressors)	A log-linear approximation of Weibull	Many	Heterogeneity is caught by an additive random component	Negative duration dependence, which is relatively robust over different monthly samples.

a. National Longitudinal Surveys of Young Men.

weeks). Models are estimated using monthly transition probabilities for March–April 1984. The control for heterogeneity is done by estimating the mean of the heterogeneity component as a function of the means of observable personal characteristics. The second-order and higher moments of the heterogeneity distribution is merged into the residuals, which is likely to produce heteroscedasticity. The reported standard errors and t ratios are, however, corrected by a consistent method. On the whole, the methodology suggested by Trivedi and Hui is innovative and deserves applications to broader samples.

The study by Atkinson *et al.* produces a negative duration dependence in all runs, but the authors do not bother much about potential biases in the α parameter, since they are primarily interested in the replacement ratio parameter. The low replacement rate coefficients may, however, also be a result of not controlling for omitted variables.

The Heckman and Borjas study, which employs a data material on workers' event histories, tests for three different kinds of structural state dependency: lagged duration dependence, occurrence dependence, and duration dependence. They find no evidence for the first two, only a positive duration dependence. The number of observations is, however, few relative to those in other studies. This results is a low precision of the estimates. As Lancaster (1979) points out, a good precision of the estimates—in particular when there are extra parameters like α, and the variance of the heterogeneity variable in the equation—seems to require a relatively large number of observations.

The Kooreman and Ridder study differs from the others in that the model is estimated on aggregate data (for the Netherlands). It also uses few variables in addition of duration (age, sex, and the unemployment rate), and on these grounds it is noteworthy that the model fails to produce a convincing negative duration dependence, when omitted variables are controlled for. Kooreman and Ridder find that the re-employment probability of males shows heterogeneity ($\sigma^2 \neq 0$) but no duration dependence ($\alpha \approx 1$). The opposite is true for females: no heterogeneity but duration dependence.

The study by Narendranathan *et al.* (1985), which uses the richest set of explanatory variables finds no duration dependence when omitted variables are controlled for, while heterogeneity and strong positive duration dependence show up in the more complete model.

This is embarrassing, since it means that 'after one year out of work the individual has a conditional probability of leaving unemployment which is more than 25 times as great as it was after he had been unemployed for a fortnight!'

In sum, there are some indications that the Weibull hazard function—although simple to use, since the specification of the expected hazard can easily be obtained by integrating out a gamma-distributed stochastic component—may not be the most suitable specification of the model.

Nevertheless, it is fair to say that empirical evidence on duration dependence—the Engström–Löfgren study will be dealt with below—does not convincingly refute the search theoretical test implication that the reservation wage falls or stays constant as a function of the duration of unemployment.

10.1. Unemployment and Duration Dependence in Sweden: The Engström–Löfgren and the Engström–Löfgren–Westerlund Studies

In this section we will report estimates of hazard functions from two subsamples of the same population of unemployed men searching for a job at the unemployment offices in the northern parts of Sweden. We will concentrate on a study of a subsample of openly unemployed men (the study by Engström *et al.* (1987)), which will be contrasted with estimates on a larger and more heterogenous subsample of disguised and openly unemployed (the study by Engström and Löfgren (1987).[5]

There are three reasons for devoting some extra time to these studies. In the first place, data were collected from the parts of the Sweden where the unemployment problems have been severe for a very long time. A priori one would guess that this improves the possibility of detecting 'involuntary unemployment' in terms of duration dependence. Second, the methodology used serves to illustrate the main technique that has so far been employed to estimate hazard functions. Third, a comparison between the results in the two studies indicates that the Weibull specification of the hazard function with a gamma-distributed random component to

---

[5] For a similar Swedish study, see Edin (1987*a*).

handle omitted variables may be unsuitable to deal with duration dependence in heterogeneous censored data.

10.1.1. Data and Model Specification

A decreasing production of steel in Europe in the late 1970s, in combination with an increased supply of iron ore from new open-cast mines, primarily in Brazil, created severe profitability problems for the dominant Swedish mining company L K A B, which has its main plants located in the most northern parts of Sweden. In 1982 it was decided that 1,800 out of 5,200 employees would be laid off, beginning in January 1983. The Government was, however, able to postpone the lay-offs until the first of July 1983.

The northern mining region (*Malmfälten*) is a region with a high employment rate, at least by Swedish standards. In 1982 (a fairly good year) the average rate of unemployment was 7 per cent (the corresponding average for Sweden was 3.1 per cent), and if disguised unemployment in terms of people in relief work or labour market programmes are added, the 'unemployment rate' rises to 13–15 per cent. The situation in 1983 was considered so severe that the government had a bill passed with policy measures that contained a special labour market programme for the laid-off miners. The data set collected by Engström *et al.* (1987) is part of an evaluation of the impact of this special labour market programme. Three inquires were sent to two groups of unemployed at three different times. One group consisted of the 1,800 employees (mainly males) who were laid off by the mining company. The other group, the control group, consisted of 1,400 males who were recorded as unemployed at the unemployment offices in northern Sweden during the months August, September, or October in 1983.[6]

One of the questions in the final inquiry—used in Engström *et al.*'s—concerned the exact length of the most recent spell of unemployment. The answers can be classified into three different categories, which are shown in Fig. 10.1.

Individual 1 had been searching for a job during T_1 weeks when he found a job. His unemployment duration S_1 therefore equals T_1 weeks. Individual 2 had been searching for a job during T_2 weeks

---

[6] The same period during which the majority of the L K A B employees were laid off.

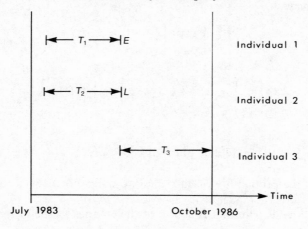

E=employed

L=left the labour force, had relief work, or took
part in labour market training

T=length of a spell of unemployment

Fig. 10.1. Estimates of bounds for the length of unemployment spells by
Engström *et al.* (1987)

when he gave up and left the labour market, received relief work, or
took part in labour market training. Hence, for individual 2 we
know that the time he had to search to find work is greater than or
equal to T_2 $(S_2 \geqslant T_2)$. Individual 3 was unemployed when he
received the last inquiry in October 1986. Hence, like individual 2 he
experienced an unemployment spell longer than T_3 $(S_3 \geqslant T_3)$.

To sum up, this means that the likelihood of the sample can be
written[7]

$$L = \mu^N \prod_{k=1}^{N} [P(S_k = T_k)]^{y_k} \cdot [P(S_k \geqslant T_k)]^{(1-y_k)}$$

$$= \mu^N \prod_{k=1}^{N} [F(T_k) - F(T_k - 1)]^{y_k} \cdot [1 - F(T_k)]^{(1-y_k)} =$$

[7] For a formal derivation the reader is referred to the Appendix. $F(T_k) - F(T_{k-1})$
is a numerically convenient approximation of $f(T_k)$.

$$\mu^N \prod_{k=1}^{N} \left\{ \exp \left[- \int_0^{T_{k-1}} h_k(s)ds \right] \right.$$

$$\left. - \exp \left[- \int_0^{T_k} h_k(s)ds \right] \right\}^{y_k} \left\{ \exp \left[- \int_0^{T_k} h_k(s)ds \right] \right\}^{(1-y_k)} \quad (27)$$

Where

y_k = $\{^1_0$ if the individual did find a job
otherwise

μds = the probability of entering into unemployment in the open interval $(s, s + ds)$

$F(\cdot)$ = the distribution function of the completed-spell length

Considering this likelihood function, it seems suitable to make a short comment on the appropriate form of the function used when estimating the re-employment probability. Some studies (e.g. Barron and Mellow (1981) and Heikensten (1984), have used a so-called logit or probit function to estimate the re-employment probability.

A logit or probit function is very similar to equation (27) above. The difference is the way the distribution function $F(\cdot)$ is modelled. To be similar is, however, not enough. Consequently, results from studies using probit or logit functions do not give estimates of the parameters in a hazard function. Even if time is included as one of the exogenous variables, nothing can be said about the possible duration dependence of an (always implicit) hazard function.

Clearly, given the assumptions related to the introduction of equation (27), the likelihood function can be divided by μ^N without any change in the fundamental optimization problem. This is, however, also true if inflow intensities differ between individuals, $\mu(x_i)$, as long as the μ:s do not depend on the same parameters as the probabilities of the unemployment histories of the individuals. The reason is that $M = \prod_{k=1}^{N} \mu_k$ factors out, and a division by M^{-1} does not change the optimization problem, only the value of maximum likelihood of the sample.

Like Kooreman and Ridder (1983), we have estimated four technically different specifications of the hazard function.

$$\text{Case 1: } h(s) = \exp(x\beta) \quad (28a)$$

This is the standard case. If the reservation wage is constant and the arrival rate of a job offer is time-independent, then the hazard is a function only of individual and labour market characteristics.

$$\text{Case 2: } h(s) = \alpha s^{\alpha - 1} \exp(x\beta) \tag{28b}$$

This is the standard Weibull hazard model. Search theory would in general predict that there is a non-negative duration dependence, i.e. $\alpha \geq 1$. However, a negative duration dependence, $0 < \alpha < 1$, may be consistent with constant or falling reservation wages, if job arrival rates decrease over time. This is so because, as was emphasized in Chapter 8, the re-employment probability is a result of the generation of job offers and the conditional acceptance of a job offer, and we cannot be sure that the specification of the hazard is complete enough to control for differences in search intensity. However, we regard negative duration dependence—particularly in Case 4—as an embarrassing observation for search theory and for the advocates of sorting as an explanation of duration dependence.

$$\text{Case 3: } h(s) = \nu \exp(x\beta) \tag{28c}$$

Here we control for omitted variables by introducing a gamma distributed random component, $G(1, \sigma^2)$. If omitted variables influence the coefficient of the hazard in Case 1 the estimates of β in (28c) should exceed the estimates of β in (28a).

$$\text{Case 4: } h(s) = \alpha s^{\alpha - 1} \nu \exp(x\beta) \tag{28d}$$

This is the most general case; obviously Cases 1–3 are special cases of Case 4. If the hazard function in (28b) reveals a negative time dependence due to heterogeneity caused by omitted variables, this would in theory be corrected for by the introduction of the gamma-distributed stochastic component.

10.1.2. Comparisons of Alternative Estimates of the Hazard Function in Engström et al.'s model

Most of the independent variables used in the hazard function are standard, such as age, age of children, education, and labour market history. Some of the other variables demand further comment. The variable for the local rate of unemployment includes persons who are unemployed and searching for a job at the unemployment offices, persons who are in relief work, and persons who take part in labour market training programmes, measured as a percentage of the population in the age class 16–64 years in the local district. An average value was calculated for each relevant district during three periods: July 1983–June 1984, July 1984–June 1985, and July 1985–October 1986. For a given individual the variable then takes on the average value of the district during the period when the person became unemployed. Season is a dummy variable, which takes on the value 1 if a person became unemployed during the winter (October to February) and is 0 otherwise.

We use a number of dummy variables to study the differences between former employees of the mining company and those in the control group. The variable *LKAB* 1 takes on the value 1 for those former LKAB employees whose latest unemployment spell was during the first period, July 1983–June 1984. *LKAB* 2 takes on the value 1 for those former employees whose latest unemployment spell was during the second period, July 1984–June 1985. *LKAB* 3 takes on the value 1 for those whose latest spell was during the last period, July 1985–October 1986.

CONT 2 takes on the value 1 for those in the control group whose latest spell was during the second period, and subsequently *CONT* 3 takes on the value 1 for those in the control group whose latest unemployment spell was during the last period. The use of dummy variables presupposes that there are observations in a so-called reference group to which the other groups are compared. The reference group consists in this case of persons in the control group who had their latest unemployment spell during the first period, which is the explanation why there is no variable *CONT* 1.

The estimations of the hazard functions in Table 10.2 were carried out on a subsample of 650 individuals. The reader may remember that there were originally 1,800 employees who were laid off from LKAB and 1,400 unemployed men in the control group. Different reasons, which are given in more detail in Engström *et al.* (1987), necessitated the exclusion of people from the subsample. The most important reasons were that 550 redundant workers were older than 55 years and/or left the company after February 1984.

The former were excluded because the Swedish retirement system does not encourage them to search for a new job, and the latter category was excluded because they became unemployed during a period different from the control group. About 400 people were excluded because they claimed that they had never actively been searching for a job. People in the control group were excluded for similar reasons. Finally, questionnaire answers amounted to only approximately 50 per cent.

The estimates in Table 10.2 show an expected, but statistically insignificant, inverse relationship between the probability of leaving unemployment and the unemployment percentage.

TABLE 10.2. *Estimates of the hazard function in Engström* et al. *'s study: Cases 1–4* [a]

Variables	Case 1	Case 2	Case 3	Case 4
Constant	−2.87	−2.95	−2.87	−2.97
	(−8.38)[b]	(−8.33)	(−14.07)	(−8.37)
Local rate of	−0.03	−0.03	−0.03	−0.03
unemployment	(−1.25)	(−1.28)	(−3.31)	(−1.31)
Children less than	0.57	0.58	0.57	0.58
18 years old	(4.45)	(4.40)	(4.48)	(4.54)
Season	0.14	0.14	0.14	0.13
	(1.17)	(1.20)	(1.26)	(1.20)
Re-employed by the	0.10	0.10	0.10	0.10
company	(0.42)	(0.44)	(0.43)	(0.47)
Contruction worker (only	0.58	0.59	0.58	0.60
some individuals in the	(3.79)	(3.81)	(3.83)	(3.72)
comparison group)				
Age				
Younger than	0.25	0.26	0.25	0.26
30 years	(1.94)	(2.01)	(2.15)	(2.02)
40–9 years	−0.41	−0.42	−0.41	−0.43
	(−2.34)	(−2.38)	(−2.43)	(−2.48)
50–4 years	−0.80	−0.81	−0.80	−0.81
	(−2.91)	(−2.88)	(−2.73)	(−2.82)
Education				
Qualification as those	−0.03	−0.03	−0.03	−0.03
leaving comprehensive	(−1.82)	(−1.70)	(−1.83)	(−0.21)
school				
Senior high school	0.18	0.19	0.18	0.18
continuation	(1.24)	(1.32)	(1.28)	(1.28)

TABLE 10.2. *Contd*

Variables	Case 1	Case 2	Case 3	Case 4
school or has been at the university without getting a degree				
Has a university	0.41	0.42	0.41	0.42
degree	(1.24)	(1.24)	(1.16)	(1.17)
Labour market history				
Had a skilled position	0.33	0.34	0.33	0.34
earlier	(1.23)	(1.27)	(1.19)	(1.24)
$LKAB\,1$	−0.25	−0.26	−0.25	−0.27
	(−1.06)	(−1.08)	(−1.08)	(−1.10)
$LKAB\,2$	−0.04	−0.05	−0.04	−0.05
	(−0.19)	(−0.19)	(−0.19)	(−0.20)
$LKAB\,3$	−0.46	−0.47	−0.46	−0.48
	(−2.23)	(−2.21)	(−2.20)	(−2.24)
$CONT\,2$	−0.29	−0.29	−0.29	−0.31
	(−1.20)	(−1.19)	(−1.21)	(−1.25)
$CONT\,3$	−0.16	−0.16	−0.16	−0.16
	(−0.87)	(−0.85)	(−0.90)	(−0.88)
α^c		1.03	—	1.05
		(0.66)		(0.60)
σ	—	—	0.006	0.22
			(0.02)	(0.61)
Log likelihood ratio	80.9	81.4	80.9	81.5
	$(17)^d$	(18)	(18)	(19)

a. No. of observed unemployment spells = 650.
b. Asymptotic *t* values in brackets.
c. The null hypothesis is $\alpha = 1$.
d. Degrees of freedom in brackets.

Contrary to Nickell (1979*a*, 1979*b*), we find a significant and positive relationship between family needs and the re-employment probability. A standard search theoretical interpretation is that increased family needs decrease the reservation wage and/or increase the search intensity, which does not sound intuitively unreasonable.

The age coefficients show a re-employment probability which decreases monotonously with age. The opposite is true for the education variable, although the differences are statistically insignificant. Both phenomena seem to be standard in the duration literature. The labour market history variable also reveals a coefficient with the expected sign.

The differences between the control group and the former employees of LKAB seem to be negligible except for the *LKAB* 3 category, which contains former employees who had their latest spell of unemployment between July 1985 and October 1986.

The most striking feature of the results is, however, how little the different specifications of the hazard function matter. The β coefficients hardly change when the generality of the model is increased. The most general specification (Case 4) shows that it is not possible to refute the hypothesis that there is no duration dependence ($\alpha = 1$), and the variable measuring the variance of the gamma-distributed heterogeneity component is also insignificant, indicating a fairly homogeneous sample. On the whole the results seem trustworthy.

The data set of Engström *et al.*'s also contains information on the number of unemployment spells experienced during the period from July 1983 to October 1986. This information can be used to obtain information about what determines unemployment risks—the function $\mu(x_i)$ which was introduced in connection with equation (27)—and, indirectly, about the inflow component of the unemployment rate.

Since the number of spells is not smaller than zero and not larger than four, we need a statistical technique that can handle a dependent variable which is bounded from both below and above. A Two-Limit Tobit can do this job. In Table 10.3 we list four runs of a Tobit model where the dependent variable is the number of unemployment spells as a function of independent variables such as age, occupation, education, and number of children. The separability property, that the coefficients of the distribution function for the duration of unemployment are independent of the inflow probability and vice versa, allows us to estimate the 'unemployment risk equation' and the distribution function independently of each other. The four regressions were run on slightly more complete variations of the subsample, including, for example, people that answered that they never had been unemployed.

Estimation 1 is done with the lower limit equal to zero, while Estimations 2–4 include only individuals who have been unemployed at least once. In connection with Estimation 3 we have excluded independent variables which had statistically insignificant coefficients in the first two equations. In the fourth equation we

TABLE 10.3.   *Two-Limit Tobit estimates of number of spells equation*

Estimation	1	2	3	4
Constant	3.59	4.76	4.55	4.68
	(15.12)[a]	(17.34)	(23.71)	(23.08)
Education variables				
Elementary school	−0.29	−0.44	−0.49	−0.79
	(0.98)	(−1.56)	(1.86)	(2.85)
High school	−0.63	−0.57	−0.68	−0.87
	(−2.68)	(−2.09)	(−2.86)	(−3.49)
College	−1.67	−0.99	−1.01	−1.22
	(−3.6)	(−1.40)	(−1.47)	(−1.73)
Had skilled positions	−1.21	−0.77	−0.66	−0.89
earlier	(−3.40)	(−1.50)	(−1.33)	(−1.68)
Construction worker	1.27	0.42	0.45	0.29
	(4.54)	(1.47)	(1.56)	(0.98)
Former employee	−1.51	−1.75	−1.70	−1.72
of LKAB	(−8.12)	(−7.86)	(−7.9)	(−7.46)
Age variables				
Younger than 29	−0.32	−0.44	—	—
	(−1.3)	(−1.62)		
Age 40–9	−0.25	−0.34	—	—
	(−0.9)	(−1.02)		
Age 50–4	0.05	0.02	—	—
	(0.14)	(0.04)		
55 years or older	−0.29	−0.11	—	—
	(−0.98)	(−0.31)		
Children at home	−0.19	−0.06	—	—
	(−0.95)	(−0.28)		

a. t ratios in brackets.

have excluded people with a total time as unemployed exceeding thirty of the total forty months of the observation period.

A priori one would not be surprised if the number of spells equation is determined by other independent variables than the corresponding unemployment duration equation. Viewed from a search theoretical perspective, the duration of unemployment is very much a variable that the individual indirectly controls through the choice of his reservation wage, while the number of spells is to a much larger extent a function of factors that cannot be controlled at the individual level (disregarding voluntary quits).

This also turns out to be the case. Variables such as age and number of children come out as being statistically insignificant, while education, branch of industry (construction), and former employee of L K A B are all statistically significant, indicating that higher education reduces the unemployment risk, while being a construction worker increases it (significantly only in equation (1)).

Important in this context is that former employees of L K A B seem to have had significantly lower unemployment risk than the people in the control group. Put differently, this may be interpreted as if the intensified employment services of the special delegation have been effective in providing more permanent jobs than otherwise would have been the case.

10.1.3. A Comparison between the Engström et al. *and Engström and Löfgren*

The subsample on which the hazard function was estimated in Engström and Löfgren (1987) differs from the above subsample in several respects. The most important difference is that the disguised unemployed (people in labour market training or those in relief work) were included in the subsample, as well as those openly unemployed.[8]

The data set consists of two groups. The first group is composed of 692 redundant male workers who were laid off from L K A B's iron ore mines during 1983. The second group consists of 351 men who were recorded as unemployed at the job-centres in Lapland during the months August, September, or October 1983. In all, this makes 1,007 observations. The individuals were followed by two inquiries—the first two of the three inquiries mentioned—and additional background information was obtained from other sources.

The inclusion of disguised unemployed people means that to the list of independent variables in the hazard function are added both a relief work and a labour market training variable. Moreover, we are controlling for the different categories of redundant L K A B workers in a slightly different manner from the Engström *et al.*

---

[8] This means that a spell of unemployment, complete or uncomplete, often consists of time spent in both open and disguised unemployment. In other words, 5 weeks in open unemployment followed by 5 weeks in a continuous labour market programme would here be counted as a 10-week uncompleted spell of open and disguised unemployment, while it would in Engström *et al.*'s study qualify as a 5-week uncompleted spell of unemployment.

study, by making use of the magnitude of the severance payments through the variables under the heading 'compensations to redundants'. Another difference that may be important is that all observations on spell lengths are censored,[9] i.e. we only know that durations are shorter or longer than some t_k. For the exact likelihood function see the Appendix.

The estimation results for the four cases listed in section 10.1.1 are given in Table 10.4.

The signs of the β coefficients are once again in accordance with the conventional wisdom and the corresponding estimates in Table 10.4. The magnitudes of the coefficients are also fairly stable with respect to the specification of the hazard function.

TABLE 10.4. *Sample 1 estimates of the hazard function*

Variables	Case 1	Case 2	Case 3	Case 4
Constant	−4.048	−1.129	−1.744	−1.375
	(−21.469)[a]	(−4.778)	(−3.326)	(−3.170)
Local rate of	−0.104	−0.053	−0.102	−0.084
unemployment[b]	(−4.650)	(−2.434)	(−1.889)	(−2.008)
Children under	0.426	0.289	0.658	0.512
18 years old	(4.545)	(3.192)	(2.846)	(3.044)
Answered an inquiry	−0.181	−0.117	−0.542	−0.396
with Finnish text	(−0.637)	(−0.455)	(−0.869)	(−0.794)
Age				
Younger than	−0.102	−0.054	−0.109	−0.074
25 years	(−0.807)	(−0.454)	(−0.349)	(−0.306)
50 years or older	−0.294	−0.138	−0.371	−0.276
	(−1.995)	(−1.008)	(−1.110)	(−1.042)
Education				
Qualified as those	0.198	0.106	0.259	0.180
leaving	(1.665)	(0.951)	(0.917)	(0.833)
comprehensive				
school				
Senior high school	0.538	0.285	0.443	0.369
(16 +)/continuation	(5.035)	(2.742)	(1.763)	(1.917)
at school or has				
been at the				
university without				
getting a degree				

[9] A misspecification of the model is more severe with respect to bias, if data is censored. See Ridder (1987) and below.

TABLE 10.4. *Contd*

Variables	Case 1	Case 2	Case 3	Case 4
Has a university	1.517	0.643	1.013	0.869
degree	(5.276)	(2.708)	(1.617)	(1.784)
Labour market history				
Had a skilled	0.667	0.492	0.966	0.752
position earlier	(3.450)	(2.845)	(2.086)	(2.108)
Compensation to redundants[c]				
Category A	−3.937	−3.330	−6.160	−4.933
	(−10.211)	(−8.774)	(−10.056)	(−9.892)
Category B	−2.152	−1.916	−3.326	−2.825
	(−5.911)	(−5.714)	(−4.845)	(−5.243)
Category C	−0.328	−0.324	−0.830	−0.646
	(−2.426)	(−2.579)	(−2.462)	(−2.541)
Participation in labour market programme				
Relief work	−2.087	−1.419	−3.377	−2.538
	(−16.489)	(−9.809)	(−12.414)	(−10.742)
Labour market	−2.079	−1.263	−3.289	−2.412
training	(−17.709)	(−10.672)	(−12.914)	(−10.288)
Former employee of the	0.481	0.270	0.664	0.523
mining company	(3.646)	(2.112)	(1.968)	(2.042)
σ^2	—	—	1.500	1.175
			(16.973)	(213.484)
α^d	—	0.360	—	0.710
		(−19.514)		(−4.806)
Log likelihood	998	1 252	1 256	1 259
ratio	(15)[e]	(16)	(16)	(17)

a. Asymptotic *t* values in brackets.

b. Definition of unemployment: a person is unemployed when searching at the job-centre or taking part in a labour market programme. Number of observed unemployment spells: 1,312.

c. Compensation to redundants is measured by three dummy variables picking up the different severance payment systems that were offered to different categories of laid-off workers at L K A B.

Category A consists of persons receiving a compensation large enough to subsist on until early retirement: either white-collar workers born between 1924 and 1925, or miners who were 58 years or older when they left the company. (Note that the severance payments were not pure lump sums, since the acceptance of the payment meant that the employed sold his possibility of becoming re-employed in addition to having to leave employment earlier than if he had rejected the offer.)

Category B includes people receiving individually different but quite large severance payments, which, however, were not large enough to live on until the age of early retirement. The persons are white-collar workers born between 1926 and 1931, who should have a very low re-employment possibility.

Those in Category C left the mining company during the summer of 1983. Most of them received compensation of 60 000 S E K (£6 000).

d. The null hypothesis is $\alpha = 1$.

e. Degrees of freedom in brackets.

It is worth noting that in comparing Case 1 to Case 3, where heterogeneity is controlled for, the estimated parameter increase is in accordance with the theoretical results in Lancaster (1985). Moreover, comparing Case 2 and Case 4 with respect to the magnitude of the duration dependence parameter, α, we find that sorting due to heterogeneity is present—α increases when heterogeneity is controlled for—but interestingly enough, α remains significantly different from one. The t value in brackets under the coefficient refers to the null hypothesis $\alpha = 1$, which is the reason why its sign is negative. In other words, data seem—contrary to Engström *et al.* (1987)—to refute the hypothesis that there is a non-negative duration dependence.

There are, however, a few flaws in the values of the estimated coefficients α and σ. First of all, $\sigma^2 > 1$, which means that the mathematical expectation of a completed unemployment spell[9] is not defined in Case 3, since a finite expected duration requires that $\sigma^2 < 1$. In Case 4 the problem is that $\sigma^2 > \alpha$, which also results in an undefined expected unemployment duration.

The precision of the heterogeneity parameter, σ^2, is extremely good—too good, it might seem, considering the small increase in the log likelihood ratio when moving from Case 2 to Case 4.

These blemishes can be remedied if the disguised unemployed in the general school system are added to the sample. Now α drops to 0.2, while all heterogeneity disappears, $\sigma^2 = 0.003$, which is contrary to what is expected. On the other hand, if we disregard people with very low re-employment probabilities (categories A and B in Table 10.4), this does not change the size of the variance, but the duration dependence variable increases to 1.3, indicating positive duration dependence.[10] During all perturbation of the sample the β coefficients remain relatively unaffected.

---

[9] There seems to be some remaining confusion in the literature in Cases 2–4, perhaps stemming from a misprint in Lancaster (1979). The correct equations are found in the Appendix below, and details in their derivation can be studied in Kooreman and Ridder (1983). In Case 3 the equation is

$$E(T) = \exp(-x\beta)(1 - \sigma^2)^{-1}.$$

[10] It should be mentioned that we have decomposed our sample into different subsamples, in attempts to eliminate the inconsistent parameter estimates, without any success worth reporting.

There is some further evidence on the possible misspecification of the hazard function in the comparison between the standard run and the run where we have excluded people with a priori very low re-employment probabilities. The coefficient which is supposed to pick up the impact of intensified employment services on unemployment duration is positive and statistically significant in the standard run, and positive but insignificant in the alternative run. In the first place, it is surprising that intensified employment services matter in a region with an extremely low demand for labour. In the second place, why should they matter in particular for people with extremely low re-employment probabilities?[11]

The important point is that the magnitudes of the duration dependence variable and the variance of the heterogeneity component certainly are non-robust with respect to the composition of the sample. One reason is probably that the Weibull hazard combined with a gamma-distributed random component is not the correct specification of the model.[12] Since other authors have reported similar problems[13] with the Case 4 model, there is a need for alternative, more simple specifications of the hazard function.

Two fundamentally different specification errors of the mixed proportional hazard models are possible. Heckman and Singer (1984*b*) have warned us of the dramatic consequences of incorrect assumptions on the distribution of the unobserved heterogeneity. Also, a misspecification of the time component of the function (the base-line hazard) will of course bias the estimates (see Clayton and Cuzick (1985)). There are, however, some recent results in Ridder (1987) which indicate that the warnings from Heckman and Singer might be somewhat exaggerated. Ridder shows that if durations are uncensored, i.e. if we are dealing with completed unemployment spells, the maximum likelihood estimates of the regression parameters are not sensitive to the mis-specification of the heterogeneity distribution. If there is censoring (uncompleted unemployment spells) there is some sensitivity, but also a considerable small sample bias. Ridder also confirms that mis-specification of the duration

[11] There is an unspoken agreement among staff at the employment offices that members of category A do not need any employment services, since they are 'retired'.

[12] Another reason might be that the exact length of unemployment durations is to some extent imprecisely measured. See Engström and Löfgren (1987) for details.

[13] See Narendranathan *et al.* (1985), who have a perfectly reasonable sample and get a perfectly unreasonable magnitude of α.

dependence usually causes a significant bias in the maximum likelihood estimates of the β parameters.

Note that these results are not entirely inconsistent with the problems encountered above. The sample in Engström and Löfgren (1987) consists exclusively of censored spell data, while the sample in Engström *et al.* (1987) consists of both censored and uncensored unemployment spell data.

11
Some 'Robust' Coefficients that Matter

The discussion so far has mainly focused on the sign and magnitude of two specific coefficients, the replacement ratio and the duration coefficient. As is obvious from Tables 10.3 and 10.4, the specification of the hazard function involves many variables. Most of these are connected with the personal characteristics of the unemployed: age, marital status, education, health condition, family dependents, etc. Moreover, for data that are collected from different regions and/or over a period of time one usually also includes some indicator of the labour market situation, such as the unemployment–vacancy ratio.

In this chapter we will briefly sum up the evidence on the qualitative impact of these variables on the re-employment probability. The general tendencies should be evident from Table 11.1. The variables listed in this table are of course not always defined in the same manner. For example, the education variable not only differs among different studies, but is also often divided into different types of education. The 'good labour market history' variable contains such things as 'not registered as unemployed in last twelve months' (Narendranathan *et al.* (1985)) and 'previous possession of qualified work' (Engström *et al.* (1987)). Also, the 'family needs' variable hides differences in definitions. On the whole, however, there is a surprising unanimity in the qualitative impact of personal characteristics and demand conditions on the re-employment probability. The signs are also the expected ones, although seldom possible to derive from a search model, and robust with respect to variations in the specification of the particular model.

An interesting question which has not been discussed sufficiently is what regressors matter the most for the expected length of an unemployment spell. Is it differences in personal characteristics, the labour market situation, or economic incentives such as the magnitude of the replacement ratio? The figures in Table 11.2, which are borrowed from one of the 'classical' 1979 papers by Nickell, cover the main tendencies, although it might be necessary to

TABLE 11.1. *Qualitative impacts on the re-employment probability from certain variables in the x vector of the hazard*

	Local labour demand	Age	Married	Female	Bad health	Family needs	Age under 30	Education	Trade member	Good labour market history
Lancaster (1979)	+	–								
Nickell (1979a, 1979b)	+	–	+							
Heckman and Borjas (1980)	(+)	(–) (+)			–					
Kooreman and Ridder (1983)	+	–				–				
Atkinson et al. (1984)	+	–	+							
Narendranathan et al. (1985)	+	–	+		–		+	+	–	+
Folmer and van Dijk (1986)	+	–	+	–				+		
Engström et al. (1987)	(+)	–			+	+	(+)	+		(+)

TABLE 11.2.   *Expected duration of unemployment in weeks in Great Britain, 1972*

Personal characteristics	Ratio	Weeks
Typical man		10.5
Replacement ratios	0.4	6.7
	0.8	12.1
	1.0	16.3
Married, 3 children		12.4
Unmarried		22.7
Age 20		7.1
Age 60		17.9
Vacancy/unemployment ratios	0.2	10.0
	0.5	8.8
	1.0	7.1

Source: Nickell (1979a)

multiply all figures by two or three to get a picture of the present situation in Great Britain.[1] It should be obvious from Table 11.2 that personal characteristics are more important than the labour market situation and the replacement ratio for expected spell lengths. Another important variable for spell lengths, not included in the table, is education (see e.g. Engström *et al.* (1987)).

Similar computations on aggregate data in Kooreman and Ridder (1983) show that the elasticity of expected unemployment duration with respect to age is more than twice as high as the corresponding elasticity with respect to the unemployment percentage.[2]

The numbers in Table 11.3 refer to a typical man in the study by Engström *et al.* (1987). He is a person living in Kiruna and a former employee of the mining company LKAB. His latest unemployment spell started during the period July 1983–June 1984, when the

[1] The figures in table 2 of Narendranathan *et al.* (1985) cover the 1978 situation in GB. For details like the one in Table 11.2 above, see also Atkinson *et al.* (1984) and Folmer and van Dijk (1986). Table 11.2 is constructed by putting all variables equal to their means, except the variable under consideration.

[2] Results like this are also to be found in the microstudy of Dutch regional unemployment by Folmer and van Dijk (1986). Green's (1985) findings are different, although his aggregate data do not allow him to control for regional differences in the composition of the labour force. Note that the elasticity discussed above translates into an elasticity for unemployment, since in a steady state the unemployment rate is linearly homogeneous in duration.

TABLE 11.3. *Expected duration of unemployment in weeks*

Variables	Case 1	Case 2	Case 3	Case 4
Typical man	18	18	18	18
Expected duration if the dummy variables instead had the following values				
Re-employed by the mining company = 1	17	16	17	16
Season = 1	16	15	16	16
Children less than 18 years old = 0	32	31	32	31
Age				
Younger than 30 years = 1	14	14	13	14
40–9 years = 1	27	27	27	27
50–4 years = 1	41	39	41	39
Education				
Qualified as those leaving comprehensive school = 1	23	22	23	22
Has a university degree = 1	14	14	14	14
Labour market history				
Had a skilled position earlier = 1	13	13	13	13
$LKAB\,1 = 0$	14	14	14	14
$LKAB\,1 = 0$ $LKAB\,2 = 1$	15	14	15	15
$LKAB\,1 = 0$ $LKAB\,3 = 1$	23	22	23	22
$LKAB\,1 = 0$ $CONT\,2 = 1$	19	18	19	19
$LKAB\,1 = 0$ $CONT\,3 = 1$	17	16	17	16

Source: Engström *et al.* (1987).

local rate of unemployment (open plus disguised) was 17.8 per cent. He has children less than 18 years old, is between 30 and 39 years old, has graduated from senior high school (16 +), and his latest unemployment spell started in the summer.

The numbers emphasize the importance of being young, having a good education, having a good labour market history, and having family needs in terms of young children for the magnitude of the re-employment probability.

One can claim—with reference to the results presented above—that the identification of risk groups through personal characteristics is more important for the design of labour market policy than a test of the economic theory underlying the length of an expected unemployment duration at which the models (in which the duration variable is used as an explanatory variable) are aimed. On the other hand, it is fair to say that we do not need a hazard function to identify risk groups. In this respect it is more straightforward to ask people active in the field. Moreover, some of the personal characteristics, such as sex, age, health, and marital status, are not easily changed through labour market policy. It is easier to change the demand for labour.

12

Conclusions and Appendix

A much-debated issue during the early stages of the research on unemployment durations was what unemployment duration measure to choose. The three main candidates, the average completed-spell length (T_μ), the average uncompleted-spell length $(\widetilde{T}_\mu)$, and the experience-weighted average spell length (T_μ^e), all have their virtues. The completed-spell measure gives us the expected length of an unemployment spell and is also one of the two components (the inflow component being the other) that constitute the unemployment rate under steady-state conditions. The uncompleted-spell measure has neat connections both to the cost of unemployment and to the experience-weighted spell length. Finally, the experience-weighted spell measure gives us the average length of an ongoing spell of unemployment, in other words the typical length of observed uncompleted unemployment spells. Since the latter statistics are reported routinely by the employment surveys in many countries, a good deal of useful information on both the cost of unemployment and the length of a typical unemployment spell already exists.

Many of the more recent efforts in duration analysis have been devoted to the empirical estimation of hazard functions, and given these, all three measures are in theory computable. On the other hand, labour policy makers want easily accessible statistics, with a reasonable information content. There are good reasons to believe that much of the routinely collected information on unemployment provides this. Increases in both the duration and inflow components are responsible for the higher unemployment rates during the late 1970s and early 1980s. However, in most countries where data is available the duration component seems to be the main culprit. The USA is a possible exception to this rule. The statistics also tell us that youth unemployment occurs with much shorter unemployment spells than the average aggregate spell length. In other words, a higher inflow into unemployment than the average (higher unemployment risks) explains why the young experience a higher unemployment rate than the rest of the working population. There are, however, some reservations. Discouraged-worker effects seem to be much more important among the young. If withdrawals from the labour force are ignored, youth unemployment spells are even longer than the average spell length.

Some early attempts were made to explain the development of the transition probability over the business cycle. The direction in which the duration component changes is not derivable from theory. Empirical evidence indicates that the favourable effect on the re-employment probability from more jobs dominates the unfavourable effect from the increased reservation wages that are likely to be the result of a recognized increase in the number of jobs. Data also seem to indicate that there is no measurable impact from a lag in the detection of better job opportunities. This is consistent with a hypothesis of rational expectations and/or a neo-Keynesian hypothesis that the transition probability falls (rises) with a more (less) biting job-rationing constraint.

One of the main themes in the unemployment duration field has been the measurement of the effects on unemployment duration of unemployment benefits. The aim of such studies is to establish whether and to what extent a more generous unemployment benefit system causes an increase in the unemployment rate. The researchers have used data and statistical methods of varying types and quality, so it is far from surprising that the estimates of the unemployment benefit elasticity ranges from zero to 3.0. However, a recent study based on a very complete cross-section data set, containing among other things exact information on the benefits received, seems to confirm early estimates that the unemployment elasticity is to be found in the interval 0.3–1.0, implying that a 10 per cent increase in real unemployment benefits increases the duration of unemployment by approximately 6 per cent.

This elasticity varies with the age of the unemployed. It is higher than average for teenagers and lower than average for older men.

On the other hand, the unemployment benefit system cannot explain much of the recent sharp rise in unemployment rates in most OECD countries. Economic models based on rational individual behaviour exclude money illusion, and since the real value of unemployment benefits has stayed fairly constant over time one cannot expect a major impact on unemployment from this source. Moreover, there is theoretical evidence indicating that the (partial)

partial-equilibrium effects from unemployment benefits exaggerate their general-equilibrium effects.

Since search is productive and social and individual pay-offs from extended search will very likely differ, the key issue is not whether we should have an unemployment benefit system or not, but rather how it should be designed and what the optimal level of the unemployment benefit is. The latter is a tricky problem, since it is likely to vary with such things as aggregate demand, age, and other personal characteristics of the employee. Existing elasticity estimates can at least help us find a second-best answer.

In its most crude form, search theory predicts that the reservation wage stays constant or falls with the duration of unemployment, implying that the constant or falling reservation wage will show up as a non-negative duration dependence, given the personal characteristics of the unemployed and a given demand for labour. On the other hand, if unemployment in major segments of the labour market is involuntary, because there is job rationing, and there are personal scars from long-term unemployment as such, this will, *ceteris paribus*, show up as a negative duration dependence.

The 'statistical problem' to refute crude search theory is created by the *ceteris paribus* clause, since an inability to control for relevant determinants of the reservation wage would bias the result from any test towards negative duration dependence. This is so because persons with low reservation wages will on average be sorted out faster than persons with high reservation wages.

A lot of econometric studies have tried to test for duration dependence. The results are mixed, but it is fair to say that following for potential biases resulting from omitted variables often eliminates an existing significant negative duration dependence.

The main test technique used is to estimate a so-called Weibull hazard function by maximum likelihood methods. There are, however, statistical indications that this is not the most appropriate way of modelling duration dependence among the unemployed. In samples where most parameters of the variables controlling for aggregate demand and personal characteristics have reasonable signs and sizes, the introduction of a stochastic component allowing for heterogeneity has sometimes produced unreasonable estimates of the duration dependence parameter. A priori considerations, however, predict that there are no reasons to be particularly surprised. The Weibull model presupposes that duration dependence is a monotonously decreasing or increasing function of time.[1]

An initial segment with positive duration dependence followed by negative duration dependence would be more intuitively reasonable. Loosely speaking, an unemployed individual would need some time to search and to find out that he is involuntarily unemployed, and, provided that his search is successful, he never will. This story also indicates another flaw in the standard model of duration dependence. It presupposes that every individual has the same kind of duration dependence, independent of personal characteristics and labour market conditions. To rephrase this more simply (although with some loss of precision): people are either voluntarily or involuntarily unemployed; search unemployment (frictional unemployment) cannot coexist with involuntary unemployment. We would instead expect that there are segments of the labour market where job rationing exists, and others where there is excess demand.

The sensitivity to *ad hoc* parametrizations of duration models that has been documented both theoretically and empirically has led some authors to ask what features of duration models can be identified non-parametrically. Recent attempts in this direction show some limited success (see e.g. Dynarski and Sheffrin (1987) and Steinberg and Monforte (1987).) The 'non-parametric' techniques[2] used in these two papers do not, however, allow a test for duration dependence. Recently, Jackman and Layard[3] suggested an ingenious and simple method to test for duration dependence on aggregate data. Jackman and Layard study the re-employment probabilities of four groups of unemployed people. The difference

---

[1] Weibull originally applied the model to fatigue resistance of steel, and the monotonicity property seems more reasonable in this context. The same monotonicity 'constant' is present in the Gompertz specification of the hazard function. A non-monotonic hazard is connected with the log-logistic distribution $F(t) = 1 - [1/(1 + \gamma t^\alpha)]$.

[2] The main references are Cox (1972, 1975), Heckman and Singer (1984a, 1984b, 1985), Kiefer (1984), Kiefer *et al.* (1984), Baker and Trivedi (1985), and Trivedi (1985). See also Kaplan and Meir (1958). The result in Elbers and Ridder (1982) that both components of the proportional hazard are identifiable means that they can be recovered also by non-parametric methods. The general idea in the seminal papers by Cox is to recover β without specifying the form of the baseline hazard (the time-dependent component), which, however, does not allow us to detect duration dependence. See also Kiefer (1988).

[3] See Jackman and Layard (1986) and also Layard's comments on this paper.

between these groups is the length of time in unemployment at the time of the interview. They examine the average re-employment probability of each group during the period 1976–85. To draw the conclusion that a negative duration dependence did exist in Britain during this period, only two assumptions are needed: that the state of the British economy has gradually deteriorated, and that the characteristics of the people entering unemployment has not changed during the period.

The signs and magnitudes of the coefficients in the hazard function of the variables relating to the personal characteristics of the unemployed and demand factors are relatively robust. It is also true that age and other personal characteristics are more important than demand variables in explaining differences in the length of unemployment spells. This does not mean that demand factors are unimportant. The policy maker can change personal characteristics such as educational status, but not age and sex. The demand for labour, on the other hand, can be more easily manipulated.

In sum, the empirical and theoretical work done so far on unemployment durations has taught us a lot from a methodological standpoint, and has also enabled us to exclude a few suggested explanations of 'the new depression' which is reflected in today's unemployment rates.

On the other hand, this means that we still lack an explanation of the higher NAIRUs (Non-Accelerating Inflation Rates of Unemployment) which has firm empirical support. Such an explanation, however, demands a broader analytical perspective than the partial and static perspective inherent in an analysis of unemployment durations. The recent dynamic modelling of so-called 'hysteresis effects', whereby the equilibrium unemployment rate depends on the initial conditions, which are due to e.g. linear dependence among the relevant dynamic equations, is at best a first step.[4] It can, for example, be argued that linear dependence of the required type has 'probability zero'. However, if it can be shown that the linear dependence is a consequence of optimal behavioural rules for the policy makers—as in Sachs (1987)—and institutional facts, this becomes a more credible story.

---

[4] The idea of hysteresis is originally due to Phelps (1972). For an explicit model producing hysteresis, see Löfgren (1982), and for a test of hysteresis that turned out negative, see Pissarides (1986).

The development of unemployment dynamics, which was initiated in connection with the 'new micro-economic foundation of macro-economics' at the end of the 1960s, was certainly halted by the takeover of the rational-expectation hypothesis. The latter is, indeed, grounded in dynamic theory, but the theory is used to trace out the equilibrium path which most often by assumption happened to coincide with the market-clearing path of prices.

Appendix: The Derivation of the Probability Distribution for an Uncompleted Spell of Unemployment and Some Related Technicalities

Let $g(t)dt$ denote the probability of observing an *uncompleted* spell of unemployment of length t, and let $\underline{t}$ denote the *completed* spell length. To observe an unemployed individual who has been unemployed exactly t periods, it must be true that he entered unemployment t periods ago ($0 \leqslant t < \infty$), and that his completed spell length is at least t periods. Formally

$$g(t)dt = Pr(in\ (-t,\ -t+dt)\ \text{and}\ \underline{t} \geqslant t \mid \text{unemployed at 0})$$

$$= \frac{Pr(in\ (-t,\ -t+dt)\ \text{and}\ \underline{t} \geqslant t)}{\int_0^\infty Pr(in\ (-s,\ -s+ds)\ \text{and}\ \underline{t} \geqslant s)}$$

$$= \frac{Pr(\underline{t} \geqslant t \mid in\ (-t,\ -t+dt))\cdot Pr(in\ (-t,\ -t+dt))}{\int_0^\infty [Pr(\underline{t} \geqslant s \mid in\ (-s,\ -s+ds))\cdot Pr(in\ (-s,\ -s+ds))]} \quad (A1)$$

Now if the probability of entering unemployment is constant over time and equal to μdt, then:

$$Pr(in\ (-t,\ -t+dt)) = \mu\ dt$$

and (A1) reduces to

$$g(t)dt = \frac{Pr(\underline{t} \geqslant t)dt}{\int_0^\infty Pr(\underline{t} \geqslant s)ds} = \frac{(1-F(t))dt}{E(\underline{t})} \quad (A2)$$

if $Pr(\underline{t} \geqslant t)$ is assumed to be independent of the time of entering unemployment. The denominator of (A2) is a consequence of equation (9) in section 7.1. The likelihood function for a sample of uncompleted spells of unemployment—equation (22) in section 9.1—now follows. Note also that under these conditions Pr (unemployed at 0) $= \mu\, E(\underline{t})$.

The data of the Engström and Löfgren study reported in section 9.1 contain both unemployed and employed people (or those out of the labour force). Hence we observe both unemployed people with uncompleted spell lengths t_i, and people with completed unemployment spells shorter than some t_j.

In order for the latter to be observed, the individual must have entered and left the stock of unemployment before the time of the survey. The probability of this event is

$$Pr(in\ (-t_j,\ -t_j+dt_j)) \cdot Pr(\underline{t} \leqslant t_j) = \mu \cdot F(t_j)dt_j. \qquad (A3)$$

In order for the former individual to be observed, he must have entered unemployment at some point of time before the survey, remain unemployed at the time of the survey, and his uncompleted spell length must be exactly t_i periods. The probability of this event is

$$Pr(\text{unemployed at } 0) \cdot$$

$$Pr(in(-t_i,\ -t_i+dt) \text{ and } \underline{t} \geqslant t_i)\,|\,\text{unemployed at } 0)$$

$$= \mu E(\underline{t}) \cdot g(t_i)dt_i$$

$$= \mu \cdot [1 - F(t_i)]dt_i. \qquad (A4)$$

Formulas (A3) and (A4) imply that the likelihood of the Engström and Löfgren (1987) sample can be written

$$L = \mu^N \overset{N}{\underset{k=1}{\pi}}\ [1 - F(t_k)]^{1-y_k} \cdot F(t_k)^{y_k} \qquad (A5)$$

where

$$y_k = \begin{matrix} 1 & \text{if the individual is employed} \\ 0 & \text{otherwise} \end{matrix}$$

In Engström *et al.* (1987) one component of the likelihood function coincides with (A4), while the other consists of the density function of the completed unemployment spell length, $f(t_k)$, which numerically is approximated by $F(t_k) - F(t_k-1)$.

To control for heterogeneity caused by omitted variables we

introduce a stochastic component, ν, in the hazard function. The modified hazard then reads

$$h(t) = \nu \exp[x'\beta]\cdot\alpha t^{\alpha-1} = \nu\phi(x'\beta) \cdot \psi(t). \tag{A6}$$

Let ν be distributed according to a gamma distribution with unit mean and variance σ^2. The distribution function of the unemployment duration given ν, and for specified x, is

$$1 - F(t|\nu) = \exp\left(- \nu \exp(x'\beta) \int_0^t \psi(s)ds \right). \tag{A7}$$

By integrating over ν, ($[0,\infty]$) the expression (A7) can be transformed into the distribution function of unemployment duration at t given only x. One obtains[1]

$$1 - F(t) = \left[1 + \sigma^2 \exp(x'\beta) \int_0^t \psi(s)ds \right]^{\frac{-1}{\sigma^2}}. \tag{A8}$$

If one derives[2] the hazard function associated with (A8)—sometimes called the 'apparent hazard'[3]—one obtains

$$h_a(t) = \exp(x'\beta)\, \psi(t)[1 - F(t)]^{\sigma^2}. \tag{A9}$$

Note that if $\sigma^2 \to 0$ the apparent hazard coincides with the 'true' hazard. Moreover, if the true hazard is independent of duration, $\psi(t) = 1$, then the apparent hazard will read

$$h_a(t) = \exp(x'\beta)[1 - F(t)]^{\sigma^2} \tag{A10}$$

with derivative with respect to time

$$\frac{\delta h_a(t)}{\delta t} = -f(t)\sigma^2 \exp(x'\beta)[1 - F(t)]^{(\sigma^2-1)} < 0. \tag{A11}$$

In other words, the heterogeneity of data, $\sigma^2 \neq 0$, will show up as a spurious negative duration dependence. Since (A11) holds with

---

[1] For more detailed calculations, see Elbers and Ridder (1982) and Kooreman and Ridder (1983).

[2] $h_a(t) = \dfrac{f(t)}{1 - F(t)}$.

[3] See McKenna (1985).

strict inequality, the apparent hazard may reveal a negative duration dependence even if the exit probability increases over time.

The four variations of the hazard considered by Engström and Löfgren (1987) are

Case 1. $\nu \equiv 1$, $\phi(x'\beta) = e^{\beta x}$, and $\psi(s) = 1$
Case 2. $\nu \equiv 1$, $\phi(x'\beta) = e^{\beta x}$ and $\psi(s) = \alpha s^{\alpha-1}$
Case 3. ν gamma$(1, \sigma^2)$, $\phi(x'\beta) = e^{\beta x}$, and $\psi(s) = 1$
Case 4. ν gamma$(1, \sigma^2)$, $\phi(x'\beta) = e^{\beta x}$, and $\psi(s) = \alpha s^{\alpha-1}$

Obviously, when $\sigma^2 = 0$ Cases 2 and 4 coincide.

The mathematical expectations of the completed unemployment spell in the four cases are:[4]

Case 1. $E(T) = \displaystyle\int_0^\infty (1 - F(s))ds = \exp(-x\beta)$

Case 2. $E(T) = \dfrac{1}{\alpha} \cdot \exp(-x\beta/\alpha)\Gamma(1/\alpha)$

   where $\Gamma(\cdot)$ is the gamma function.

Case 3. $E(T) = [\exp(-x\beta)(1 - \sigma^2)]^{-1}$

Case 4. $E(T) = B\left(\dfrac{1}{\alpha}, 1/\sigma^2 - 1/\alpha)/\alpha(\sigma^2 \exp(x\beta)\right)^{1/\alpha}$

   where $B\left(\dfrac{1}{\alpha}, 1/\sigma^2 - 1/\alpha\right)$
   $= \Gamma(1/\alpha)\ \Gamma(1/\sigma^2 - 1/\alpha)\ [\Gamma(1/\sigma^2)]^{-1}$

---

[4] For a derivation, see Kooreman and Ridder (1983).

13

Comment

Richard Layard

This is a very useful survey paper, with important original results added in. It deals with matters of profound importance to modern European society—the effects of unemployment benefits, and the effect of long-term unemployment.

Long-term unemployment

Let me begin with long-term unemployment. As the authors show, the recent rise in unemployment in Britain and elsewhere has been mainly associated with increases in unemployment duration rather than with an increased inflow into unemployment. One reaction to this fact is to say, 'So what?' The other is to say, 'Can this help to explain why unemployment seems to be so persistent after a shock?' I believe the latter reaction is right.

After all, crude exit rates from unemployment *are very much lower* among those with long durations of unemployment. Let us assume for a moment that this was entirely *due* to the effect of long-term unemployment upon a person's skill, motivation, and acceptability to an employer. Then the effective number of job-seekers would not be the number of unemployed (U) but that number times the average effectiveness of each job-seeker ($\bar{c}$). And average effectiveness in turn would depend on the structure of the unemployed by duration.

Hence the duration structure of unemployment would affect the short-term NAIRU (non-accelerating inflation rate of unemployment). The NAIRU is that rate of unemployment (U/N) at which the planned mark-up of wages over prices is consistent with the planned mark-up of prices over wages. The first mark-up (of wages over prices) depends on the rate at which effective job-seekers are finding work, i.e. on $A/\bar{c}U$, where A is the outflow from unemployment. But in equilibrium the outflow from unemployment (A) equals the inflow (sN). Hence the wage mark-up depends positively on $s/\bar{c}(U/N)$. The more effective the job-seekers (the higher $\bar{c}$), the lower unemployment can be with no increase in wage pressure.

When effectiveness ($\bar{c}$) is low, unemployment has to be high to contain wage pressure. And effectiveness is low when the unemployed have been out of work for long. In Layard and Nickell (1987) we show clearly how long-term unemployment raises wage pressure. The 'hysteresis' element in European unemployment is, we argue, mainly due to the long-term unemployment caused by earlier shocks, rather than to the reduction in the number of 'insiders'.

But this whole line of argument *assumes* that long-term unemployment affects behaviour, and that the lower exit rates are not simply a reflection of heterogeneity among those who become unemployed. Can this be proved? As Löfgren and Engström show, the cross-section evidence is inconclusive. But, as Jackman and I (1988) argue, it *can* be proved from time-series evidence. Suppose there was pure heterogeneity, and that for a given unemployed individual the exit probability from unemployment is, independent of duration, given by[1]

$$p_{it} = c_i g_t \tag{1}$$

where c_i reflects only antecedent individual characteristics and g_t reflects the state of the job market. Suppose too that, since the inflow to unemployment is fairly stable, so also is the density of c, $f(c)$, among new entrants.

---

[1] This follows from the simple theory of matching. The number of matches (A) depends on the number of vacancies (V) and the number of effective job-seekers ($\bar{c}U$). Hence

$$A = g(V, \bar{c}U)$$

This process exhibits constant returns so that

$$\frac{A}{U} = \bar{c}g\left(\frac{V}{\bar{c}U}, 1\right)$$

and for the ith class of job-seekers

$$\left(\frac{A}{U}\right)_i = c_i g\left(\frac{V}{\bar{c}U}, 1\right)$$

or

$$p_{it} = c_i g_t.$$

It follows that, when the economy turns down and g_t falls, the quality of the unemployed does not change, for the stock of each type of unemployed person is given by the inflow times the duration, $1/c_i g_t$. In a downturn, all durations increase in proportion, so all stocks increase in proportion. Quality is unchanged. All that happens is that the overall exit rate, $\bar{p}$, falls in proportion to g. The same happens to the exit rate of new entrants, $\bar{p}_N$. Hence[2]

$$\frac{\bar{p}_t}{\bar{p}_{Nt}} = \text{constant (all } t)$$

What are the facts? The British data are shown in Table 13.1. Between 1979 and 1985 the exit rate of new entrants fell by less than a third, and the overall exit rate fell by over a half. This is inconsistent with pure heterogeneity.

TABLE 13.1. *Exit rates from unemployment (quarterly rates, males, Britain)[a]*

	$\bar{p}_{Nt}$ (1)	$\bar{p}_t$ (2)	$\bar{p}_t/\bar{p}_{Nt}$ (3)	$\bar{c}_t/c_N$ (4)
1969	241	588	244	288
1979	152	219	144	159
1985	107	103	96	100

a. Index 1984 = 100.
Source: Jackman and Layard (1988).

The difference was due to duration dependence. In fact the ratio of exit rates at different durations is very stable over time in Britain. Though we *know* there is some heterogeneity, let us for simplicity proceed as though there were not. We then replace (1) by

$$p_{dt} = c_d g_t \tag{2}$$

where d is duration. It follows that the exit rate of new entrants is

$$\bar{p}_{Nt} = c_N g_t \tag{3}$$

[2] $$\bar{p}_{Nt} = E(c)g_t$$

where E is the expectation using $f(c)$.

$$\bar{p}_t = E\left(cg_t \cdot \frac{1}{cg_t} \Big/ E\left(\frac{1}{cg_t}\right) \right) = E\left(\frac{1}{c}\right)^{-1} g_t$$

and the overall exit rate

$$\bar{p}_t = \Sigma f_{dt} c_d \cdot g_t = \bar{c}_t g_t \tag{4}$$

where f_{dt} is the fraction of the unemployed at duration d. As the proportion of long-term unemployed rises, so $\bar{c}$ falls. Hence the overall exit rate ($\bar{p}$) falls relative to the exit rate of new entrants ($\bar{p}_N$), since

$$\frac{\bar{p}_t}{\bar{p}_N} = \frac{\bar{c}_t}{c_N}$$

How does this story hold up? To answer this, we need to construct an index of $\bar{c}_t / c_N$. Since the ratios of the p_ds are similar in every year, we can find these ratios by comparing the p_ds in *any* year. For example, if we wish to use the p_ds in 1984 as the weights for the index, we simply note that

$$\frac{\bar{c}_t}{c_N} = \frac{\Sigma f_{dt} c_d}{c_N} = \frac{\Sigma f_{dt} c_d g_{1984}}{c_N g_{1984}} = \frac{\Sigma f_{dt} p_{d,1984}}{p_{N,1984}}$$

We show this index in column (4) of Table 13.1. By construction, in 1984 it has to equal column (3). But there is no logical reason why this should hold in any other year, unless equation (2) held as an empirical fact. Yet the equality holds closely in the earlier years too.

So a simpler theory based on duration dependence does extremely well at explaining the movement in relative exit rates over time. As I have said, we know there is *some* heterogeneity among unemployment entrants. But, when planning economic policy, it seems sensible to assume that there is also a substantial degree of duration dependence as well. Swedish policy has been more sensible than most in this respect (Layard, 1986).

13.1. Unemployment Benefits

My own feeling is that the importance of unemployment benefits is underestimated in Löfgren's and Engström's paper. I fully accept that, in the neighbourhood of existing benefit levels, the elasticity of duration with respect to benefits is below unity. I also recognize that this may exaggerate the general-equilibrium effect of benefits.[3]

---

[3] Any search theory model that produces an ambiguity in the sign of the total effect should be ruled out, on the ground that subsidies never reduce the level of an activity.

TABLE 13.2. *Duration of unemployment benefits and duration of unemployment*

	Duration of benefit	% of unemployed over 1 year (1985)	Unemployment rate (1987)
Belgium	indefinite	68	$11\frac{3}{4}$
Britain	indefinite	41	11
Netherlands	indefinite	55	$12\frac{3}{4}$
Germany	indefinite	31	8
France	30 months	47	$11\frac{1}{2}$
Sweden	14 months	11	$2\frac{1}{4}$
USA	6 months	9	$6\frac{3}{4}$

Source: Burtless (1987); OECD *Employment Outlook*; OECD, *Economic Outlook*.

But this says nothing about the effect of having *no* benefits, or of refusing to give benefits except to people who satisfy a stringent work test. To get a hint of the possible effects of benefits, one has only to look at Table 13.2. This shows in the first column the period for which benefits are available to a typical unemployed person, other than on some fragmentary basis. There is an inevitable element of simplification in the presentation, but the broad impression given by the column is valid.[4] The second column shows the proportion of the unemployed who are long-term unemployed. The relationship between the two columns is certainly striking. Long-term unemployment is very low in Sweden and the USA, where benefits cease after fourteen or six months respectively. It is much higher in the EEC countries, where benefits are long-lived. Since the total unemployment rate is in general higher where unemployment lasts longer, it is difficult not to conclude that unemployment is profoundly affected by whether or not benefits are available.[5]

Indeed, my own interpretation of the rise in EEC unemployment would be roughly as follows. After 1980, the USA, Scandinavia, and the EEC were hit by high real interest rates, compounded in the EEC by a fiscal deflation. In the USA unemployment rose sharply,

---

[4] The information is mainly based on Burtless (1987).

[5] For micro-evidence on the effects of entitlement see Holen (1977).

but then fell as poverty drove the unemployed back to work at stable real wages. In Scandinavia (north of the Baltic) manpower policy was used to prevent unemployment rising. But in the EEC unemployment was allowed to rise and there was no labour market mechanism available, as in the USA, to promote a bounce-back.

Thus European benefit systems play an important role in explaining European unemployment. But the remedy is not in my view for Europe to follow the USA. Instead it should follow Sweden, and guarantee to the long-term unemployed the legal right to work or training.

14

Comment

Anders Björklund

The study of Löfgren and Engström is an impressive exposition of recent research on a topic which fascinates scientists, policy makers, and the general public. The emphasis on the *duration* of unemployment is particularly relevant because there are strong reasons for believing that the welfare consequences of unemployment are related to the duration component of unemployment. And it is the concern about negative welfare consequences of long-term unemployment which makes the topic so central in the public discussion.

The analysis by Löfgren and Engström helps us understand the nature, causes, and consequences of unemployment duration. Such positive analysis is a prerequisite for future welfare-oriented research about appropriate policies to combat unemployment. Löfgren and Engström confine themselves to one type of consequence for individuals experiencing long-term unemployment: the effect of ongoing unemployment on the probability of leaving unemployment (for employment). A declining exit probability is termed negative duration dependence, in contrast to positive duration dependence in case of rising exit probabilities.

Because of the methodological difficulties involved in testing this hypothesis, the literature does not provide a clear-cut answer. Löfgren and Engström argue, however, that the available empirical evidence speaks in favour of no or (possibly) of positive duration dependence. The mechanism most likely to produce such a pattern is declining reservation wages of the unemployed. This in turn is predicted by many versions of standard search theory.

A (too) quick reading of the paper might give the impression that there are no permanent scars of long-term unemployment, and that the public concern about unemployment is exaggerated. Before such conclusions are drawn, the picture has to be complemented by another type of individual welfare consequence of unemployment, namely the effect on subsequent wages. If an unemployed person reduces his reservation wage during job search his expected subsequent wage will decline. The scars of long-term unemployment will show up in lower wages rather than in declining exit probabilities. My view of the literature on unemployment and subsequent wages is that most studies have found deleterious effects. Swedish studies of relevance are Björklund (1981), Björklund and Holmlund (1987) and Edin (1987b). Björklund (1981) used two waves of panel data from 1968 and 1974 and found that ten weeks of unemployment reduced subsequent wage rates by 7 per cent. The analysis was based on a representative sample of the Swedish population and hence included all types of unemployment.

A weakness of the study was, however, that neither work experience nor unemployment was carefully measured during the period between the two interviews. This drawback was eliminated in Björklund and Holmlund (1987), where the authors could use a new set of panel data with carefully measured labour market histories between 1984 and 1986. Work experience as opposed to unemployment and non-market activity turned out to have significantly positive effects on wage growth. Indeed, the quadratic term was positive too, even though estimated with low precision.

Edin (1987b) used individual earning data for the period 1971–80 pertaining to workers who were made redundant owing to a plant closing 1977. The estimated earnings equation is based on pooled cross-section and time-series data, allowing for individual-specific effects as well as autocorrelated errors. For the particular plant closure under consideration, the job loss was associated with a drop in earnings (relative to other industrial workers) of about 14 per cent. No evidence of a catch-up effect was found.

The only study on British data I know of is Nickell (1982). He estimated models of average hourly earnings for a sample of men aged 16–64 over the period 1965–75. He used the potential of panel data to control for individual effects, and found that spells of unemployment lasting at least three months had a negative effect on hourly earnings. The effect was strongly significant from zero. The specification allowed spells of sickness, training, and unemployment to affect earnings. The interpretation of the unemployment coefficient must then be that being unemployed rather than employed (or out of the labour force for other reasons than schooling or sickness) has a deleterious effect on subsequent earnings.

Not surprisingly most studies have used US data. Chowdhury and Nickell (1985) estimated models very similar to Nickell (1982) and found that unemployment spells have a considerable negative effect on earnings that can be as high as 14 per cent for a ten-week spell. The losses decay rapidly, but there is some slight evidence of a small permanent impact. The study was based on a sample of male heads of household aged 25–55 in 1968. The panel data covered the period 1968–76.

In a comprehensive volume on youth unemployment in the USA, Freeman and Wise (1982) summarize the results from three studies on the effect of present unemployment on future unemployment and wages. They conclude: 'In fact, there is little evidence that time spent out of work early in a youngster's career leads to recurring unemployment. Rather, the cost of not working is the reduction in wages persons suffer later because they failed to accumulate work experience, something employers reward.' An early study by Lazear (1976) also found that work experience among youth had an effect on wage growth which could be separated from aging *per se*. This indicates that there is a cost of long-term unemployment in terms of lower subsequent earnings.

The only study I know of which has produced opposite results concerning effects of unemployment on subsequent earnings is Becker and Hills (1983). They find that *short* periods of unemployment are associated with higher wages some eight to ten years later. However, the net effect of teenage labour market experience is positive for youth in this study too.

To summarize, the picture provided by Löfgren and Engström should be complemented by the available evidence on unemployment and subsequent wages. The studies show quite uniformly that there is a cost of long-term unemployment in terms of lower future earnings. This scarring effect shows that the public concern about the welfare consequences of unemployment is justified. Somewhat surprisingly, the results also support search theory, because the mechanism which most probably produces a combination of rising exit probabilities from search theory and lower subsequent wages is declining reservation wages, which are predicted by the theory.

References for Part II

Akerlof, G.A., and Main, B.G. (1980). 'Unemployment Spells and Unemployment Experience', *American Economic Review*, 70.

—— and —— (1981). 'An Experience Weighted Measure of Employment and Unemployment Duration', *American Economic Review*, 71.

Albrecht, J.W., and Axell, B. (1984). 'An Equilibrium Model of Search Unemployment', *Journal of Political Economy*, 92.

——, ——, and Lang, H. (1986). 'General Equilibrium Wage and Price Distributions', *Quarterly Journal of Economics*.

——, Holmlund, B., and Lang, H. (1986). 'Job Search and the Transition to Employment: Theory', FIEF Working Paper No. 26, Stockholm.

Atkinson, A.B., Gomulka, J., Micklewright, J., and Rau, N. (1984). 'Unemployment Benefit, Duration and Incentives in Britain', *Journal of Public Economics*, 23.

Axell, B., and Lang, H. (1986). 'The Effects of Unemployment Compensation in General Equilibrium with Search Unemployment', FIEF Working Paper No. 13, Stockholm.

Axelsson, R., Holmlund, B., and Löfgren, K.G. (1977). 'On the Length of Spells of Unemployment in Sweden: Comment', *American Economic Review*, 67.

—— and Löfgren, K.G. (1977). 'The Demand for Labor and Search Activity in the Swedish Labor Market', *European Economic Review*, 9.

——, ——, and Nilsson, L.G. (1987). *Den svenska arbetsmarknadspolitiken under 1900-talet*, Stockholm: Prisma.

Baker, GM., and Trivedi, P.K. (1985). 'Estimation of Unemployment Duration from Grouped Data: A Comparative Study', *Journal of Labor Economics*, 3.

Barlow, R.E., and Proschan, F. (1975). *Statistical Theory of Realiability and Life Testing*, New York: Holt, Rinehart & Winston.

Barron, J.M. (1975). 'Search in the Labor Market and the Duration of Unemployment: Some Empirical Evidence', *American Economic Review*, 65.

—— and Mellow, W. (1981). 'Changes in Labor Force Status among the Unemployed', *Journal of Human Resources*, 16.

Becker, B., and Hills, S. (1983). 'The Longrun Effects of Unemployment and Job Changes Among Male Teenagers', *Journal of Human Resources*, 18.

Björklund, A. (1978). 'On the Duration of Unemployment in Sweden, 1965–1976', *Scandinavian Journal of Economics*, 79.

—— (1981). *Studies in the Dynamics of Unemployment*, Stockholm: EFI (Economic Research Institute).

—— (1983). 'Measuring the Duration of Unemployment: A Note', *Scottish Journal of Political Economy*, 30.

—— and Holmlund, B. (1981). 'The Duration of Unemployment and Unexpected Inflation: An Empirical Analysis', *American Economic Review*, 71.

—— and —— (1986). 'The Economics of Unemployment Insurance: The Case of Sweden', FIEF Working Paper No. 25, Stockholm.

—— and —— (1988). 'Job Mobility and Subsequent Wages in Sweden', Working Paper No. 192, Industrial Institute for Economic and Social Research, Stockholm.

Blau, D. M., and Robins, P. K. (1986*a*). 'Labor Supply Response to Welfare Programs: A Dynamic Analysis', *Journal of Labor Economics*, 4.

—— and —— (1986*b*). 'Job Search, Wage Offers and Unemployment Insurance', *Journal of Public Economics*, 29.

Brännäs, K. (1986). 'Small Sample Properties in a Heterogenous Weibull Model', *Economic Letters*, 21.

Burdett, K. (1979). 'Unemployment Insurance Payments as a Search Subsidy: A Theoretical Analysis', *Economic Inquiry*, 27.

—— (1981). 'A Useful Restriction on the Offer Distributions in Job Search Models', in G. Eliasson, B. Holmlund, and F. P. Stafford (eds.), *Studies in Labor Market Behaviour: Sweden and the United States*, Stockholm: IUI (Industrial Institute of Economic and Social Research).

Burtless, G. (1987). 'Jobless pay and high European Unemployment', in R. Z. Lawrence and C. L. Schultze (eds.), *Barriers to European Growth*, Washington, DC: Brookings Institution.

Carlsson, J. A., and Horrigan, M. W. (1983). 'Measures of Unemployment Duration as Guides to Research and Policy: Comment', *American Economic Review*, 73.

Chowdhury, G., and Nickell, S. (1985). 'Hourly Earnings in the United States: Another Look at Unionization, Schooling, Sickness, and Unemployment Using PSID Data', *Journal of Labor Economics*, 3.

Clark, K. B., and Summers, L. H. (1979). 'Labor Market Dynamics and Unemployment: A Reconsideration', *Brookings Papers on Economic Activity*, 1.

Clayton, D., and Cuzick, J. (1985). 'Multivariate Generalizations of the Proportional Hazards Model', *Journal of the Royal Statistical Society*, series B, 34.

Cox, D. R. (1972). 'Regression Models and Life Tables', *Journal of the Royal Statistical Society*, series B, 34.

—— (1975). 'Partial Likelihood', *Biometrika*, 62.

Cubbin, J.S., and Foley, K. (1977). 'The Extent of Benefit-Induced Unemployment in Great Britain: Some New Evidence', *Oxford Economic Papers*, 29.

Danziger, S., Haveman, R.H., and Plotnik, R. (1981). 'How Income Transfers Affect Work Saving and the Income Distribution', *Journal of Economic Literature*, 29.

Dynarski, M., and Sheffrin, S.M. (1987). 'New Evidence on the Cylical Behaviour of Unemployment Duration', in K. Lang and J. Leonard (eds.), *Unemployment and the Structure of Labour Markets*, Oxford: Blackwell.

Edin, P.A. (1987*a*). 'The Labor Market Dynamics of a Plant Closure', Department of Economics, Uppsala University (mimeo).

Edin, P.A. (1987*b*). 'Individual Consequences of Plant Closures', dissertation, Department of Economics, Uppsala University.

Ehrenberg, R., and Oaxaca, R. (1976). 'Unemployment Insurance Duration of Unemployment and Subsequent Wage Gain', *American Economic Review*, 66.

Elbers, C., and Ridder, G. (1982). 'True and Spurious Dependence: The Identifiability of the Proportional Hazard Model', *Review of Economic Studies*, 49.

Engström, L., and Löfgren, K.G. (1987). 'Disguised and Open Unemployment, Intensified Employment Services, and Unemployment Durations', Stockholm: FIEF (mimeo).

——, ——, and Westerlund, O. (1987). 'Intensified Employment Services, Unemployment Durations, and Unemployment Risks', Department of Economics, University of Umeå (mimeo).

Feinberg, R. (1977). 'Search in the Labor Market and the Duration of Unemployment: Note', *American Economic Review*, 67.

Feldstein, M.S. (1975). 'The Importance of Temporary Layoffs: An Empirical Analysis', *Brookings Papers on Economic Activity*, 3.

—— (1976). 'Temporary Layoffs in the Theory of Unemployment', *Journal of Political Economy*, 84.

Folmer, H., and van Dijk, J. (1986). 'Differences in Unemployment Durations: A Regional or a Personal Problem?', Faculty of Economics, University of Groningen (mimeo).

Fowler, R.F. (1968). 'Duration of Unemployment on the Register of the Wholly Unemployed', Studies in Official Statistics Research Series No. 1, London: HMSO.

Frank, R.H. (1978). 'How Long is a Spell of Unemployment?', *Econometrica*, 46.

Freeman, R. and Wise, D. (eds.) (1982). *The Youth Employment Problem: Its Nature, Causes and Consequences*, Chicago, Ill.: University of Chicago Press.

Friedman, M. (1968). 'The Role of Monetary Policy,' *American Economic Review*, 58.

Green, A. E. (1985). 'Unemployment Duration in the Recession: The Local Labor Market Area Scale', *Regional Studies*, 19.

Grubel, H. G., and Maki, D. (1974). 'The Effect of Unemployment Benefits on US Unemployment Rates', Dept of Economics, Simon Fraser University (mimeo).

——, —— and Sax, S. (1975). 'Real and Induced Unemployment in Canada', *Canadian Journal of Economics*, 8.

Hall, R. (1970). 'Why is the Unemployment Rate so High at Full Employment?', *Brookings Papers on Economic Activity*, 3.

—— (1972). 'Turnover in the Labor Force', *Brookings Papers on Economic Activity*, 3.

Hasan, A., and De Broucker, P. (1982). 'Duration of Concentration of Unemployment', *Canadian Journal of Economics*, 15.

Heckman, J. J., and Borjas, G. J. (1980). 'Does Unemployment Cause Future Unemployment? Definitions, Questions and Answers from a Continuous Time Model of Heterogeneity and State Dependence', *Economia*, 47.

—— and Singer, B. (1984a). 'Econometric Duration Analysis', *Journal of Econometrics*, 24.

—— and —— (1984b). 'A Method of Minimizing the Impact of Distributional Assumptions in Economic Models for Duration Data', *Econometrica*, 52.

—— and —— (1985). 'Social Science Duration Analysis', in J. J. Heckman and B. Singer (eds.), *Longitudinal Analysis of Labour Market Data*, Cambridge: Cambridge University Press.

Heikensten, L. (1984). *Studies in Structural Change and Labor Market Adjustment*, Stockholm: EFI (Economic Research Institute).

Henry, S. G. B., Payne, J. M., and Trinder, C. (1985). 'Unemployment and Real Wages: The Role of Unemployment, Social Security Benefits and Unionization', *Oxford Economic Papers*, 37.

Holen, A. (1977). 'Effects of Unemployment Insurance Entitlement on Duration and Job Search Outcome', *Industrial and Labour Relations Review*, 30/4.

Holmlund, B. (1986). *Vägar ut ur arbetslöshet: Stockholmsungdomars erfarenheter 1981-1982* [*Ways out of Unemployment: Youth's Experiences in Stockholm*], Forskningsrapport no. 4, Stockholm: FIEF.

Jackman, R., and Layard, R. (1986). 'Does Long-Term Unemployment Reduce a Person's Chance of a Job? A New Test', Centre for Labour Economics, London School of Economics, Working Paper No. 883.

—— and —— (1988). 'Does Long-Term Unemployment Reduce A Person's Chance of a Job? A Time-Series Test', Centre for Labour Economics, London School of Economics, Discussion Paper No. 309.

Johnson, G., and Layard, P.G.R. (1986). 'The Natural Rate of Unemployment and Labor Market Policy', in O. Ashenfelter and P.R.G. Layard (eds.), *Handbook of Labor Economics*, Amsterdam: North-Holland.

Jovanovic, B. (1979). 'Job Matching and the Theory of Turnover', *Journal of Political Economy*, 87.

Kaitz, H. (1970). 'Analyzing the Length of Spells of Unemployment', *Monthly Labor Review*, 93.

Kalbfleisch, J.D., and Prentice, R.L. (1980). *The Statistical Analysis of Failure Time Data*, New York: Wiley.

Kaplan, E.L., and Meir, P. (1958). 'Nonparametric Estimation from Incomplete Observations', *Journal of the American Statistical Association*, 53.

Keeley, M., and Robins, P.K. (1985). 'Government Programs, Job-Search Requirements, and the Duration of Unemployment', *Journal of Labor Economics*, 3.

Kiefer, N.M. (1984). 'A Simple Test for Heterogeneity in Exponential Models of Duration', *Journal of Labor Economics*, 2.

—— (1988). 'Economic Duration Data and Hazard Functions', *Journal of Economic Literature*, 26.

——, Lundberg, S.J., and Neuman, G.R. (1984). 'How Long is a Spell of Unemployment? Illusions and Biases in the Use of CPS Data', Cambridge, Mass., National Bureau of Economic Research, Working Paper No. 1467.

—— and Neuman, G.R. (1979). 'An Empirical Job Search Model', *Journal of Political Economy*, 87.

—— and —— (1981). 'Individual Effects in a Nonlinear Model: Explicit Treatment of Heterogeneity in the Empirical Job-Search Model', *Econometrica*, 49.

Kooreman, P., and Ridder, G. (1983). 'The Effects of Age and Unemployment Percentage on the Duration of Unemployment', *European Economic Review*, 20.

Lancaster, T. (1976). 'Redundancy, Unemployment and Manpower Policy', *Economic Journal*, 86.

—— (1979). 'Econometric Methods for the Duration of Unemployment', *Econometrica*, 47. pp 939–56.

—— (1985). 'Generalized Residuals and Heterogeneous Duration Models', *Journal of Econometrics*, 28.

—— and Nickell, S.J. (1980). 'The Analysis of Re-employment Probabilities for the Unemployed', *Journal of the Royal Statistical Society*, 143.

Lang, H. (1985). 'On Measuring the Impact of Unemployment Benefits on the Duration of Unemployment Spell', *Economic Letters*, 18.

Layard, R. (1981). 'Measuring the Duration of Unemployment: A Note', *Scottish Journal of Political Economy*, 29.

—— (1982). 'Youth Unemployment in Britain and the United States Compared', in R. Freeman and D. Wise (eds.), *The Youth Labor Market Problem*, Chicago, Ill.: Chicago University Press.

—— (1986). *How to Beat Unemployment*, Oxford: Oxford University Press.

—— and Nickell, S. (1987). 'The Labour Market', in R. Dornbusch and R. Layard, (eds.), *The Performance of the British Economy*, Oxford: Oxford University Press.

Lazear, E. (1976). 'Age, Experience and Wage Growth', *American Economic Review*, 66.

Lindbeck, A. (1981). 'Work Disincentives in the Welfare State.' Nationalekonomische Gesellschaft Lectures, Vienna: Manz.

Lippman, S., and McCall, J. J. (1976). 'The Economics of Job Search: A Survey: Part I', *Economic Inquiry*, 14.

Löfgren, K. G. (1976). *An Indirect Approach to Determine the Average Duration of Unemployment*, Umeå Economic Studies No. 31, University of Umeå.

—— (1982). 'Contract Theory and the Phillips Curve,' *Zeitschrift für Nationalökonomie*, 42.

Lucas, R. E. (1972). 'Expectations and the Neutrality of Money', *Journal of Economic Theory*, 4.

MacKay, D. I., and Reid, G. L. (1972). 'Redundancy, Unemployment and Manpower Policy', *Economic Journal*, 82.

McKenna, C. J. (1985). *Uncertainty and the Labour Market: Recent Developments in Job Search Theory*, Brighton; Sussex: Wheatsheaf.

Main, B. G. (1981). 'The Length of Employment and Unemployment in Great Britain', *Scottish Journal of Political Economy*, 28.

—— (1982). 'Three Summary Measures of the Duration of Unemployment', *Scottish Journal of Political Economy*, 29.

Maki, D., and Spindler, Z. A. (1975). 'The Effect of Unemployment Compensation on the Rate of Unemployment in Great Britain', *Oxford Economic Papers*, 27.

Mavromaras, K. G. (1987). 'Unemployment Benefits and Unemployment Rates Revised: A General Equilibrium Job Search Model', *Journal of Public Economics*, 32.

Meyer, B. (1988). 'Unemployment Insurance and Unemployment Spells', Cambridge, Mass.: National Bureau of Economic Research, Working Paper No. 2546.

Minford, P. (1983). 'Labor Market Equilibrium in an Open Economy', *Oxford Economic Papers*, Special Issue on Unemployment.

—— (1985). 'Unemployment and Real Wages: The Role of Unemployment,

Social Security Benefits and Unionisation (Labour Market Equilibrium in an Open Economy)', *Oxford Economic Papers*, 37.

Mortensen, D. T. (1970). 'Job Search, the Duration of Unemployment and the Phillips Curve', *American Economic Review*, 60.

Muth, J. (1961). 'Rational Expectations and the Theory of Price Movements', *Econometrica*, 29.

Narendranathan, W., Nickell, S., and Stern, J. (1985). 'Unemployment Benefits Revisited', *Economic Journal*, 95.

Nickell, S. (1979a). 'Estimating the Probability of Leaving Unemployment', *Econometrica*, 47.

—— (1979b). 'The Effect of Unemployment and Related Benefits on the Duration of Unemployment', *Economic Journal*, 89.

—— (1982). 'The Determinants of Occupational Success in Britain', *Review of Economic Studies*, 49.

—— (1984). 'A Review of *Unemployment: Cause and Cure* by Minford et al.', *Economic Journal*, 94.

OECD, *Employment Outlook*, Sept. 1983.

——, *Employment Outlook*, Sept. 1986.

Perry, G. L. (1972). 'Unemployment Flows in the US Labor Market', *Brookings Papers on Economic Activity*, 1.

Phelps, E. S. (1967). 'Phillips Curves, Expectations of Inflation, and Optimal Unemployment over Time', *Economica*, 34.

—— (1972). *Inflation Policy and Unemployment Theory*, New York: Norton.

Pissarides, C. (1986). 'Unemployment Flow in Britain: Facts, Theory and Policy', Centre for Labour Economics, London School of Economics, Working Paper No. 86.

Ridder, G. (1987). 'The Sensitivity of Duration Model to Misspecified Unobserved Heterogeneity and Duration Dependence', Department of Actuarial Science and Econometrics, University of Amsterdam (mimeo).

Sachs, J. D. (1987). 'High Unemployment in Europe: Diagnoses and Policy Implications', in C. H. Siven (ed.), *Unemployment in Europe: Analysis and Policy Issues*, Stockholm: Timbro.

Salant, S. W. (1977). 'Search Theory and Duration Data: A Theory of Sorts', *Quarterly Journal of Economics*, 91.

Sargent, T. (1979). *Macroeconomic Theory*, New York: Academic Press.

Sidder, H. (1985). 'Unemployment Duration and Incidence: 1968-82', *American Economic Review*, 75.

SOU [Swedish Government Committee Report] (1984:31). Arbetslöshetens effekter för individen—en granskning av den svenska forskningen av A. Björklund.

Ståhl, I. (1978). 'Unemployment Insurance: The Swedish Case', in H. Grunel and M. Walker (eds.), *Unemployment Insurance: Global Evidence of its Effects on Unemployment* (Vancouver: Fraser Institute).

Steinberg, D., and Monforte, F.A. (1987). 'Estimating the Effects of Job Search Assistance and Training Programs on the Unemployment Durations of Displaced Workers', in K. Lang and J. Leonard (eds.), *Unemployment and the Structure of Labour Markets*, Oxford: Blackwell.

Stigler, G.J. (1962). 'Information in the Labor Market', *Journal of Political Economy*, 70.

Taylor, J. (1977). 'A Note on the Comparative Behaviour of Male and Female Unemployment Rates in the United Kingdom, 1951-1976', University of Lancaster (mimeo).

Topel, R.M. (1983). 'On Layoffs and Unemployment Insurance', *American Economic Review*, 73.

Trivedi, P.K. (1985). 'A Note on Estimating Unemployment Duration', *Australian Economic Review*, 69.

—— and Baker, G.M. (1983). 'Unemployment in Australia: Duration and Recurrent spells', *Economic Record*, 59.

—— and Hui, W.T. (1987). 'An Empirical Study of Long-Term Unemployment in Australia', *Journal of Labor Economics*, 5.

Weibull, W. (1951). 'A Statistical Distribution Function of Wide Applicability', *Journal of Applied Mechanics*, 18.

Index